T0335201

—————————— 2004-05 ——————————

EDITORS
Sidney Gottlieb and Richard Allen

EDITORIAL ADVISORY BOARD
Charles Barr   Lesley Brill
Paula Marantz Cohen   Leonard J. Leff
Thomas M. Leitch   James Naremore

Founding Editor
Christopher Brookhouse

Editorial Assistant
Renata Jackson

Cover Design
Deborah Dutko

The *Hitchcock Annual* (ISSN 1062-5518) is published each spring. Editorial, subscription, and advertising correspondence should be addressed to: Sidney Gottlieb, Editor, *Hitchcock Annual,* Department of Media Studies, Sacred Heart University, Fairfield, CT 06825-1000. E-mail address: spgottlieb@aol.com

The cost for continuing subscribers is $10 per volume for individuals (outside the U.S. add $5.00 for postage) and $25.00 for institutions. Make checks payable to: *Hitchcock Annual.* All back issues are available, as are offprints of individual articles. Inquire for prices.

We invite articles on all aspects of Hitchcock and his work, and encourage a variety of approaches, methods, and viewpoints. For all submissions, follow the guidelines of the *Chicago Manual of Style,* using full notes rather than works cited format, and include two copies of the essay to be considered (only one of which will be returned) with return postage. Submissions may also be made by e-mail as attached files. The responsibility for securing any permissions required for publishing material in the essay or related illustrations rests with the author. Authors of articles with illustrations will be asked to contribute to covering the additional printing charges incurred by such illustrations.

The *Hitchcock Annual* is indexed in the *Film Literature Index* and *MLA International Bibliography.*

The publication of this volume has been supported by grants from the Graduate School of Arts and Sciences and the Tisch School of the Arts, New York University, and from the Department of Media Studies and Digital Culture, Sacred Heart University.

HITCHCOCK ANNUAL
2004–05

CHARLES BARR

Deserter or Honored Exile?
Views of Hitchcock from Wartime Britain

There is a formula used by old-fashioned schoolteachers, in Britain at least, when rebuking children for bad behavior: ''You've let the school down, you've let your friends down, and worst of all, you've let yourself down.'' A comparable kind of public criticism was levelled at Alfred Hitchcock following his move from Britain to Hollywood at the end of the 1930s, by some of his fellow-countrymen—a minority, but an articulate and influential one. This aspect of his career is, I think, worth closer study than it has received hitherto.

Hitchcock was nearly forty, and had directed more than twenty British films, when he moved to America in March 1939 to take up a contract with David O. Selznick. When war broke out in Europe six months later, on September 3, he was on the point of shooting his first Hollywood film, *Rebecca*, and he remained from then on a Hollywood director. Since the United States did not join the war until December 1941, he was based for more than two years in a neutral country while his own was at war. Although he subsequently came back to visit Britain from time to time, he never again made his home there, and when, occasionally, he filmed there, it was as a visitor from Hollywood who stayed in luxury London hotels.

There were those who saw his move out of Britain, at that particular time, or at least his failure to return home after the war started, as a form of betrayal, and between them they echoed the schoolteacher's threefold rebuke. He had let his country down, by leaving it at a time when it was clearly moving towards war. The most pointed attack on him in these terms came from the veteran actor Sir Seymour Hicks, who in 1922 had given Hitchcock his very first commission as a director.[1] He had let his friends down: his colleagues in the British film industry which had nurtured him, and which needed him at this time of extreme crisis and challenge. The man who articulated this attack most persistently was Michael Balcon, now head of Ealing Studios, who had produced many of Hitchcock's best British films.[2] And, not least, he had let himself down: cut himself off from his cultural roots, betrayed his distinctive talents, sold out to the sheltered opulence of America. The classic statement of this view came at the end of the decade from the critic, later filmmaker, Lindsay Anderson, in an article that made a lasting impact.[3]

When starting to look at this topic of British responses to Hitchcock's move to Hollywood, I was surprised to find how little it had been investigated. One reason for the gap is surely the fact that the bulk of the serious biographical and historical research on Hitchcock's career has been done by scholars based in America. I'm referring to books like the two major biographies by Donald Spoto and Patrick McGilligan; the massive annotated bibliography by Jane Sloan; *Hitchcock: The Making of a Reputation*, by Robert Kapsis; and the study of Hitchcock's first decade in Hollywood by Leonard Leff, entitled *Hitchcock and Selznick*.[4] The Kapsis book, for instance, even though it traces the graph of Hitchcock's reputation across his whole career, has little to say about the key transitional decade of the 1940s, and ignores altogether the British perspective on it; he doesn't even mention Lindsay Anderson, whose article undeniably helped to fix a view of Hitchcock's decline that was dominant for at least a decade in English-language criticism.[5] The two major biographies don't ignore the British angle, but they tend to take an over-simple and second-hand line. I say this not to put down any of these writers, whose scholarly ambition in so many ways puts their British colleagues to shame, but their American perspective clearly does create some imbalances.

McGilligan's recent biography makes two main points about the view from 1940s Britain. He refers to the attacks on Hitchcock made by Balcon early in the war for staying in Hollywood, and dismisses them as hasty and misguided; and he quotes Lindsay Anderson's 1949 account of the decline in Hitchcock's work after he went to America, and treats it as being typical:

> In England the director's reputation had [as of 1943] predictably declined, with a general feeling among critics that Hollywood had not only robbed England of Hitchcock, but Hitchcock of his individuality . . . Lindsay Anderson, like other English critics, embraced little of what Hitchcock did after he left home.[6]

This is probably the impression of Hitchcock's status in 1940s Britain that most people have, and I tended to share it myself until recently: the impression that there was some initial resentment of Hitchcock's absence, but that it was quickly shown up as being misguided; and that most serious British critics of the time were less than enthusiastic about the actual films that Hitchcock made in his first few years in Hollywood.[7]

On both issues, however, the reality is rather more complicated. This decade of the 1940s was easily the most turbulent and eventful one in the intertwined histories of British film production and British film culture, and the contested public image of Hitchcock and of his films not surprisingly reflects this. Before going further, I need to acknowledge, more prominently than in an endnote, a share of responsibility for McGilligan's corner-cutting, in that I read much of his draft and had the chance to raise queries; but it was only after taking on this piece of research, in the context of a wider survey of British wartime cinema, that I realized how partial were the received views.[8] So this essay is offered as a belated postscript. The reception of two films in particular, with topical war themes, will help to illustrate the debates: *Foreign Correspondent*, made between the start of the war and America's entry into it, and released in August 1940, and the other made at the end of the war, *Notorious*, released in America in 1946 and in England early in 1947.

The main attacks on Hitchcock and other so-called deserters came in the spring and summer of 1940—a period that spanned the fall of France, the superseding of Chamberlain by Churchill as Prime Minister, and the airborne Battle of Britain. The attack by Seymour Hicks was published in May 1940, and included the proposal that Hitchcock should direct Charles Laughton and other Hollywood-British actors in a film entitled "Gone with the Wind Up."[9] This echoes some of the attacks that were being made on other absentees such as the poet W.H. Auden, the novelist Christopher Isherwood, and the musician Benjamin Britten. But the weekly fan magazine, *Picturegoer*, had already, from the start of the war, been discussing the issue of what the Hollywood British should do, presenting both sides of the argument. On October 7, 1939, the magazine's editor, Malcolm Phillips, reported on the urgent campaign to, in the words of his headline, "Keep The Home Cameras Turning," and approved the action of those who were coming back to assist this. While their Hollywood correspondent W.H. Mooring was broadly sympathetic to those who stayed, Maurice Cowan took a less friendly line. In a two-page spread on January 27, 1940, "Call Up for Hollywood," he sardonically invited them to come back and work for military rates of pay: among the illustrations is the one of Hitchcock used on the cover of this issue. "Here's Alfred Hitchcock as he'd look as a major-general. Pay £4 10s 6d a day plus allowances."[10]

Of course there was no serious suggestion that Hitchcock should volunteer for active service; he was, like Laughton, unfitted both by age and by physical condition, and his potential contribution lay elsewhere. On May 11, the same month as the Hicks article, came Michael Balcon's first main intervention, in a *Picturegoer* interview published under the heading "Call Up the Hollywood Britons." Hitchcock is unmentioned, but is implicitly contrasted with another filmmaker who had returned after starring in two films produced by Selznick immediately prior to *Rebecca*: ''Leslie Howard, for instance, has come back to work here, and immediately the money is forthcoming for him to produce pictures.''[11]

Though outspoken, this piece is less prominent and less violent than the full-page article, ''Deserters,'' published as the main feature article in the *Sunday Dispatch* on August 25, 1940. Here, the central text by Balcon is backed up by inserts from four others with film connections: the comedy star George Formby, the actors Owen Nares and (again) Sir Seymour Hicks, and the writer J.B. Priestley. A variety of points are made, ranging from hysterical to thoughtful, but one passage from Balcon stands out:

> I had a plump young junior technician in my studios whom I promoted from department to department. Today, one of our most famous directors, he is in Hollywood, while we who are left behind are trying to harness films to the great national effort. . . . I do not give this man's name as I have decided not to mention any of the deserters by name.

The name was hardly needed, and Hitchcock was provoked into a sharp reply, published two days later. He hit back at Balcon, accusing him of jealousy and insisting that ''The British government has only to call upon me for my services. The manner in which I am helping my country is not Mr. Balcon's business.''[12]

Hitchcock's second Hollywood film, *Foreign Correspondent*, opened in America on the very day of his reply to Balcon, and in early October it reached Britain. It supplied the most vivid and timely illustration of the way in which Hitchcock had chosen to ''help his country,'' in that it mounted, in the format of a suspense thriller, a stirring attack on American isolationism, and could thus be seen as doing an important propaganda job. Joel McCrea plays an American reporter in

Europe, Huntley Haverstock, who moves from naive disinterest to commitment during the countdown to war; the main action ends with his return to America on the eve of war, but a tacked-on coda shows him a year later in London, broadcasting to America from a BBC studio while the bombs fall. Like Chaplin's *The Great Dictator*, released early in 1941, the film ends with a set-piece speech directed in effect at the audience, and specifically the American one, as Hitchcock and his writers construct from 6,000 miles away the experience of a blitz that was still in the future as they filmed it, but was very real to the first British audiences who viewed it:

> I can't read the rest of the speech I had because all the lights have gone out—so I'll just have to talk off the cuff. All that noise you hear isn't static. It's death coming to London. Yes, they're coming here now. You can hear the bombs falling on the streets and the homes. Don't tune me out. Hang on a while, this is a big story—and you're part of it. It's too late to do anything here now except stand in the dark and let them come. It's as if the lights are out everywhere— except in America. Keep those lights burning there. Cover them with steel—ring them with guns. Build a canopy of battleships and bombing planes around them. Hello, America! Hang onto your lights. They're the only lights left in the world!

An intense debate about the film and about this climactic speech is played out in the columns of the polemical film magazine of the time, *Documentary News Letter*, whose title speaks for itself, though it covers wider issues than actual documentary production.[13] The film is reviewed by a committed long-term member of the British documentary movement, Basil Wright, co-director of the classic *Night Mail* (1936). If anyone, at that time, can be said to have been dedicated to the realist aesthetic and to the support of indigenous production close to the daily realities of British wartime life, this is the man. The journalistic output of

Wright and his close associates is filled with references to the importance of getting ordinary people and their struggles and their aspirations onto the screen. And yet he is also a champion of Hitchcock's Hollywood work, right from the start:

> In *Rebecca* Alfred Hitchcock showed that Hollywood had supplied for him two essentials which had been markedly lacking in his long and successful career in British studios. The first was full and unstinted film-making facilities. The second was good producership. *Rebecca*, for all its faults, had qualities both of technique and imagination which transcended anything Hitchcock had achieved over here. Apparently the long traditions of Hollywood really do mean something.
>
> Certainly in *Foreign Correspondent* this always talented director has made his best film; and it is no detraction from Hitchcock's own qualities to emphasise the fact that it was made under the producership of Walter Wanger, one of the most enlightened and talented of the younger school of Hollywood tycoons.[14]

So Wright is not just opposing Balcon's already well-publicized line on Hitchcock's exile, he is suggesting that Hitchcock was held back in Britain by the low quality of his producers, of whom the dominant one had, of course, been Balcon himself. He goes on to praise the robust propaganda value of the film, and especially its ending. A letter appears in the next issue from an equally prominent member of the documentary movement, like Wright a critic as well as a filmmaker, Paul Rotha.[15] He places on record his "deep resentment" of the final speech and of the magazine's support of it. The lights over here are still burning; the sequence could only have been made by people who didn't understand British democracy and British morale. And the letter is endorsed by a total of seven other journalists and filmmakers, including Michael Balcon and the Brazilian-born director Alberto Cavalcanti.[16]

Cavalcanti had recently joined Balcon at Ealing, but he had spent the previous seven years at the GPO Film Unit, taking over the running of it when John Grierson resigned in 1937, and was strongly identified with the documentary ethos—indeed this was precisely why Balcon recruited him. Two short films made by his colleagues at the unit shortly after his departure can be seen as, among other things, a filmic reinforcement of the protest letter. While *Foreign Correspondent* was circulating, vivid images of the actual bombing of London were already being widely shown in Britain and overseas, and not only in newsreels. The GPO team put together, at high speed, a powerful documentary report, *London Can Take It*, with introduction and commentary by a genuine American foreign correspondent, Quentin Reynolds of *Collier's Weekly*; Reynolds flew to Washington to deliver a copy personally to the President, and it was shown in hundreds of American cinemas during October, as well as throughout Britain. It is possible that Reynolds and the filmmakers had seen *Foreign Correspondent* by the time he finalized the commentary, which repeatedly emphasizes the reality of all the material—"These are not Hollywood sound effects"—and it seems very probable that the unit's quick follow-up film, *Christmas Under Fire*, was designed partly as a corrective to the rhetoric of the final speech by Joel McCrea. Reynolds again narrates the film, introducing it on-camera as a report on English life in Christmas 1940 which he is taking to America; and the climax of his commentary, spoken over evocative images of blackout and family celebrations, foregrounds the same imagery of lights burning in the darkness:

> There is no reason for America to feel sorry for England this Christmas. England doesn't feel sorry for herself. Destiny gave her the torch of liberty to hold and she has not dropped it. She has not allowed the strong waves of terrorism which are sweeping over the world from Berlin to let that bright light even flicker.[17]

For *Foreign Correspondent*, and for Basil Wright, it could be argued that the crudity both of the BBC setting and of the final speech was offset by, and justified by, the force of the message delivered to audiences in neutral America, and in other neutral countries. Indeed, the relation between *Foreign Correspondent* and the documentaries can be seen as complementary rather than oppositional, in that the same audiences evidently responded positively to both—to melodrama backed up by ''Hollywood sound effects,'' and to the documentary record that was in its own way just as artfully manipulated.

Even so, it could still be argued, and would continue to be argued by Balcon, that Hitchcock could have made equally effective, and more convincing, films in Britain if, like Leslie Howard, he had come back from Hollywood, and that his work would have been crucial, among other things, in helping to open up the American market for British wartime films in a way that went beyond the very intermittent success that would be achieved by a few of them. He had just reached the point, with the critical and box-office triumph of *The Lady Vanishes* (1938), of having developed an image, both in his person and in his films, that had genuine international currency, and Balcon and others were deeply frustrated that he didn't fully exploit it in the service of Britain at war, and the British cinema at war. This viewpoint can be respected, particularly if we shake off the wisdom of hindsight and think ourselves back into that period when the survival of a strong British film industry and even (after the fall of France, and before either the U.S.S.R. or the U.S.A. joined the war) of an independent Britain remained precarious.

Hitchcock would, as McGilligan points out, make contributions to the British cinematic war effort in two minor ways: he handled the re-dubbing of two British films with soundtracks more accessible to American audiences, and he came over in early 1944 to make two French-language short films for the Ministry of Information, films of marginal importance.[18] But apart from that he made no film after *Foreign Correspondent* that engaged directly with the war in Europe, the focus of both *Saboteur* and *Lifeboat* being essentially American.

Meanwhile, British audiences flocked to this film almost as eagerly as they would do two years later to MGM's *Mrs Miniver*. On October 15, at the height of the German bombing of London, the *Evening Standard* noted:

> Queues were seen at West End cinemas for the first time for a month. People lined up to see Hitchcock's *Foreign Correspondent* at the Gaumont. Takings on Sunday were only £50 below *Rebecca* on a similar day six weeks ago. Customers will face the blitz if the cinemas will give them the right films.

However, the debate rumbled on, notably in the pages of *Picturegoer*, where W.H. Mooring continued to send consistently upbeat news from Hollywood about the activities of Hitchcock and his fellow-exiles. One of these despatches provoked Balcon into another response, which filled a page in the issue of May 10, 1941, under the title ''You're Wrong, Mr. Mooring.'' The claim that these exiles are working positively to ''serve the cause of democracy'' is, he insists, unconvincing when, like Victor Saville (*Bitter Sweet*) and Herbert Wilcox (*No No Nanette*), and like Hitchcock since *Foreign Correspondent* (*Mr. and Mrs. Smith, Suspicion*), they are making films unrelated to the war, however good those films may turn out to be:

> These producers are simply following their normal occupation and manufacturing films. What has this to do with war effort and fighting for democracy?
> If they were making them here, they *would* be doing good work, whether the subject of the films was propaganda or not. This would be the case, because their films would earn American dollars for the British Treasury, and because they would be helping to preserve an industry whose very existence is now threatened.

And there, more or less, it rests. Letters from *Picturegoer* readers fill a page of a subsequent issue (June 7), mainly supporting Balcon, though one of them makes the point that we are doing all right without the exiles, so good riddance. Soon, it became apparent that the indigenous film industry ''whose very existence is now threatened'' was growing progressively more confident. At the same time, Britain and its Dominions ceased to be so isolated, since in this year of 1941 first the U.S.S.R. (in June) and then the U.S.A. (in December) joined the war. The targeting of propaganda at neutral countries ceased to be a main concern, though it was still significant for maintaining morale at home and impressing allies. A number of made-in-Britain propaganda features had a big success in the home market and earned unusually wide distribution in the U.S., films such as the GPO Unit's *Target for Tonight*, Powell and Pressburger's *49th Parallel* and *One of Our Aircraft is Missing*, Noel Coward's *In Which We Serve*, the Army Film Unit's *Desert Victory* (recording the defeat of Rommel in North Africa) and, later, Olivier's prestige production with a clear topical slant, *Henry V*. Hitchcock's renewed presence in Britain might have strengthened this output considerably, given it more weight in the export market, and thus cut down the proportion of box-office receipts being remitted to the U.S. This is hypothetical, but it helps to explain the hostility of men like Balcon and the less excitable Priestley.

It may also, it has been suggested, help to explain the failure of the British establishment to honor Hitchcock with a knighthood until close to the end of his life.[19] Though this whole honors system was, and continues to be, one of the most offensive elements in British public life, encouraging snobbery, subservience, and subtle forms of corruption, its operations can be revealing. Among British filmmakers active in the war years, Laurence Olivier was knighted in 1947, primarily as a stage actor, but his work as director/star of *Henry V* in 1944 must have helped; Carol Reed followed in 1952. Among producers, Balcon, who had campaigned tirelessly in support of indigenous production throughout the war while running a busy and successful operation at Ealing, became Sir Michael in 1948.[20] These cases seem fairly predictable, but more surprising was the knighthood given to Alexander Korda as early as June 1942. Balcon had been critical of him as well for basing himself for long periods in Hollywood, not Britain, but made amends to him in his autobiography, as he pointedly did not to others:

> Certainly I misunderstood his departure to Hollywood, with other members of his family, early in the Second World War. I was wrong then about Korda but perhaps not so wrong about some of the others who left with unseemly haste immediately before or after the war began.[21]

Korda had directed a strong anti-isolationist film in Hollywood—*Lady Hamilton* (1941), which exploited to the full the historical lessons of Nelson's resistance to Napoleon—but so had Hitchcock, so what was the difference? Well, Korda had previously produced a high-profile propaganda film in Britain (*The Lion Has Wings*, started immediately on the outbreak of war and released within two months); he had made it clear he was not leaving the country for good; and he was extremely busy in the anti-isolationist cause, both in Hollywood and to some extent beyond it. Whether or not he was technically some kind of undercover British agent, he was sufficiently active in the film community to attract the odium of the Senate committee that was trying to root out pro-British propaganda in Hollywood, and was due to appear before them, and to defend *Lady Hamilton*, in December 1941; the attack on Pearl Harbor then rendered the Senate hearings redundant, but the summons could itself be seen as a badge of honor. And Korda kept in regular touch with Churchill, whom he had cultivated for years, who adored *Lady Hamilton*, and to whom he clearly owed the knighthood.[22]

It is possible that Churchill saw *Foreign Correspondent*, but there seems to be no record of it (as there is of much of his prolific film viewing), and none of the other pro-Korda factors apply.[23] Hitchcock was not cut out for the kind of diplomatic wheeling and dealing that Korda relished. Indeed, in contrast to the sentimental anglophilia of the Hungarian-born Korda, Hitchcock seems basically quite happy to have turned his back on his native country, even though he returned a few times in and after the war to attend to family matters and, now and then, to direct. The producer John Houseman, who was involved in early discussions of *Saboteur* (1942), has left a revealing account of their meetings:

> What I was unprepared for was a man of exaggeratedly delicate sensibilities, marked by a harsh Catholic education and the scars from a social system against which he was perpetually in revolt and which had left him suspicious and vulnerable, alternately docile and defiant.[24]

In the end, like Chaplin, and like the comic writer P.G. Wodehouse, two other distinguished expatriates, Hitchcock did receive what was virtually a deathbed honor from his native country. The black marks against Chaplin were both sexual and political, and Wodehouse had been in trouble for making some naive broadcasts from captivity in Germany early in the war which were construed as unpatriotic.[25] Thorold Dickinson, a contemporary of Hitchcock who played a central role in British cinema throughout the war as both director and producer, insisted that the authorities never forgave him for his absence at that critical time.[26] Had he been determined to interrupt or renegotiate the Selznick contract, he could assuredly have done so, just as David Niven put aside his contract with Goldwyn for the duration. Nor does the argument that he and others had been advised by the government to stay on in Hollywood carry much weight, since that advice came at an early stage from the Chamberlain government, which had still not decided whether a British film industry was even worth maintaining in time of war. And it was certainly unwise of him to let it be known that he had sounded out the British studios about a return, but that they had been unable, in war conditions, to guarantee his former level of salary.[27] The bottom line was that, having finally made the move to America which had so much to be said for it in career terms, he was determined not to reverse it, and the attacks seem only to have increased his determination and, even more, that of his wife, Alma Reville, always an equal partner in his decisions.[28]

□   □   □   □   □

These controversies, however, scarcely seemed to impinge on those who reviewed films week by week in newspapers and magazines. Rarely do they even refer to the attacks on Hitchcock for making films in Hollywood rather than in Britain. His move is soon taken as a *fait accompli*, and most of them refer to the films with a degree of respect, affection, and even pride, even if they have mixed feelings about the success of some of them. They especially welcome *Shadow of a Doubt* in 1943: Dilys Powell of the *Sunday Times* speaks for many in finding it ''delightful,'' in that it marks a full return, in his new environment, to the assurance of *The Lady Vanishes*.[29]

His next film, *Lifeboat*, makes the headlines in advance: a front-page story in the *Sunday Chronicle*, ''Film Angers America,'' is linked to the syndicated weekly column by the American journalist Dorothy Thompson, who protests that

> It shows a typical Nazi as a superman, and a cross-section of American society as morons. . . . A lot of Americans are asking whether Hitchcock would have dared, in the middle of the war, to have presented a cross-section of British society in the same light.[30]

One of those who defends Hitchcock most vigorously, when the film opens in Britain, is Richard Winnington, film critic of the daily *News Chronicle*:

> Wild complaints that [the Nazi's] superior competence and resourcefulness cast a slur on democracy strike me as foolish. . . . As a portrait of

the Nazi make-up it is a relief after the succession of swaggering imbeciles we are accustomed to. I find this good and timely propaganda. The film is a virile, polished and workmanlike job.[31]

And yet, when he next reviews a Hitchcock film, *Spellbound*, in 1946, Winnington's line has changed:

Year after year we go on expecting things from Alfred Hitchcock through a deep-rooted gratitude for his "early" and "middle" British periods. And year after year we see him becoming more and more dedicated to that empty polish which is the standard achievement of the Hollywood director.[32]

This line is very close to that of Anderson in the 1949 *Sequence* article, and may even have influenced him. Winnington was, of all British critics, the one most respected by the "young Turks" who founded the magazine in 1947, a respect that he reciprocated. Here he has in effect repudiated his praise for *Lifeboat*, without admitting it. I see this not as dishonesty but as a response to what had been happening in the intervening period—he may well have forgotten what he wrote two years earlier. Those years from 1944 to 1946 were momentous ones for British cinema, with a whole string of films seeming to establish both a distinctive British film aesthetic, based primarily on restraint and realism, and a more promising basis for commercial prosperity than ever before. In his survey of 1945, Winnington called it "Britain's most dazzling year of film-making," and detected a shift in the power relations of Britain and Hollywood:

British films have taken an unprecedented leap forward in the last year both in entertainment value and in techniques. . . . Considering the relative sizes of the two industries and the appalling restrictions of space, apparatus and personnel that still afflict her

studios, Britain's achievement is nothing less than
epic. The British cinema has been truly born.[33]

This is not the place for further elaboration of these
developments, destined to be short-lived, but the context
does help to explain this critic's change of attitude to a
Hitchcock who had by now fully committed himself to
Hollywood and its ways. *Notorious* follows in early 1947,
opening in London in the same week as the re-release of a
celebrated Duvivier film of the 1930s, and Winnington's
verdict on it begins thus:

> If *Poil de Carotte* sparkles, *Notorious* can be said to
> glitter with a deadly slickness. Alfred Hitchcock has
> gone out, at all costs, for polish, at the price of
> originality and suspense and story. . . . He seems
> bent on refuting his previous theories of
> condensation by dallying with close-ups and
> irrelevant sequences.[34]

Compare the socialist political weekly *Tribune*: their critic,
Simon Harcourt Smith, reviews *Notorious* alongside another
momentous film of that year, *The Best Years of Our Lives*,
characterizing the pair of them as

> a couple of large, glossy, slightly self-important
> pictures from Hollywood. . . . The one has been
> directed by Alfred Hitchcock, the other by William
> Wyler. Both provide uninspired but quite competent
> entertainment.
> *Notorious* is perhaps the worse film of the two
> because of what we used to expect from Hitchcock.
> Looking back, I am inclined to think we expected too
> much. . . . No Hitchcock film has any point of view
> to give it substance; and when the quickness of his
> hand no longer takes us in, there is very little to do
> but doze. Certainly there is little sleight of hand in
> the new Hitchcock picture. . . . Nevertheless, the film

is just worth seeing if only for the hearty appetite with which Miss Bergman eats Mr. Grant in one of the earlier sequences.[35]

Little sleight of hand, no point of view, irrelevant sequences, gratuitous close-ups and gloss—these now seem extraordinary comments to make on a film which stands up as well as any film, by Hitchcock or anyone else, to analysis as a model of tight, rigorous, organic construction. Whether you like the film or not, it seems perverse to criticize it in those terms, as being slack and rambling. Harcourt Smith's witticism at the expense of the long kissing scene is an accurate indication of his dilettantism, but Winnington was a critic of admirable care and seriousness whom Philip French, the longest-serving and most professional of his successors, has aptly compared with George Orwell.[36] On the basis of these confidently scornful views of *Notorious*— Winnington the true enthusiast writing for a popular paper, Harcourt Smith the general arts man writing for a minority one, plus Anderson, voice of a new generation of cineastes— it's easy to infer that in those days, in this British milieu, the critics just didn't get it: didn't begin to understand the new and productive directions that Hitchcock's work was taking, perhaps because they were too caught up in the euphoria of a new dawn for British cinema, and of the non-Hollywood aesthetic associated with it. Even when that new impetus petered out, neither Winnington nor Anderson would soften their severity towards the Hollywood Hitchcock.

Another influential voice was Paul Rotha, who had orchestrated the resentment against the ending of *Foreign Correspondent*. Like the *Sequence* critics, he had links with Winnington—they were drinking companions, and, after his friend's death, Rotha set up an annual prize in his memory and later published a selection of his work.[37] An updated edition of *The Film Till Now* was published in 1949, with new material written by Richard Griffith but approved by Rotha: it too records a decline in Hitchcock's work in Hollywood, where his ''cinematic construction has had to be subordinated to pseudo-romantic conflicts involving the highlighting of principal players.''[38]

Yet this is by no means the whole story. The Anderson-Winnington-Rotha axis was an influential one, but it cannot be said to have represented, to use McGilligan's phrase, a ''general feeling.'' Rotha's view diverged, as we have seen, from that of his documentary colleague Basil Wright. Likewise, Anderson's main colleague on *Sequence*, Gavin Lambert, who did not write on Hitchcock for the magazine, would later come out as a keen champion of his Hollywood films.[39] And even at the time the *Sunday Chronicle*, sister paper to Winnington's, called *Notorious* ''magnificent,'' and supported the judgment in prose that seems as miraculously modern as that of those other critics is off-beam:

> Not a word, look nor gesture but has its proper place and point in this melodrama's vehement unravelling. Not a shot nor sequence but its length is cut brilliantly to correct measure: not a performance but touches minor peaks of which I had thought even those competent actors, Cary Grant and Ingrid Bergman, incapable.[40]

The reviewer is Paul Dehn, now settling into a tenure that will be comparable to Winnington's, after whose death in 1953 he takes over the daily paper's film column.[41] And clearly he does get it, perceiving and celebrating exactly those qualities of the film that are picked up by, for instance, François Truffaut and William Rothman.[42] And a survey of the reception of *Notorious* finds just as much of that kind of positive comment as negative, albeit not so brilliantly articulated as it is here by Dehn.

All of this is just a sample of the complexities of the discourse about Hitchcock in 1940s Britain. Regularly, his work divided critics, like those of the two *Chronicles*, and divided documentary activists, like Basil Wright and Paul Rotha, and divided industry people like Michael Balcon and Sidney Bernstein, Hitchcock's past and future collaborators.[43]

The debates highlight genuine issues that were important at the time and still have a residue of meaning today. Was it more useful at the start of the war to have Britain's strongest filmmakers working in Britain, or to have a strong British presence on the ground in Hollywood helping to build up pro-British sentiment over there? Was it more effective diplomatically, particularly in neutral countries, to have vigorous propaganda films coming directly from Britain, or from ostensibly still-neutral America? And there was, and is, a perennially interesting debate as to whether Hitchcock's films had on balance gained or lost aesthetically by the move to Hollywood. The point is that there were strong and articulate voices in Britain at the time, on both sides. That is the broad picture that I hope to have established; abundant material remains for fuller research. But let's give the last word, for now, to the audience, who voted with their feet for *Foreign Correspondent* as they had done for *Rebecca* and as they would do for *Spellbound* and *Notorious*. The Granada cinema chain conducted polls of audience opinion every few years, and one question was ''Who is your favorite director?'' In the last pre-war poll Frank Capra topped the list, and Hitchcock was fourth. In the next poll, in 1946, half of the top twelve were British directors working in Britain, but the name at the top was Alfred Hitchcock.[44] Audiences at least didn't seem to feel that he had let them down.

Notes

1. As writer/star of the two-reel comedy *Always Tell Your Wife* (1922), Hicks had invited Hitchcock, then a junior studio employee, to complete it after the departure of the original director, Hugh Croise.

2. Balcon had employed Hitchcock at Gainsborough, promoted him to director in 1925, and—after his departure in 1927 to BIP for a higher salary—welcomed him back to Gaumont-British in 1934 to make *The Man Who Knew Too Much* and its four successors, the series of thrillers which decisively established his international reputation.

20   CHARLES BARR

3. Lindsay Anderson, "Alfred Hitchcock," *Sequence* 9 (autumn 1949); reprinted in Alfred LaValley, ed., *Focus on Hitchcock* (New Jersey: Prentice-Hall, 1972).

4. Donald Spoto, *The Life of Alfred Hitchcock: The Dark Side of Genius* (London: Collins, 1983), published in the U.S. in the same year as *The Dark Side of Genius: The Life of Alfred Hitchcock*; Patrick McGilligan, *Alfred Hitchcock: A Life in Darkness and Light* (Chichester: John Wiley, 2003); Jane Sloan, *Alfred Hitchcock: A Filmography and Bibliography* (Berkeley and Los Angeles: University of California Press, 1995); Robert Kapsis, *Hitchcock: the Making of Reputation* (Chicago: University of Chicago, 1992); Leonard Leff, *Hitchcock and Selznick* (London: Weidenfeld and Nicolson, 1988). The earlier book by the British critic John Russell Taylor, *Hitch: The Life and Work of Alfred Hitchcock* (London: Faber and Faber, 1978), is a relaxed authorized biography whose value comes from its direct access to Hitchcock more than from historical research.

5. See Sloan, *Alfred Hitchcock: A Filmography and Bibliography*, 18.

6. McGilligan, *Alfred Hitchcock: A Life in Darkness and Light*, 326 and 327.

7. See the Epilogue chapter in Charles Barr, *English Hitchcock* (Moffat: Cameron and Hollis, 1999), 207-10, for some discussion of the first of the two issues.

8. My book on *The Film at War: British Cinema 1939-1945* is due for publication by the British Film Institute in 2006.

9. The Hicks article is referred to by several writers, without any source or precise date being given. No doubt an initial citation was unreferenced, and a succession of later writers have taken it over without trying, or managing, to track it down directly—nor have I yet succeeded in doing so. From the start of the war in 1939 Hicks had a leading role in organizing the Entertainments National Service Association (ENSA), which put on live shows for the troops.

10. This is £4.52p in decimal coinage, or around $18 at 1940 rates of exchange. The director Ken Annakin recalls, in an interview, his work on a recruiting film in 1942, "with important actresses like Flora Robson working for £5 a day"—a precise index of the financial sacrifice they were ready to make for the war effort. See Ken Annakin, in Brian McFarlane, ed., *Sixty Voices* (London: BFI Publishing, 1992), 5.

11. Howard had starred with Ingrid Bergman in *Intermezzo* and played Ashley Wilkes in *Gone with the Wind*; these were his last two Hollywood films, both released in 1939. His first and best British

war film, as star and director, was *Pimpernel Smith* (1941), released
in the U.S. as *Mister V*. Howard died in a plane crash in 1943.

12. *New York World-Telegram*, August 27, 1940, quoted by Spoto,
The Life of Alfred Hitchcock: The Dark Side of Genius, 235-36.

13. *Documentary News Letter* was the successor to two earlier
voices of the minority film culture centered on the documentary
movement founded by John Grierson: *Cinema Quarterly* (1932-35)
and *World Film News* (1936-38). It published 60 issues between
January 1940 and December 1947, and continued for a time as
Documentary Film News before ending in 1949.

14. *Documentary News Letter*, November 1940. The review is,
following the magazine's normal practice, unsigned, but its
closeness to the argument and phraseology of Wright's signed
review of the same film in the political weekly, *The Spectator*
(October 18, 1940), establishes its authorship beyond any doubt.
Wright was a long-term member of the *Documentary News Letter*
editorial board.

15. Rotha was well known as the author of a wide-ranging
history of the medium, *The Film Till Now* (London: Jonathan Cape,
1930), reissued with updates several times in the following decades.
He had since published *Documentary Film* (London: Faber, 1936),
and had begun a career as a documentary producer and director,
which he continued throughout the war.

16. The other five are Dilys Powell, film critic of the *Sunday
Times*; Aubrey Flanagan, of the *Motion Picture Herald*; and three
prominent journalists who were not film specialists, Ritchie Calder,
Michael Foot, and Alexander Werth.

17. Neither of these two GPO films carry individual credits for
anyone except Reynolds, but Harry Watt evidently worked on both,
and Humphrey Jennings and Pat Jackson were among the other
prominent members of the unit who shot material for *London Can
Take It*. See Watt's autobiography, *Don't Look at the Camera* (London:
Paul Elek, 1974), 138-45. Details of the quick U.S. distribution of
London Can Take It are given in, for instance, Kevin Jackson's critical
biography of *Humphrey Jennings* (London: Picador, 2004), 231-34; it
also had rapid and wide exposure in countries as distant as New
Zealand. In Britain, the two films had at least as extensive a
showing as *Foreign Correspondent*. The Ministry of Information had
by then set up a system whereby a single official short film was
released each week, free of charge, to all cinemas: *London Can Take
It* was the weekly release on October 21, 1940—using, for home

consumption, the rather more tactful title of *Britain Can Take It*—and *Christmas Under Fire* was the weekly release on January 6, 1941.

18. See McGilligan, *Alfred Hitchcock: A Life in Darkness and Light* 280-81, for Hitchcock's involvement, at his own expense, in the revision of two films produced by the GPO Film Unit, which had by now been taken over by the Ministry of Information: *Men of the Lightship* (1940) and *Target for Tonight* (1941). *Bon Voyage* and *Aventure Malgache* were made in French in early 1944, at Welwyn Studios, for distribution after the Liberation, but in the event they were hardly shown. Hitchcock came to London again in 1945 to supervise the production of a film based on concentration camp newsreels, but the changing political context caused the project to be aborted.

19. He was made Sir Alfred on New Year's Day 1980, four months before his death.

20. For a summary of the range of Balcon's campaigning activities, of which the pressure on Hitchcock was only a small part, see the chapter "Retrospect 1993" in the updated edition of Charles Barr, *Ealing Studios* (Moffat: Cameron and Hollis, 1999).

21. Michael Balcon, *A Lifetime of Films* (London: Hutchinson, 1969), 93-94.

22. For the range of his contacts with Churchill, see Charles Drazin, *Korda* (London: Sidgwick and Jackson, 2002). The Churchill Archive in Cambridge, England, contains many exchanges between the two men, including several cables about *Lady Hamilton* (CHAR 2/419) and a warm handwritten letter of thanks from Korda in Hollywood, dated July 19, 1942, following his knighthood (CHAR 2/443).

23. See D.J. Wenden and K.R.M. Short, "Winston S. Churchill: Film Fan," in *Historical Journal of Film, Radio, and Television* 11, no. 3 (1991): 197-214. Despite extensive research, the authors did not claim to have established anything like a complete record of Churchill's extensive viewing even during the war years, for which sources are abundant. Since then, new documents have come to light, including lists of recommended films supplied to Churchill by the film critic of the *Observer*, C.A. (Caroline) Lejeune. One list of twenty-eight films supplied in 1942 includes both *Foreign Correspondent* and *Suspicion;* some titles are annotated by his secretary as "seen already," but they don't include either of these, and I have found no evidence that he ever did see them (Churchill Archive, CHAR 2/444).

24. John Houseman, *Run-Through* (London: Allen Lane, 1973), 479.

25. For full and judicious coverage of this episode, see Robert McCrum, *Wodehouse: A Life* (London: Viking, 2004). The Wodehouse scandal overlapped with the last phase of the attacks on Hitchcock, in mid-1941, and there are some suggestive similarities, pointed out to me by Victor Perkins.

26. I am indebted, again, to Victor Perkins for this information, drawn from a conversation he had with Dickinson in 1975. During the war, Dickinson directed both propaganda shorts and feature films, the best-known being the original *Gaslight* (1940), and was founding director of the Army Kinematograph Service, set up to produce high-quality training films.

27. This statement by Hitchcock is quoted in *Picturegoer*, August 10, 1940.

28. For Alma Reville's influence at this time, see Taylor, *Hitch: The Life and Work of Alfred Hitchcock*, 164.

29. *Sunday Times*, March 28, 1943, reprinted in Dilys Powell, *The Golden Screen: Fifty Years of Films*, ed. George Perry (London: Pavilion Books, 1989), 36-37.

30. *Sunday Chronicle*, February 13, 1944.

31. *News Chronicle*, March 19, 1944.

32. *News Chronicle*, May 18, 1946.

33. *News Chronicle*, December 29, 1945.

34. *News Chronicle*, February 15, 1947.

35. *Tribune*, undated cutting from early 1947, included on the microfiche on *Notorious* held by the British Film Insitute's library.

36. Philip French, review of the collection edited by Paul Rotha (see next note), *The Observer*, January 23, 1976. French has been film critic of *The Observer* since 1978.

37. Richard Winnington, *Film Criticism and Caricatures, 1943-53*, ed. Paul Rotha (London: Paul Elek, 1975). The Richard Winnington Award, given to "the film which best reflected his ideals of artistic and social integrity," lapsed in the early 1960s.

38. Paul Rotha, *The Film Till Now* (London: Vision Press, 1963), 557.

39. See the chapter on Hitchcock, "The Benefits of Shock," in Lambert's *The Dangerous Edge* (London: Barrie and Jenkins, 1975).

40. *Sunday Chronicle*, February 16, 1947.

41. Dehn began to write for the cinema alongside his reviewing, with original scripts for two British films in *Seven Days to Noon* (John Boulting, 1950) and *Orders to Kill* (Anthony Asquith, 1958), before becoming a full-time screenwriter in the early 1960s. He contributed

to the James Bond and *Planet of the Apes* series, and adapted *Murder on the Orient Express* for Sidney Lumet (1974).

42. William Rothman, in *Hitchcock: The Murderous Gaze* (Cambridge: Harvard University Press, 1982), calls *Notorious* "the first Hitchcock film in which every shot is not only meaningful but beautiful" (246). See also François Truffaut, *Hitchcock* (London: Secker and Warburg, 1968), 139.

43. Bernstein was an adviser to the Films Division of the Ministry of Information for most of the war, and commissioned the films Hitchcock made for them in 1944. The two men then formed Transatlantic Pictures, whose first production was *Rope* (1948).

44. Statistics from Guy Morgan, *Red Roses Every Night* (London: Quality Press, 1948), 100.

R OBIN W OOD

Hitchcock and Fascism

The following represents an attempt to draw together numerous ideas, perceptions, and suggestions from my previous work on Hitchcock. Readers of my two books will consequently encounter much here that is familiar, but what I have attempted is the reorganization of the material into new patterns that place it in a somewhat different light, producing an overall view, the "figure in the carpet" (to borrow a phrase from Henry James), that some may find controversial and which hopefully will never become merely redundant.[1] The attempt has led me, ultimately, to a new discovery of *Lifeboat* a film I now find that I, like so many others, have consistently underestimated—as one of the key works of the Hitchcock *oeuvre*.

What is Fascism?

In its strict sense, the term "Fascist" refers to certain repressive political movements developed within advanced capitalism, characterized by the glorification of power and domination and claiming the right to rule by force, without "democratic" consultation. I have been told by certain people that this is the *only* sense in which the word should be used, or its impact becomes weakened, but they are already much too late: the word has entered the language, and is now commonly used to describe, not only the policies of right-wing politicians like Thatcher and Reagan, but the behavior-patterns of some individuals. When using it in its "pure" sense, as I define it above, I shall distinguish it with a capital F, in the popular sense with a small one; there is of course a very close connection between the two. The differences and the similarities are equally important.

Fascism (strict sense) can be readily defined, pigeonholed and set apart: the Reagan and Thatcher administrations were not "Fascist." On the other hand fascist *tendencies* pervade the whole of Western culture (and, as far as I know, every other existing culture, in some form); consequently, the possibility of an escalation into Fascism is continuously present. For most of us, Fascism is something *out there*, the political philosophy of a few somewhat ridiculous (if hateful and dangerous) extremists within our own countries or "foreigners" outside them. We can repudiate it and keep it at a distance without acknowledging that fascist tendencies (the raw material out of which Fascism, given propitious circumstances, can develop) are all around and *inside* us, inherent in the very roots of our social formations, the two founding principles of which are definable only in two words that I have found to be very unpopular and which the culture at large seems to want to suppress: patriarchy and capitalism. While the culture remains founded in these principles (and there seems no great hope of their demise in the immediate future), the escalation into Fascism will remain a possibility: we can't expect to eliminate it without first eliminating *them*, since both are grounded in, and continuously foster, principles of power and domination. I am thinking of, for example, the domination of employees by employers, of women by men, of children by parents and educators. Many today are trying to free themselves from these patterns (the dominators as well as the dominated, since both are in a sense victims of the system), often with remarkable and surprising success, at least in personal relationships. Yet it is unlikely that anyone living within a patriarchal capitalist culture can escape contamination: without radical change in the fundamental social/political structures, the individual can only go so far.

My argument here is that in Hitchcock the contamination runs very deep, but that this, far from invalidating his work, is central and definitive to its distinction.

Hitchcock: Method and Thematic

One way (there are of course others) of defining the immense value of Hitchcock's work is to examine the ways in which it is pervaded on every level by fascist tendencies to a degree of clarity and explicitness unequalled (so far as I am aware) in the work of any other Hollywood filmmaker, and then go on to examine the ways in which those tendencies are exposed, worked through and denounced within the films' thematic. We have here something very different from what one might term the ''casual fascism'' of so much mainstream contemporary Hollywood cinema, which the complicit spectator can enjoy without a twinge of conscience, and equally different from the explicitly anti-Fascist films of the 1940s, which gave the spectator a reassuring sense of being ''on the right side.'' Hitchcock, on the contrary, disturbingly involves the spectator in the lure of tendencies, the seductive power of which is quite frankly admitted (they are, after all, initiated at birth, when the newborn infant is slapped on the ass, then bundled up in wrappings that constrain all movement, and developed continuously throughout childhood, a period during which issues of power and powerlessness are central to human experience as we know it), before the consequences of the seduction are confronted.

It seems clear that the fascist tendencies in Hitchcock arose from neurosis, and certainly not from any political convictions. He seems never to have associated them on any conscious level with Fascism, to which he was strenuously opposed. Yet his preoccupation with control, and the corresponding dread of its loss, undoubtedly amounted to an obsession and must be read as a form of paranoia. It is evidenced in every aspect of his method: in his approach to production work (particularly script writing, shooting, and editing), and in his attitude to actors, although his practice in such things is a more complex matter than his much-quoted statements (often deliberately hyperbolic and provocative) would suggest.

Script/Shooting/Editing

Hitchcock claimed repeatedly that the actual shooting of a film was really somewhat boring and mechanical: he had the entire film in his head, shot by shot, when the shooting script was completed. This view gains some support from Andre Bazin's testimony that, when he visited the set (on location in the South of France) of *To Catch a Thief*, Hitchcock appeared quite uninterested in what was going on and was happy to sit and chat while the action was staged and filmed.[2] (Bazin, film theory's staunchest devotee of *mise-en-scène*, was predictably appalled). However, the scene in question involved a simple chase through a flower market, and Hitchcock was working with a team of technicians in whose professionalism he could have complete confidence. Would the story have been quite the same had Hitchcock been working on one of the intimate scenes between, say, Joseph Cotten and Teresa Wright in *Shadow of a Doubt*, Grant and Bergman in *Notorious*, Stewart and Novak in *Vertigo*, Perkins and Leigh in *Psycho*? (Further, although I'm afraid equally inconclusive, consideration of this will follow in my discussion of Hitchcock and actors).

The practice of storyboarding (which Hitchcock seems to have carried further than any other director) is another obvious aspect of this obsession for control: ideally, he wanted every image—framing, direction of movement or the look, composition—drawn on paper before it was transferred to the camera. ("Ideally" here is intended to acknowledge the evident impossibility of carrying this to perfection, the variables of shooting being infinite; again what is to be stressed is the inevitable limit of control). Also relevant is his repeatedly expressed preference for shooting in a studio rather than on location (which may also partly account—aside from interests of economy—for the frequent use of often somewhat "clunky" back-projection, although the practice was certainly not uncommon in classical Hollywood).

Actors and Cattle

Hitchcock's notorious remark (that he never said that actors were cattle, he only said they should be *treated* like cattle) has of course to be taken with more than a few grains of salt: it is contradicted by the very large number of remarkable performances and complex characterizations in the films. Yet the fact that he made the remark at all (and with evident, if again hyperbolic and provocative, pride and satisfaction) is highly suggestive. What exactly he meant seems illuminated by the testimony of Kim Novak and Janet Leigh, who were responsible for two of the many unforgettable performances in his films: both have expressed their pleasure in working for Hitchcock because of the unusual amount of freedom he gave them in interpreting their roles, so long as they "made their marks" and turned their heads in the right direction. The cattle analogy works well enough here: so long as the animals go their predetermined routes (across the prairie, toward the milking-shed, into the slaughterhouse . . .), the good herdsman lets them alone to express themselves as they please. Again, however, more grains of salt: this helps to explain the occasional bad performances, from unresponsive or limited actors (the two leads in *Saboteur* for example, or three of the four leads in *Stage Fright*), but it emphatically does *not* explain the great ones. It is impossible to believe that Novak's Judy/Madeleine was entirely her own unguided invention—not because one doubts Novak's ability and intelligence, but because it is so integral, moment for moment, to the overall concept of the film. I don't think this is contradicted by another favorite Hitchcock anecdote—that when Novak asked him about her motivation in a given scene, he replied "Your paycheck." It seems likely that Hitchcock did not (as Sternberg, for example, apparently did) instruct his actors directly, imposing on them his own demand for the one "right" expression or intonation and rehearsing them until they got it exact. Rather, he succeeded in powerfully communicating his own overall conception, drawing them into his vision, so that what they gave was a rich amalgam of what he wanted and what they individually contributed. (Again, such a method obviously wouldn't work with unresponsive or self-centered actors; it also wouldn't work if Hitchcock's own vision of the film was shaky or relatively weak, which may have been the case with *Stage Fright*).

Fascism, Fascist Tendencies, and Villains: Uncle Charlie and Brandon

Hitchcock's villains are quite diverse, but for present purposes two main groups can be distinguished; the one factor connecting the two is charm, but the charm is of very different kinds. One (relatively uninteresting) group might be exemplified by Professor Jordan (Godfrey Tearle) in *The 39 Steps*, Stephen Fisher (Herbert Marshall) in *Foreign Correspondent*, and Charles Tobin (Otto Kruger) in *Saboteur*. The charm of this group is superficial, a consciously adopted mask concealing *politically* evil intent: Tearle is the head of a spy ring, Marshall and Kruger are both Fascists masquerading as good citizens, a further demonstration of how easily and glibly Fascism (unlike fascist tendencies) can be discredited and disowned. They are played by British or European actors and they have aristocratic personalities, hence are automatically suspect, upper-classness being equally suspect in middle-class Britain and Middle America, the films' main audience. In short, they are stock figures.

There is, however, one highly complex figure who belongs in certain respects to this group: Phillip Vandamm (James Mason) of *North by Northwest*. We have again a European actor, and an emphasis upon charm, suavity, sophistication; there is also, obviously, an obsession with control and power. There is an important difference, however: although a spy for some at most only vaguely suggested foreign power, he appears—unlike, for example, Otto Kruger in *Saboteur*—quite innocent of any actual political commitment; his obsession with control seems more personal, its primary object Eve Kendall (Eva Marie Saint). He is, one might say, more fascist than Fascist, and has as strong a resemblance to Gavin Elster (Tom Helmore) in *Vertigo* as to the explicitly Nazi villains of the World War II movies.

Those in the second group, which chiefly concerns me here, are nearly always played by American actors and their charm is complex, insidious, and seductive: the most complete incarnations are Uncle Charlie (Joseph Cotten) in *Shadow of a Doubt*, Brandon (John Dall) in *Rope*, and Bruno Anthony (Robert Walker) in *Strangers on a Train*, although one must add (as idiosyncratic variant) Norman Bates (Anthony Perkins) in *Psycho*. Three characteristics distinguish them decisively from the former group: they are all (in various ways and to varying degrees) clearly vulnerable from the outset; they are *introduced* as morally dubious or worse (there is no surprise revelation), and they are neurotic, with hints of a (usually non-specific) sexual deviancy, not necessarily gay but certainly ''queer'' in the sense of that word in current circulation.[3] All three (and Norman Bates less obviously) are obsessed with power and control, and with the corresponding terror of impotence (the sexual connotations of the word seem appropriate). All three exert a fascination (on the other characters, and certainly on the spectator) that severely undermines the simple satisfaction we feel at the downfall of the villains of the first group. We may note here that a number of Hitchcock's minor villains share some of the same characteristics, especially the vulnerability: Rowley (Edmund Gwenn) in *Foreign Correspondent*, Fry (Norman Lloyd) in *Saboteur*, Keller (O.E. Hasse) in *I Confess*, Gromek (Wolfgang Kieling) in *Torn Curtain*. And we may also note that this catalog of male villains is in fact initiated by a woman. Although she never appears, Rebecca (in Hitchcock's first Hollywood film) fully embodies all the components: charm and fascination, sexual ambiguity and charisma, ultimate vulnerability (represented by her cancer). One may even claim a marginal fascism in her cruelty to the mentally retarded Ben.

If I concentrate here on Uncle Charlie in *Shadow of Doubt* and Brandon in *Rope* it is because they make explicit the link

between fascist tendencies and Fascism, in speeches delivered
when they get "carried away" and unwarily expose the
corruption that underlies the charm, and its roots in neurosis.

Uncle Charlie

Immediate context: Family dinner, complete with
"Sparkling Burgundy." Young Charlie (Teresa Wright)
describes (very pointedly) a supposed dream about her uncle
leaving on a train; Uncle Charlie realizes that she knows at
least a part of his secret. The conversation shifts to his
projected talk to his motherly elder sister Emma's "Ladies
Group," and what his subject will be:

> CHARLIE: Women keep busy in towns like this. In the
> cities it's different. The cities are full of women,
> middle-aged, widows, husbands dead, husbands
> who've spent their lives making fortunes, working
> and working, and then they die, and leave their
> money to their wives, their silly wives. And what do
> the wives do, these useless women? You see them in
> the hotels, the best hotels, every day by the thousands,
> drinking the money, eating the money, losing the
> money at Bridge, playing all day and all night, smelling
> of money, proud of their jewelry but of nothing else.
> Horrible. Faded, fat, greedy women . . .
> YOUNG CHARLIE: But they're alive, they're human
> beings.
> CHARLIE: (now in close-up, turning into camera, as if
> addressing the audience) Are they? Are they,
> Charlie? Are they human or are they fat, wheezing
> animals, hmm? And what happens to animals when
> they get too fat and too old?

Brandon

Immediate context: Brandon's party, David Kentley's
body in the chest on which the food (now mostly eaten) was

set out. The party small talk turns to movies, to which Rupert Cadell (James Stewart), Brandon's teacher at university, humorously expresses his intellectual superiority. Mr. Kentley (Sir Cedric Hardwicke) is becoming increasingly anxious because his son is so late. From movies, the conversation shifts to murder, the tone still apparently humorous: Rupert puts forward the theory of one's right to kill anyone who is behaving inconveniently—those before on in a movie line-up, recalcitrant, headwaiters, and so on—insisting all the time that he is quite serious, while preserving his easygoing, good-natured smile and manner. He sits beside Mr. Kentley, and as he ends his speech the camera moves right (on the words ''as such''), passing Mr. Kentley as he turns (uneasy at the conversation as much as at his son's failure to appear) to look out of the window, finally framing Kentley and Brandon.

RUPERT: Murder is—or should be—an art . . . and as such the privilege of committing it should be reserved for those few who are really superior individuals . . .
BRANDON: (cuts in) And the victims—those inferior beings whose lives are unimportant anyway . . .
MR. KENTLEY: You're not serious about these theories.
BRANDON: Of course he is . . . A few of those men of such intellectual and cultural superiority that they're above the traditional (sneering) moral concepts. Good and evil, right and wrong were invented for the ordinary average man, the inferior man, because he needs them.
MR. KENTLEY: Then obviously you agree with Nietzsche and his theory of the superman.
BRANDON: Yes, I do.
MR. KENTLEY: So did Hitler.
[Brandon instantly dissociates himself from the Nazis, but purely on the grounds that they were ''stupid.'' Then:]
BRANDON: I'd hang all incompetents and fools anyway; there are far too many in the world.

MR. KENTLEY: Then perhaps you should hang me, Brandon, for I confess I'm so stupid I don't know whether you're all serious or not.

A number of issues are involved here. First, neither of the speeches quoted above is strictly Fascist. Brandon's is Fascist in spirit, but it explicitly disclaims any political extension, being a personal apologia for his (assumed) right to murder anyone who annoys him by falling short of his (again assumed) level of intellectual development; at most it would be the philosophy of a few "superior" individuals, not of a political movement. Charlie's is grounded in misogyny, and so is even further from any directly political application (except of course for *sexual* politics, which demands a section to itself). Unlike, however, the general misogyny of which Hitchcock has often been accused (misguidedly, but not without some plausible foundation), Charlie's misogyny is severely restricted, directed against women of a highly specific age (old), class (wealthy), social status (widow), physical type (fat), character (silly), and social value (useless). The terms exclude both his niece and his sister, the former corresponding to none of the criteria, Emma only marginally to a few: she is plump and middle-aged, and her apparent foolishness is presented not as silliness but as the pathetic self-deception so common to pre-feminist mothers of nuclear families, whose sense of worth and meaning depends upon the credo that "It will all come right in the end."

Charlie's idealization of Emma, far from connecting her to the "merry widows," suggests that to him she is their opposite: a kind of touchstone of what women *ought* to be, endlessly nurturing and self-sacrificing, asking for no rewards. (Like all idealizations, this is a false view of Emma, the "typical" American mother whose typicality is characterized by a profound disturbance and unhappiness a little below the cheerful, all-accepting surface. The portrayal, with its remarkable insights, deserves to be placed beside the equally remarkable portrayal by Helen Hayes of the equally disturbed mother in Leo McCarey's *My Son John*). The "merry widow" member of her ladies' club, on the other hand, fulfills them perfectly, the film suggesting that she will be Charlie's next victim, and calling into question his distinction between cities and small towns. If Brandon's "fascist tendencies" are extremely close to Fascism, Charlie's are much more plainly and simply pathological. (His subsequent speech to his niece in the Til Two bar should be recalled here: ". . . the world is a foul sty . . .").

If both Charlie and Brandon are psychopaths, the psychological formations that have produced their conditions are clearly as diverse as the manifestations. The film places the blame for Charlie's sickness on two causes: explicitly, on a childhood accident (skidding into a streetcar on his bicycle); implicitly, on being spoiled and over-mothered (primarily, it is implied, by Emma who is therefore an innocent contributor to his condition). With a little ingenuity the two can in fact be reconciled. The accident (while clearly offered as a "real" incident) lends itself readily to interpretation in terms of Freudian dream symbolism: riding a bicycle/sexual activity, skidding and crashing/orgasm. Further, he was riding the bicycle (a Christmas gift) for the first time (he "took it right out"), and the photograph that evokes the memory shows a boy just around the age of puberty.

We have, then, the shock (for a "well brought up" child of the early part of the century) of discovering sexuality, combined with the film's clear enough hints of embryonically incestuous feelings for his sister/mother-figure (his first action on their reunion is to "unmarry" her, calling her by her maiden name and wanting to see her just as she was in the past). May we see Charlie's sexual (self-)disgust displaced on to his idealized Emma's opposite, the "merry widows" he murders? There is also his ambivalent relation to his niece, whom he also idealizes as an image of the innocence he has lost, although clearly relishes the destruction of that innocence: the word that springs to one's mind during the scene in the Til Two bar is "violation," and his first action when he arrived and was given her bedroom (plucking a rosebud from a bouquet) can be read as symbolic "deflowering."[4]

Charlie murders "silly," "useless" old women; Brandon, with his accomplice Philip (Farley Granger), murders a handsome young man. If the two characters are in some respects related (by the common quasi-fascist power motivation, a false empowerment compensating for the dreaded impotence, by their seductive charm and superficial self-confidence, by the fascination they arouse in the spectator and presumably aroused in Hitchcock), their specific psychopathological formations could scarcely be more contrasted. The more I think about *Rope,* the more it seems to offer itself for reading as a film about being gay within a certain cultural period and milieu. It is very curious that (as far as I am aware) Hitchcock was never asked about this. It is true that he seemed consistently reluctant to discuss his films in terms of their thematic content, habitually deflecting dialogue toward formal and technical concerns, and it is particularly a pity that Truffaut, granted the opportunity of a lifetime, made so little attempt to challenge this: in the celebrated interview book the discussion of *Rope* deals exclusively with the enclosed space, the long takes, the use of color.[5] Yet few doubt that Brandon and Philip are a gay couple, presented as such as explicitly as the Motion Picture Production Code (which forbade all reference to homosexuality) allowed. The "few" occasionally ask me, "Can you prove it?" and of course I can't: if I could, the film would never have been made.[6]

I have argued in the chapter on "Hitchcock's Homophobia" in *Hitchcock's Films Revisited*) that Brandon and Philip may not necessarily be lovers in the physical sense (David's murder can be read as a grotesque substitution for the sexual act), or, if they are, their lovemaking must be characterized by self-loathing and disgust, probably sado-masochistic (with Brandon of course as the sadist).[7] In other words, they would be viewing their condition precisely as their culture taught them to. It appears to be difficult for people today—and especially for gays of the present generation—to grasp this fully; as Brandon and Philip's near contemporary I can testify personally to the sense of total disempowerment with which gays grew up, the sense of being something less than fully human, one's inner being kept strictly unknown, or, if known, unmentionable.

None of the characters in the film refers even obliquely to the nature of Brandon and Philip's relationship. They couldn't, of course. Yet the silence imposed by the Motion Picture Code is merely the concrete manifestation of the silence (the ''gentlemen's agreement'') imposed by the culture. One might even say that Brandon and Philip are fortunate to exist within a relatively sophisticated milieu where they are neither ostracized nor excoriated. It is, however, clear that Brandon's malice cannot be explained purely in terms of his embrace of the superman philosophy: the film shows that it is directed not only against his immediate victim but against heterosexuals, and specifically young heterosexual lovers, against Kenneth (Douglas Dick) and Janet (Joan Chandler), where it takes the form of spiteful practical jokes (we sense, indeed, that Kenneth might easily have substituted for David as victim). Not every gay man, happily, has found it necessary to over-compensate for this sense of abject disempowerment with fantasies of the superman and the right of life and death over other human beings. I have never murdered anyone, but the self-disgust which was a determining aspect of my life had many consequences, none of them positive. Today, Brandon and Philip could join Act Up and march with the hundreds of thousands on Gay Pride Day. For my part, I have trained myself to feel at ease with referring casually to myself as a gay man before classes of a hundred and more students. (The students seem at ease with it too, although of course I don't know what they say to each other afterwards, and they have their grades to worry about). But in 1948 I could identify totally with Brandon's position (while being appalled at his actions), and I saw the film repeatedly, almost obsessively. I think I understand it (and Brandon) better than anyone else seems to, although what I understand may well be the film rather than "Hitchcock's intentions': perhaps *he* didn't understand it either, and preferred not to, seeing it as a somewhat academic exercise and aesthetic challenge.

There seems to me little doubt, however, that on some level (out of the many that operate within his great films) Hitchcock identified with Brandon, and also with Uncle Charlie. Indeed, in *Shadow of a Doubt* he seems playfully and teasingly aware of this, as one of his best and most elaborate personal cameos suggests. On the train to Santa Rosa (the place of innocence, to which both Charlie and Hitchcock will bring experience and corruption), Charlie lies concealed in a bunk, pretending to be ill. He is incognito, as "Mr. Otis." Hitchcock sits across the aisle from him, exactly parallel, incognito as an anonymous Bridge player. His opponents are a doctor and his wife. When a porter comes to tell Charlie they are arriving at Santa Rosa, the wife tells him her husband is a doctor. The porter says: "He's a very sick man . . . I haven't set eyes on him myself since he first got on the train." Similarly, we are not allowed to set eyes on Alfred Hitchcock: all we get is a view of the back of his head, and if we were not watching out for his personal appearance we wouldn't recognize him. The doctor looks across the table at Hitchcock: "Why, *you* don't look very well yourself." We see that his hand consists of all thirteen spades. Like Uncle Charlie (at least through the first part of the film) he is "holding all the cards." But they are the cards that signify death, and thirteen was the number on the door of Uncle Charlie's rooming house in New York.

Hitchcock's identification with Brandon is less explicit but more pervasively suggested: Brandon, like Hitchcock, is the *metteur-en-scène*, obsessed with the control he presumes to exert over every detail, both in the decor and in the manipulation of the actors in his macabre scenario. It seems to me that Hitchcock (whether consciously or not) acknowledges this partial identification in his own *mise-en-scène*.

Victor Perkins has described one such moment with his customary sensitivity and precision:

Early in the film Brandon, the dominant partner in the scheme, walks from sitting-room to kitchen carrying the murder weapon, a length of rope. The camera follows him at a distance and directs our attention to the exhilarated arrogance of his walk. It stops at the kitchen door, but Brandon walks through and in the brief moment of the swing-door's rebound we see him drop the rope into a drawer. Here the flashy precision of the camera effect informs our view of Brandon; the split-second control of the image becomes a projection of Brandon's evil assurance and calculation.[8]

Hitchcock's identification with Charlie and Brandon is never more than partial and provisional. It is qualified in three ways, of which the most obvious and least interesting is that they both get their comeuppance by the end of the film, this being inevitable and demanded by the Motion Picture Code. In Hitchcock's case, however, this comeuppance is never a mere afterthought, tacked on in the interests of censorship demands and conventional morality after the audience has been permitted thoroughly to enjoy the experience of identifying with outrageous antisocial behavior for ninety minutes or so of Saturnalia. This is ensured by the other two qualifications:
1. Identification, far from being established or even suggested at the outset, is initially denied. Charlie is introduced as a criminal hiding out (unsuccessfully) from the police in a dingy boarding-house. We don't know, of course, that he is ''the Merry Widow Murderer,'' but there is never a shadow of a doubt in the audience's mind of his criminality, the ''shadow'' of the title being cast over Young Charlie as her suspicions are aroused. As for Brandon, we know from the film's second shot (after the opening credit shot) that he is the murderer of a nice-looking young man (whom we may also have seen in the film's theatrical trailer, now available as part of an appendix to the laserdisc and DVD of The Birds). The principle on which identification is

built is precisely the combination of charm and the assumption of potency and prestige accompanied by vulnerability and the constant fear of losing it (the police surveillance of Charlie; Brandon's stammer): feelings rooted in the founding structures of patriarchal/capitalist culture.

2. The presence in each film of a counterbalance, an alternative identification figure: in *Shadow of a Doubt*, Young Charlie; in *Rope*, Rupert Cadell (though, in the latter case, less because he is a university professor than because he is Jimmy Stewart).

One might well argue that what makes *Shadow of a Doubt* unique in Hitchcock's work is the presence in a central role of an authentically *pure* identification figure, so that here weight and counterbalance are precisely matched. I don't think this effect is quite reproduced anywhere else in Hitchcock (the closest is Stevie [Desmond Tester] in the bomb-on-the-bus sequence of *Sabotage*), and perhaps this is why *Shadow of a Doubt* remains the most perennially disturbing of all his films (which does not necessarily mean the best). What disturbs us, surely, is less the revelation that Uncle Charlie is the Merry Widow Murderer than the gradual erosion of Young Charlie's innocence: if Charlie loves her (which he clearly, in highly complicated ways, does) he also resents her (as representing the innocence which he has lost and longs to recover). The scene in the Til Two bar is clearly a violation, a perverse and brutal enactment of the symbolic "deflowering" when he first entered her bedroom. Through its dual identification the film becomes a kind of collision course for all the contradictory imperatives and impulses of patriarchal/capitalist culture.

The dual identification in *Rope* is clearly quite other. As Brandon's charismatic teacher and transmitter of Nietzschean theory, Rupert Cadell is undoubtedly implicated in Brandon's crime, even though we believe, with Brandon, that Rupert would not have been capable of committing it. (One might see him as a transitional step in Stewart's evolution from the idealistic Capra hero to his "impure" roles in the films of Hitchcock and Anthony Mann in the 1950s.) This claim has been argued brilliantly and definitively by Victor Perkins, in an article originally published in *Movie* and reprinted in *The Movie Reader*, the strength of his analysis residing partly in the fact that the demonstration is grounded not only in the action and dialogue but in Hitchcock's formal procedures (the climactic positioning within the frame of Rupert as the third point in the triangle).[9] The final effect is complex: Rupert is at once a sort of accessory-before-the-fact, unwitting but guilty, and the impassioned and appalled denouncer of the crime, the obvious sincerity of the denunciation given an edge by the hysteria that became so integral to Stewart's persona, here expressing Rupert's half-awareness of his own responsibility. (Hitchcock provides a second counterweight to the lure of fascism in Mr. Kentley, arguably more impressive because absolutely pure, with no personal axe to grind. This is clear from the dialogue quoted above, but is given its force by Hardwicke's marvelously precise, perfectly judged performance).

Gender Fascism

It should come as no surprise—given the constituting inequalities of our culture—that the obsession with power and the correspondingly intense fear of its loss would find their strongest expression (beyond the purely economic) in heterosexual relations. It is a part of the supreme distinction of Hitchcock's work that in his best films all the little subterfuges, pretenses, minor concessions, by which men have disguised the fact, through so many centuries, of women's subordination and oppression, are ruthlessly stripped away, exposing the mechanisms whereby gender fascism has been perpetuated in all its ugliness.

Again, there is no ''pure'' denunciation, no self-righteousness, no attempt by Hitchcock to position himself outside ''all that'': the films' disturbing power derives from the degree to which he is implicated in the processes and brutalities (often reaching physical expression but primarily psychological) of male domination. They are denounced, not by the filmmaker from some lofty position of superior moralist, but *by the films*—by their overall movement, and through the complexities of identification upon which they are built, both structurally and in the minutiae of shooting/editing. If the films contain few suggestions as to how men *should* treat women, they are devastatingly eloquent about the disastrous consequences (for both sexes) of the ways in which they typically *do*, and they achieve this by involving the spectator directly in the sources and mechanisms of male egoism. I have argued this at such length elsewhere that it would be foolish to repeat it here in detail. I shall simply direct interested readers to the latter part of *Hitchcock's Films Revisited*, and especially to the sections dealing with *Notorious* and *Vertigo*.[10] I want also to refer them to Tania Modleski's *The Women Who Knew Too Much*, the best book on Hitchcock I have read (the chapter on *Vertigo* is obligatory reading for anyone seriously interested in Hitchcock).[11] Surprisingly, given the differences in our methodologies, Modleski's conclusions coincide to some extent with my own. Modleski's book and *Hitchcock's Films Revisited* were written at the same time, quite independently, so there is no question of direct influence either way). I wouldn't presume to summarize Modleski's argument, so the brief account offered here addresses only my own.

Central to it is the sense of Hitchcock's very strong identification, in many films running from *Blackmail* to *Marnie*, with the woman's position, the "feminine"—an identification which, carried beyond a certain point, can become terrifying for a man as deeply enmeshed in patriarchal culture as Hitchcock. The identification is therefore "answered" by a corresponding violence *against* women, the excesses of that violence testifying precisely to the intensity of the identification. The clearest, almost schematic, enactment of this psychological process is the first half of *Psycho*. If I single out *Notorious* and *Vertigo*, it is partly because they can be seen as complementary, in the sense that the spectator's primary identification figure in the former is a woman, Alicia (Ingrid Bergman), while in the latter it is a man, Scottie (James Stewart), yet both films carry what I have called gender fascism well beyond the point where its consequences are fully felt, its drives relentlessly exposed.

The processes whereby identification is built are far more complex than has been generally acknowledged; they cannot be reduced to anything as simplistic as "the male gaze," nor to the straightforward use of point-of-view shots. The latter cannot, in themselves, *establish* identification: Hitchcock commonly uses them to clinch it after it has been established by other, less obvious and obtrusive, means. A good example is the opening of *Psycho*: it seems to be generally agreed that Hitchcock constructs a strong identification with Marion Crane (Janet Leigh), but the first unambiguous point-of-view shot (precisely adopting the character's line of vision) occurs when, through the car windshield, she sees her boss crossing the street in front of her. Identification in the first part of *Psycho* is relatively clear cut; elsewhere it is far more complex. During the opening scenes of *Notorious*, Alicia is presented fairly consistently as the "object of the gaze" (that of the male characters, and also the spectator's), but it is *her* emotions and reactions to which we are given access, attaching us sympathetically. (Do we *really*, as some would claim, identify with the back of a man's head, before we are even certain that he is Cary Grant?). Here identification with the male gaze and emotional identification are established (by different means and on different levels) in terms of sharp conflict, a conflict which is sustained and developed throughout the film, accounting for the pervasive tension and disturbance it arouses. (Another, rather different, instance of a sustained dual identification is *Shadow of a Doubt*).

Hitchcock's strategy in *Vertigo* is different again. Here, identification can be established immediately, and instantly confirmed by point-of-view shots. We identify with Scottie's terror because he is clinging to a gutter at a great height, just as we identify with Fry at the end of *Saboteur*: it scarcely matters that Fry was marked as "villain" and that Scottie is Jimmy Stewart, although that helps. Yet our identification with Scottie throughout the first two-thirds of the film does not remain untroubled. To be sure, "Madeleine" is constructed as an ideal male fantasy figure, desirable yet mysterious, vulnerable, and helpless, profoundly in need of male protection, a "pair of good strong arms." But we are also made aware that Madeleine is just that—a fantasy— through the presence of Midge. Some of us may also become troubled by Scottie's tendency to dominate, to force perceptions and explanations on Madeleine, although we cannot but be aware that she invites this, apparently wants and needs it. There is, however, another dimension to our involvement with Scottie, the matter of knowledge: we are never allowed to know more than *he* knows, and share intimately in everything he finds out (more precisely, in everything he *believes* he has found out). It is the completeness of this identification with Scottie's restricted point of view that makes the sudden shift in our knowledge so shattering so devastating. It is not only that we are put in possession of knowledge that he doesn't have access to: the particular nature of the knowledge exposes the basis of Scottie's obsession as illusion, a skillfully constructed fantasy. (Gavin Elster has in common with other potent Hitchcock villains a clear hint of the diabolic: his intimate understanding of the workings of Scottie's psyche goes far beyond the factual knowledge of his vertigo into areas unlikely to be accessible to a mere casual "college chum.")

The last third of *Vertigo* remains, after multiple viewings, one of the most disturbing experiences in cinema, partly because of its actual, immediate content, but also because of the new harsh light it casts backward over the earlier scenes, revealing Scottie's concern for Madeleine, his desire to save her, as at bottom simply a more benign form of "gender fascism," the drive for power and possession. And, in the excruciatingly painful scenes in which he attempts to transform Judy into Madeleine, all benignity disappears, as the male desire to dominate women, to mold them into a desired submissive image, becomes fully manifest. The turning-point is of course the moment when Scottie leaves Judy's apartment and the camera remains behind. Up to that

point he has been present in every scene in which Kim
Novak appears, and we have watched her (whether as
Madeleine or Judy) strictly through his consciousness.
Suddenly our central identification figure is removed from
the image and we are left alone with a woman of whom we
know almost nothing except that she left Salina, Kansas, a
few years ago (as the character played by Novak did at the
end of *Picnic*). After Judy's revelation, our identification with
Scottie is shattered beyond repair: not only do we now know
things that he doesn't, but the knowledge calls into question
everything that has preceded it. After the letter scene
Hitchcock returns us, on the level of the gaze, to Scottie's
consciousness (he continues to be given many point-of-view
shots; Judy is permitted only one, of the lovers on the bank
beside the lake) but identification is split as it was in
Notorious, although much more drastically: our *emotional*
identification is with Judy, and Scottie's behavior (in any case
increasingly pathological) is subjected to an intense and
devastating scrutiny. We are never invited simply to despise
him, however: if his tormenting of Judy is brutal and
unforgivable, we are kept fully aware that it is the product of
his own torment.

Vertigo is now generally acknowledged to be Hitchcock's
most personal (as well as most profound) film. We don't
need scandalous anecdotes about his treatment of certain
female stars in real life to convince us of the inwardness and
intimacy of his understanding of the mechanics of ''gender
fascism'' and its masquerade as ''romantic love.'' If there is
a film that more movingly, ruthlessly, and beautifully
exposes its sources and its consequences, I haven't seen it.
It's worth remembering that Hitchcock didn't *have* to give us
Judy's revelation, its abrupt transformation of everything that
preceded it, and the shift in viewpoint that follows it: he
could simply have followed more faithfully the nasty little
novel by Boileau and Narcejac, *D'Entre les Morts*, from which
the film was adapted and in which the secret is kept until the
final pages, allowing us no insights into the female character
and no reflection back beyond a vague sense of disillusionment.

The Anti-Nazi Movies

One might expect, from Hitchcock's intimate and highly personal understanding of the power/domination drive and its consequences, that the wartime films dealing directly with Nazism would reveal particular insights into political Fascism. One would be, on the whole, disappointed.

The five war movies can be divided into two groups: the three set in Europe (*Foreign Correspondent* and the two short propaganda films in French, *Bon Voyage* and *Aventure Malgache*). and the two set either in America itself (*Saboteur*) or in a microcosm of American society (*Lifeboat*), the latter being by far the more interesting. The two French shorts are workmanlike pieces that more readily fulfil their limited function; *Shadow of a Doubt, Rope*, or *Vertigo* tells us far more about fascism. *Foreign Correspondent* belongs generically with the series of ''commitment'' films (in which a seemingly irresponsible American individualist is brought to recognize the necessity of engagement) produced in Hollywood between 1940 and 1944, of which *Casablanca* is the most celebrated and McCarey's ever-astonishing *Once Upon a Honeymoon* the best. I have not forgotten *To Have and Have Not*, but it barely qualifies, coming right at the end of the cycle when ''commitment'' was no longer an issue, and Hawks showing only minimal interest in the theme, marginalizing it in favor of his own idiosyncratic concerns. *Foreign Correspondent* has the distinction of coming right at the beginning (1940), before America entered the war and at a time when ''engagement'' was a matter of heated controversy. Not surprisingly, the film somewhat hedges its bets: it's final message seems to be ''Terrible things are happening—join the fight,'' but it is possible to read the message of the ending as ''America is the one safe haven left, and its function should be to remain that way.'' Hence the ''commitment'' theme (though clearly there) receives somewhat perfunctory treatment, Hitchcock using it as a thread on which to hang a series of his most brilliant set pieces: the ''umbrellas in the rain'' assassination, the extended windmill episode, the Westminster Cathedral sequence, the climactic struggle for survival on the wing of a plane in the middle of the Atlantic. The film belongs essentially with his picaresque adventure films, an undemanding ''entertainment'' rather than a serious challenge. As such it is continuously enjoyable.

Saboteur

"The normal are normally cold-hearted."
—Bones, the "human skeleton"

"This is an easy country to lose your way in."
—The blind hermit

Saboteur is one of Hitchcock's most underrated and neglected films. Customarily seen as a link between (but inferior to) *The 39 Steps* and *North by Northwest* because of what Andrew Britton and others have called the ''double-chase'' narrative (shouldn't it be *triple* chase?—the falsely accused hero pursues the villains to clear his name and is then pursued by the police, but he is also pursued, in turn, by the villains, who see him as a threat), it has more in common thematically with the superficially very different *Lifeboat*. The neglect has perhaps two causes. Aside from the celebrated Statue of Liberty climax for which it is mostly remembered, *Saboteur*'s set pieces compare unfavorably (in originality and ingenuity, and most of all in pictorial quality) with their equivalents in *Foreign Correspondent*. But its real drawback is the casting: Robert Cummings cannot suppress his apparently irreducible aura of blandness and smugness, and Priscilla Lane is perhaps the one female star from whom even Hitchcock could not elicit an interesting performance.

One might posit, tentatively (as it is purely speculative), that Hitchcock, confronted with the political realities of Fascism, temporarily repressed his habitual fascination with power/domination (it would scarcely have been possible for him, had he even wanted to, to make a film in the 1940s in which the audience is subtly drawn into and identified with Nazism in order to be punished for the identification, although *Lifeboat* comes dangerously close). He therefore turned his perennially subversive attention elsewhere, toward his newly adopted country America, on which the films can be read as a devastating assault. Their acceptance (precarious, in the case of *Lifeboat*) by the American public is quite remarkable.

Identification in *Saboteur* is not primarily with power (the film's Fascists are generally unattractive, although Tobin holds a certain allure) but with its victims: a hero under threat from the film's first minutes right up to its last, and finally Fry, our sense of his helplessness and terror intensified by the smug confidence he has displayed throughout. Aptly named, he dwindles from the creator of the immense conflagration that is the narrative's starting-point to mere ''small Fry'' (Pat [Priscilla Lane]: ''Fry . . . he's so *small''*). The film gradually reveals that power in America is *literally* Fascist: all the rich and powerful are committed to Fascism, and the police are their support (the cops believe the wealthy Tobin unquestioningly and refuse even to listen to the factory worker Barry Kane (Robert Cummings); the sheriff Pat runs to after escaping from Soda City is ''a particularly good friend of the Nazis''). Mrs. Sutton's elaborate ''charity affair'' is a front for a Fascist organization and, presumably, a means of supplying it with funds, while her guests are either Fascists or mindless dupes. Even Pat is, if not a dupe, then initially incapable of recognizing Barry's honesty and innocence.

Most interestingly, Hitchcock presents his Fascists and their saboteurs as perfectly ''normal'' good citizens, committed to the ideal of the American family. Tobin just adores playing with his little granddaughter; Freeman (another apt name) wants Barry to admire the photograph of his two kids; the saboteur in the ''American Newsreel'' office (another Fascist front) has ''promised to take my kid sister to the Philharmonic,'' and so hopes the ship they are blowing up will sink quickly. Mrs. Sutton, while not explicitly connected to any family, is clearly one of the pillars of New York society.

Conversely and without exception, all the film's sympathetic characters, all those who believe in and help Barry, are outsiders to American bourgeois culture: the truck driver who gives him a lift and subsequently deceives the police to enable him to escape; the blind hermit (a clear debt to *The Bride of Frankenstein*) who, possessing the sixth sense movies habitually attribute to the blind, understands immediately that he is innocent; above all, with the exception of the midget, who is a miniature Fascist, the circus ''freaks,'' the ultimate outsiders, who, although divided amongst themselves, by democratic vote decide to conceal him from the police and lie for him. Given Hitchcock's habitual skepticism toward ''normality,'' one might connect Bones' statement that ''The normal are normally cold-hearted' to his subsequent pronouncement: ''In this situation I find a parallel for the present world predicament. We stand defeated at the outset.''

Lifeboat

In the context of the Hitchcock *oeuvre*, *Lifeboat* has generally been regarded as something of a ''sport'' (in the botanical sense), a project motivated primarily by interests of topicality, little more than an interesting footnote to his career. Insofar as it has been regarded as central, it is (with Hitchcock's encouragement) on strictly formal grounds: the challenge of shooting in a severely restricted space while remaining ''cinematic'' (compare, most obviously, *Rope* and *Rear Window*, but also *Dial M for Murder* and *Under Capricorn*). It seems to me to occupy an important position among his dozen most important films, both for its intrinsic achievement and for what it contributes to everything the name ''Hitchcock'' means today; and it is the one film that enables me to draw together the disparate threads of this discourse, finally reuniting Fascism and fascism.

The question of identification is again crucial, and helps to define *Lifeboat*'s distinctness from any other Hitchcock film. Again, his intention can be discerned from his own cameo, one of his wittiest and most ingenious: the advertisement for "Reduco" in a newspaper, exhibiting a (relatively) slender Hitchcock next to the familiar fat one, slimmed down presumably as a result of depriving himself of food. It is his signal that his identification here is with the survivors (*all* the survivors), who are perilously short of food and water and (by the film's end) close to extreme starvation. Depending on how one understands the term, one could say either that the film forbids identification altogether (no one is singled out in the manner of Bergman in *Notorious* or Stewart in *Vertigo*), or that identification is dispersed throughout the lifeboat's passengers, that it flickers intermittently from character to character, each of whom elicits a degree (usually transitory) of sympathy or admiration. In fact (with the possible exception of Mrs. Higley (Heather Angel), who commits suicide early in the narrative) every character is undercut, all are subjected to an astringent scrutiny and criticism.

The scenario offers numerous possible identification figures, of which the least probable is Mr. C.J. Rittenhouse (Henry Hull)—" 'Rit' to you"—the oil tycoon, to whom I shall return later. Most obviously, there are the two tentatively formed "romantic couples," neither of which is likely to strike us as particularly romantic. First (because they are "lead" rather then "supporting" characters) Constance Porter (Tallulah Bankhead), the tough career woman and star reporter, and Kovak (John Hodiak), the Communist stoker. We understand from the outset that the relationship has no possible future and that its powerful erotic charge is based upon challenge and a sort of fascinated mutual contempt (as the psychiatrist tells us in *Bringing Up Baby*, "the love impulse frequently expresses itself in terms of conflict"). Kovak could be the film's hero (the U.S.S.R. being at that time an ally), were it not for his ruthlessness, brutality, and readiness to take command in a way that constitutes an affront to the democratic system; if it seems to us today, in retrospect after the McCarthy period, audacious to make a Russian Communist a potential hero-figure, it was perhaps more audacious in 1943 to suggest that Communism under Stalin had become merely another form of Fascism.

Connie could be its heroine were it not for her irresponsibility, her assumption that a "story" has clear priority over human feeling, and her commitment to such accoutrements as jewelry and mink coats. (The narrative systematically deprives her of all of them and thus humanizes her, but Hitchcock is clear-sighted—or, if you are sentimental, cynical—enough to see that she returns to her earlier persona at the imminence of rescue). Their relationship is summed up in the passionate, but frantic and desperate, kiss at the moment they think the lifeboat is going under in the storm and they are both about to die, an extraordinary moment that simultaneously celebrates the urge to live and defines the only conditions under which they can come together.[12]

The other couple, "Sparks" (Hume Cronyn) and Nurse Mackenzie (Mary Anderson), *do* appear to have a potential future: unlike Connie and Kovak, they are ideally matched (in contemporary terms they must have signified the alliance of America and Britain). Hitchcock gives full credit to their decency, their humanity, their gentleness, but he also (being the cinema's great realist, skeptic or cynic, as you choose) makes us aware of their ineffectuality. Sparks, who is (as Kovak asserts) the most qualified to take charge and chart the course, refuses such a responsibility, saying that he has "no executive ability'; Nurse Mackenzie explicitly disclaims any political awareness whatever ("I don't understand any of it. I don't understand people killing each other")—she has enlisted as a nurse solely in order to put the injured back together. At the film's climax she also betrays her own principles, in one of the film's most shocking moments.

Gus (William Bendix), the "jitterbug" with the severely injured leg, Sparks's American counterpart as a working-class man, although quite unlike him in character and level of awareness, shares this humility: Kovak's first choice for "skipper" (on the very shaky grounds that he is an "able" seaman) he reacts to the suggestion with astonishment,

instantly denigrating himself ("I'm a *dis*abled seaman").
While he elicits compassion, he also elicits, in about equal
measure, annoyance, and it is difficult for viewers to
dissociate themselves from Connie's well-meant but
patronizing attitude toward him; certainly, he is not an
identification-figure.

Startling as it may seem, perhaps the most plausible
identification-figure in the entire film is Joe (Canada Lee), the
black steward. That he comes so close is underlined by the
way in which he is regarded by the film's two most socially
privileged characters, the "underdog" being one of the most
elementary identification-figures: Connie Porter has nick-
named him "Charcoal," and Rittenhouse habitually (until at
last corrected) addresses him as "George." Furthermore, Joe
is consistently treated as an outsider to "democratic"
American capitalism, which the film consistently deconstructs.
In one of the film's many remarkable moments (but the more
times I see it the more *every* moment seems remarkable), it is
the leading exponent of "democratic capitalism," Mr.
Rittenhouse (all these other nice people having failed to
notice), who suggests that "George" might have a vote as to
whether or not they throw Willy overboard; his response is
a surprised "Do *I* get to vote too?" followed by "Guess I'd
rather stay out of this." This is very different from Nurse
Mackenzie's pacifism (which is based on political ignorance
rather than enlightened feminist commitment): Joe has been
raised to know that he is not expected to have a voice in any
political decisions. He continues to be treated as a servant by
all the other characters (even the gentle working-class
Sparks), and when he at last (in the film's final third) joins
spontaneously in the "white" conversations, it is with
reference to that common cultural refuge of American blacks,
the one area from which they have not felt excluded, sports
("Pittsburgh's the team to watch"). He becomes an active
participant in events only after his past career (pickpocket)
has been exposed: it is Joe who is enlisted to "lift" Willy's
compass, and who, at the film's climax, grabs his secret
water flask from "right under his shirt."

Joe, however, is also undercut, and in the one scene where he "takes over": the burial at sea of Johnny, Mrs. Higley's baby. Rittenhouse ("Well . . . I suppose any prayer will do") has begun Psalm 23, but falters after the first lines; Joe (his head entering the frame from screen right in close-up) completes the recitation, reminding us that religion has traditionally been another refuge of American blacks from the systematic deprivations of capitalist democracy. But Hitchcock does not leave it at that: immediately after the final lines ("Surely goodness and mercy shall follow me all the days of my life; and I shall dwell in the house of the Lord forever"), the camera tracks in to a medium close-up of Mrs. Higley, her face fixed in an expression of despair and torment, arms still extended as if still holding her baby, a figure whom goodness and mercy have conspicuously *not* followed, and whose subsequent suicide merely confirms the absoluteness of her despair. If the staging of the scene of the baby's burial appears to elicit from the audience a sentimental response, this is subsequently undercut by the remaining passengers' response to the death of his mother: no ceremony, no prayer, just the swift slicing of the rope that holds the body to the lifeboat.

One might view *Lifeboat* as a cinematic kaleidoscope: the perspective changes at every turn of the narrative. But a kaleidoscope requires a center from which it makes some sort of sense, and the center of *Lifeboat* is the U-Boat captain Willy (Walter Slezak). Superficially, he is another of Hitchcock's charming villains ("That one may smile and smile and be a villain"), although the infinitely tougher Hitchcock does not succumb to Slezak's charm to the degree McCarey did in *Once Upon a Honeymoon* (Willy never reminds one of Oliver Hardy). The film establishes an extremely complex relationship to him, both our own and the other characters' (the two are not identical). When he first appears, we are offered, through the various dramatized reactions, a spectrum of attitudes from which to choose, ranging from "Throw him overboard," through instinctive compassion, to Rittenhouse's notion that he might be reformed, reconstructed, and taught "the American way." He may seem initially to embody something of the seductive charms of a Brandon or an Uncle Charlie, and Hitchcock shows him seducing the other survivors in precisely this manner, but for the audience any such possibility is undercut early on, before he is exposed as the captain of the U-boat: while, after the baby's burial at sea, we may be invited to view the characters' behavior as "sentimental," we are clearly *not* asked to associate ourselves with his vast yawn of boredom as they tie Mrs. Higley down to prevent her from following her child overboard. From that moment on there is no question of identification with him, and when he becomes strategically ingratiating we see through him even when the characters don't.

Hitchcock, in fact, uses Willy increasingly to distance us farther from the Americans, by letting us in to Willy's secrets: we know long before they find out that he has a compass, and subsequently a water supply; we are even allowed to suspect that he understands English, when (shortly before the amputation of Gus's leg), he seems to be responding to a remark by Nurse Mackenzie. And, most disturbingly, we can't help admiring him even in his duplicity and callousness: he is stronger, both mentally and physically, than any of the other passengers, with a stamina that derives not only from his secret supplies but from what he refers to as "right living"—the Nazi discipline; his cunning, foresight, and pragmatism are precisely the qualities needed for survival. Yet an indispensable component of the seductiveness of Charlie and Brandon is their patent vulnerability, and this Willy (at least until quite late in the film) entirely lacks; even in his death (horrifying as it is) he conspicuously lacks pathos, a "human" dimension we know he would repudiate. His chief function is quite other: he is the magnet that attracts and organizes the dispersed particles of potential American Fascism.

One way (there are many) of looking at *Lifeboat* is to see it as a development of the essential theme of *Saboteur*: that "capitalist democracy" is a contradiction in terms, that such a "democracy" can never be based upon "government by the people for the people . . ." but will inevitably degenerate into "government by the rich and powerful for the rich and powerful," and thereby, with the same inevitability, gravitate toward Fascism. The Americans of *Lifeboat* are not members of an explicitly Fascist conspiracy, but only Kovak (the only one supported by an alternative and adversarial political ideology) is able to see through Willy from the outset. Of the rest, the rich are irresistibly drawn to and seduced by Willy's charisma, his authority, his certitude, while the less privileged are rendered impotent by their deeply indoctrinated sense of humility and inferiority. Hence, Willy's most enthusiastic supporters are Connie and Rittenhouse.

One of the film's central paradoxes is that it is the latter who speaks most explicitly and confidently for "the American way"; another is that it is Connie (the film's ostensible "heroine" insofar as it can be said to have one) who is Willy's most fervent supporter, even after she has intuited that he was the U-boat's captain and therefore knows that he has already lied to them. It is Rittenhouse who, after insisting upon a democratic vote (in which even a black man should have a voice, even if "Rit" can't remember his name), automatically takes over, allotting everyone his/her appropriate duty. The less privileged are unable to protest openly, but can grumble among themselves (Nurse Mackenzie, quietly: "Who elected Mr. Rittenhouse?"; Sparks: "Mr. Rittenhouse"). But, when it comes to plotting the course (not merely of the lifeboat, perhaps, but the "course" of the American future), Rittenhouse is helpless; it is Connie who appeals to Willy for a decision, which Rittenhouse then accepts, despite Kovak's objections. Kovak challenges his assumption of authority, and this leads to a debate as to who should be the "captain." Connie supports Rittenhouse ("He owns a shipyard"; Kovak: "Has he ever been in it?"), then transfers her vote to Willy (whom she now tricks into revealing himself as a "real" captain), Rittenhouse seconding her. Kovak takes over, abruptly and peremptorily, his *coup* ratified by a quick referendum in which Rittenhouse, with his "official" commitment to democratic process, casts the decisive vote: "Well, if the rest agree . . ." As he speaks the words we see Joe in the background of the shot, unasked, ignored, and the full force of his earlier "Do I get to vote too?" becomes apparent.

The remainder of the film is structured upon two contrary developments which partly overlap: that whereby Willy takes over the boat, and that whereby the others see through him and eventually kill him. The former culminates *after* the discoveries that Willy has a compass and speaks English, when, after the storm that destroys not only the remaining food and water supplies but the mast, Willy personally rows the boat toward the German supply ship; the latter culminates in Willy's death, after the discovery that he made no attempt to save Gus when he went overboard (they never find out that he pushed him) and, unforgivably, that he has water. We can trace the steps in this double movement:

The amputation. Is the amputation of Gus's leg necessary? Hitchcock leaves it ambiguous. Nurse Mackenzie examines the leg, and her reaction suggests the seriousness of its condition, but it is only Willy who instantly insists that it must be removed. Hitherto relegated to an ignominious position in the boat, and denied a voice despite the support of Connie and Rittenhouse, he is quick to make the most of his opportunity to establish himself: as a surgeon in civilian life (I take it we believe this, although we only have his word for it?), he is the only one qualified to carry out the operation. Its apparent success is his first step in gaining general respect and acknowledgment.

The course. From the moment when he is exposed as the U-boat's captain, Willy consistently asserts his knowledge of the correct course to Bermuda, but is initially overruled by Kovak, who follows the course suggested by Sparks. After the operation, his strategy is to continue to undermine all confidence that the course adopted is correct, until, finally, the only passenger who supports Kovak is Gus, whose opinion is clearly based upon allegiance to a "buddy" and has no rational backing. So even Kovak capitulates ("All right, Sparks. Follow the German's course"). The "German's course," it turns out, is the direct one to a Nazi supply ship. *Storm: Willy Takes Control.* It is Sparks's recollections of a nocturnal conversation with the ship's navigator (the indirect product of his sudden intimacy with Nurse Mackenzie) that lead to his realization that they are headed in the wrong direction; this leads in turn to Alice's memory of Willy examining his "watch" when he already knew the time, thence to the conscription of Joe as pickpocket and the discovery that Willy's "watch" is a compass. As the storm blows up, Kovak demands Willy's execution. Gus is swept overboard and Willy, the instant pragmatist, grabs the tiller and saves his life, the others all helpless. Willy, with renewed confidence in his multiple abilities (to dominate, to manipulate, to impress), shouts out to them in English ("You fools, thinking about yourselves. Think about the boat"). Rations and mast go over. Willy, the only one with the stamina to row, promptly transforms his nadir into his zenith: Hitchcock cuts to a calm sea, Willy rowing and singing popular German songs (including the Goethe/ Schubert *Heidenröslein*)—to Rittenhouse's accompaniment on Joe's "penny whistle." Everyone has accepted that Willy is right: Bermuda is too far. It is best to row to the supply ship. Only Kovak, now helpless, points out that they are now all Willy's "accompanists," and are on their way to a concentration camp.

Death of Gus; water. While Willy rows on, steadily and imperturbably, multiple squabbles break out among the "allies." During the night Gus, now delirious (Willy knows he has been surreptitiously drinking sea water and has not intervened), cries out repeatedly for water and sees Willy drinking from his secret flask. Gus half-awakens Sparks to tell him, but is by now quite incoherent; Sparks attributes his words to delirium and turns back to sleep. But Gus has become too dangerous. After engaging him in friendly conversation that leads to talk of Gus's girlfriend and jitterbug partner, Rosie, Willy persuades Gus that Rosie is waiting for him "out there" and gives him the necessary push. When the others wake up and find Gus gone, Willy tells them he went overboard in the night, defending his failure to stop him, Nazi rationalism thinly masked as humanist compassion: ''A poor cripple dying of hunger and thirst. What good could life be to a man like that?'' But then nature takes over: Willy sweats, and you can't sweat if you've gone without water. Sparks remembers Gus's nocturnal ramblings and Joe, showing more initiative than ever before, dramatically intervenes, pulling out the flask from Willy's shirt. Willy then makes one of his rare misjudgments, defiantly admitting that he not only has water but food tablets, and justifying himself with brutal Fascist realism and common sense (''You should be grateful to me for having the foresight to think ahead''). They beat him savagely as they push him overboard.

The murder of Willy is the film's most audacious sequence. Far from making it palatable to his contemporary audience by playing it as justifiable rage against Fascist dehumanization (hence downplaying or sanitizing the violence), Hitchcock stages it as his messiest murder scene prior to Torn Curtain's one great sequence, sparing us nothing. A number of aspects can be singled out:

1. Despite Joe's attempt to stop her (''Please. Please Miss Alice''), it is the gentle pacifist Nurse Mackenzie, the film's spokesperson for compassion who announced at the outset that she doesn't ''understand people killing each other'' and enlisted only to ''help put them together,'' who leads the attack.

2. Most prominent behind her are Connie and Rittenhouse. The point is clear enough: they are the two who were most taken in and they feel betrayed, made fools of. They are killing Willy out of personal pique.

3. When, after much battering with any implements ready to hand, they get Willy overboard, we see his fingers still desperately clinging to the side of the boat, with Nurse Mackenzie and Rittenhouse still beating his head. It is Rittenhouse who finishes him off, with (as a nice touch of some rough sort of ''poetic justice'') the boot discarded from Gus's amputated leg.

4. At the end, the camera pulls back to reveal Joe standing apart, the only non-participant: as an American black he knows all about lynch mobs. Which of course brings home to the audience precisely what is going on here: one form of Fascism is being answered by another of its manifestations. Again, for a moment at least, Joe becomes the nearest we are offered to an individual identification-figure—except that we, unlike him, are also deeply implicated in Willy's murder, the impulse to yell "Yes, go on, beat the bastard to death" being scarcely far below the level of consciousness. Again, although here in a way somewhat remote from the "gender fascism" movies or the seductive charm of Charlie and Brandon, Hitchcock is at once implicating us (and himself) in fascist tendencies in order to evoke a profound disturbance.

5. Willy, while he may never achieve pathos, reveals himself as human in his vulnerability, and it seems impossible for the spectator not to feel for him somewhat as we feel for Fry at the end of *Saboteur*: the moment when Willy, unable, for all his "superman" strength, to control physical reactions, sweats, immediately establishes a shift in our relation to him, and the shift is confirmed both by his "human" misjudgments and by his evident terror of death as his fingers cling to the lifeboat. It is important that his death is reserved for the film's climax: *Torn Curtain* (and our relation to its ostensible "hero") never recovers from the murder of Gromek.

6. We are left with the question of why, exactly, do they kill Willy? Because he killed Gus? But they don't know that—only the spectator knows it. Because, then, he didn't prevent Gus from going over? But the immediate provocation, the thing that can't be tolerated, is the fact that Willy had a secret supply of water and food tablets, which (presumably) he had in his possession before his U-boat went down, having had the foresight to be prepared for emergencies. Don't all the other characters (except Joe?) wish that *they* had thought of such things?—they were, after all, on a ship crossing the Atlantic in the middle of a ruthless

war. And, if any of them *had* had such foresight, would they
have shared their possessions? And, even if they had, would
they really have wanted to? Don't they, ultimately, kill Willy
because he was smarter and more ruthless than they were?
But then, doesn't his ''smartness'' derive from a totally
unacceptable ideology?

All this seems clearly *there* in the film. But there is one
more point the film can't afford to make too clear. Gus had
become a burden and a nuisance, his delirious rantings
painful; unless a miracle happened he would anyway be
dead before they were saved; his whole life seemed centered
on winning jitterbugging contests, so where would he have
been anyway with a leg missing? An even more disturbing
question is raised, implicitly, by this most disturbing of
filmmakers: How do we, as spectators, feel when Willy
pushes Gus overboard? Horrified, certainly. But also possibly
just a little relieved and released, because we shan't have to
listen to his agonized rantings any longer? So perhaps Willy
is, after all, somewhat closer to certain of Hitchcock's other
villains than I have hitherto acknowledged? Isn't he, like
Bruno Anthony in *Strangers on a Train* or Thorwald in *Rear
Window*, the agent who fulfills the repressed and shameful
wishes of the protagonists (here multiple), and arguably of
the spectator? Or, to put it another way, do we all secretly
wish to become (or are we in essence already) either Fascists
or fascists?—*Lifeboat* representing the point where the
distinction between the two becomes blurred. F(f)ascism is,
as I began by saying, inherent in our upbringing and our
conditioning. Hitchcock's films bring such questions—and
such questioning of our culture and of our selves—more
insistently and urgently to the surface than any others in my
experience.

How could Hitchcock end such a film, which is not so
much a statement as an amazingly complex and coherent
organization of contradictions irreconcilable within
capitalism? Just as they reach the supply ship, an American
warship comes to the rescue; everyone returns to normal.
Alice and Sparks are by now engaged; Connie (after losing

her last prestige symbol, her Cartier bracelet, to a fish) redoes her hair and puts on lipstick; Rittenhouse again addresses Joe as "George." But Hitchcock introduces two disturbances. First, the boat from the supply ship, filled with their supposed rescuers, helpless and presumably unarmed, is blown out of the water by a shell, answering the Nazi destruction of a lifeboat full of survivors against which Kovak protested so vehemently early in the film. Second, another Nazi, a survivor from the supply ship, surfaces from the water at the lifeboat's side like the collective unconscious of all its passengers, exactly as Willy did at the film's beginning. This time it's a young seaman, desperate and terrified, but still ready to pull a gun on his rescuers. The questions this most disturbing of films raises and orchestrates with such concentrated intelligence will continue similarly to resurface as long as capitalist culture continues to exist.

Notes

1. My first book was published as *Hitchcock's Films* (London: Tantivy Press, 1965). This was republished, along with a series of new essays articulating a different view of his achievement, as *Hitchcock's Films Revisited* (New York: Columbia University Press, 1989), further revised and expanded in 2002.

2. See André Bazin, "Hitchcock contra Hitchcock," *Cahiers du Cinéma*, 39 (October 1954); translated into English as "Hitchcock versus Hitchcock," in *Focus on Hitchcock*, ed. Al LaValley (Englewood Cliffs, NJ: Prentice Hall, 1972).

3. Obviously, at this stage of cultural evolution, "queerness" is inevitably associated with evil; for a positive incarnation of a queer character, compare Johnathan Schaech's Xavier in Gregg Araki's *The Doom Generation*.

4. If readers think this is just my dirty mind, I can shift the blame to Deborah Thomas, from whom I stole most of this material many years ago.

5. François Truffaut, *Hitchcock* (New York: Simon and Schuster, 1967), 130-37.

6. Arthur Laurents, who worked on *Rope*, suggests that it was clearly the intention of the writers to portray a homosexual on

screen. Hitchcock himself was thoroughly complicit in this, although according to Laurents, he never referred explicitly to homosexuality, preferring the euphemism "it." See "Working with Hitch: A Screenwriter's Forum with Evan Hunter, Arthur Laurents, and Joseph Stefano," ed. Walter Srebnick, *Hitchcock Annual* (2001-02), 3. In *Original Story by Arthur Laurents: A Memoir of Broadway and Hollywood* (New York: Applause, 2000), Laurents writes, "The actual word *homosexuality* was never said aloud in conferences in *Rope* or on the set, but [Hitchcock] alluded to the subject so often—slyly and naughtily, never nastily—that he seemed fixated if not obsessed" (124).

7. Wood, "The Murderous Gays: Hitchcock's Homophobia," in *Hitchcock's Films Revisited*, revised edition, 336-57.

8. V.F. Perkins, *Film as Film* (London: Penguin, 1972), 88-89. I am using this quotation here quite unscrupulously: Victor uses it to make a somewhat different point ("In Hitchcock's *Rope*, for example, camera movements are employed to deepen our knowledge of each of the main characters"). To digress here for a moment (because I think this is an important issue in art criticism), I think it is fair to say that Victor and I have a long history of mutual respect and distrust. I have learnt a great deal from his writings, but I think our ways of experiencing films are quite different and probably incompatible. His criticism gives the impression (which may of course be false) that he watches films with a kind of detached judgmental objectivity, which he then projects on to the director: hence Hitchcock, here, is not expressing identification with Brandon but simply using a particular technique to "deepen our knowledge" of the character. I, on the contrary, get hooked into a film as soon as it begins, and it takes an extremely bad film to make me detach myself. I identify instantly with whatever character(s) I am encouraged to identify with, and then, like Victor, project *that* on to the director, assuming that s/he identified in the same way.

The point of the digression is that no critic should ever be regarded as an oracle of truth, and this goes for even the most insistently "scientific" of semiotic/structuralist/psychoanalytic theorists. If the critic (as opposed to the casual reviewer) has an advantage over the half-inebriated viewer of a Saturday night Late Movie on TV, it is because s/he has seen a great many movies and spent many hours meditating on them and formulating what seems to him or her a responsible position. The importance of the

digression is that everyone (except myself?) seems to be looking for
a god (or goddess), and none exists, not Freud, not Marx, not Jesus
Christ, not even Pauline Kael. The correct attitude is precisely that
mutual respect (if it is deserved) and distrust (always) that I have
come to see as exemplary in the professional relationship between
myself and Victor.

   9. V.F. Perkins, "*Rope*," *Movie* 7 (February/March 1963): 11-13;
reprinted in *The Movie Reader* (New York: Praeger, 1972), 35-37.

   10. See "Star and Auteur: Hitchcock's Films with Bergman,"
and "Male Anxiety, Male Desire: The Essential Hitchcock," in
Wood, *Hitchcock's Films Revisited*, 303-35, and 371-87.

   11. Tania Modleski, *The Women Who Knew Too Much: Hitchcock
and Feminist Theory* (New York: Routledge, 1989).

   12. This recalls a similar scene in *Rich and Strange*, where a man
and a woman, after going through a lengthy process of getting to
know one another and experiencing many hard times, consolidate
their relationship as a couple with a kiss as they face (but then are
miraculously rescued from) death at sea.

JAMES M. VEST

Metamorphoses of Downhill:
From Stage Play to Cinematic
Treatment and Film

The developmental history of the 1927 silent
Gainsborough feature *Downhill* is underrepresented in
Hitchcock scholarship for several reasons. Primary
documentation is sparse, scattered, and difficult to recover.
Copies of the film remain relatively inaccessible for viewing,
and it counts among the least appreciated of Hitchcock's
works. Consequently, discussions of the transition from
source play to film have often been scant, generalizing, and
rather wide of the mark. Critics and biographers from Peter
Noble to Patrick McGilligan have suggested that *Downhill* is
merely a straightforward adaptation of a successful theatrical
production.[1] In counterpoint, Charles Barr and Ken Mogg
have prepared the way for reconsiderations of such claims,
and Michael Williams has set the stage for a thorough
examination of frequently overlooked contemporary
sources.[2]

Several of those sources can clarify the evolution from
stage to screen. One is a typescript of the play *Down Hill* in
the Manuscripts Division of the British Library. Another is a
preliminary cinematic treatment, "Down Hill," archived at
the British Film Institute. A third, a narrative synopsis titled
"Downhill," published to coincide with the commercial
release of the film, also illuminates the process of media
transposition. Finally, surviving prints of *Downhill* in the film
collections of the Museum of Modern Art in New York and

the British Film Institute document numerous accommodations made as the basic story line evolved cinematically.[3] In all versions, the narrative kernel remains essentially unchanged: unjustly expelled for a classmate's misbehavior and rejected at home, a British schoolboy named Roderick Berwick wanders through increasingly tawdry circumstances, first in England and then in France, until at last he returns for a second chance. However, the array of characters and arrangement of events differ considerably among the versions, as do details of the denouement. A comparison of these diverse renderings reveals substantial variations in terms of plot development, character portrayal, tone, and thematic emphasis.

The Stage Play: Down Hill

Although the film's credits begin with a somewhat misleading statement that the movie is "by David L'Estrange"—the collective pen name of Ivor Novello and Constance Collier—in fact it is a rather loose adaptation of their 1925 play, *Down Hill.*[4] The typescript of the play registered with the Lord Chamberlain's Office runs to 155 pages, encompassing nine scenes in three acts, followed by an alternate 70-page version of Act II. The protagonist's name varies with his circumstances: he is "Rod" to school chums, "Roddy" to actress Julia Blue, "Roddie" or "Roddy" to his family, and "Rodingo" or "Rigo" in Marseilles.

The play opens with a comic routine set "in a Public School" dormitory where Rod is cleaning up after a muddy soccer match while his roommate Tim Wakeley is cramming for a history test covering influential French women (*Down Hill*, 4). When Tim complains, "Montespan—Maintenon—which came first? Maintenon—Montespan?—Blast!" (4), Rod replies sardonically, "Girl friends aren't allowed in this seminary" (5). Their talk turns to a girl named Mabel and "that fateful Thursday" (8). Rod states glibly that when she tried to get him to kiss her he told her to "go have a nice clean wash" (8) and acknowledges that it was his idea that the two boys should break the school rules and visit Mabel (9). Shortly thereafter, when the pair receive a summons to the headmaster's office, Tim haltingly confides to Rod, "In there in the dark—I—we—" (11). To Rod's pressing question, "You didn't make a fool of yourself?" Tim can only nod assent (12).

In a well-appointed office, the audience sees Mabel for the first time as she is quizzed by the headmaster, Doctor Dowton. He asks bluntly "You're going to have a child?" and she replies "Yes," then adds "I'm not going through it without some help" (15). When the two boys arrive, Rod does most of the talking, explaining how he and Tim have met Mabel on three occasions after hours at the shop where she worked. Pointing to Rod, Mabel identifies him as father of her child and expresses her expectations for financial support (18). Doctor Dowton reluctantly confirms that he must expel Rod for breaking what he has called "a rule of God" (17) and hands him a pound note for train fare (19-20). The scene ends with the following exchange:

ROD: I can't come and play for the Old Boys, sir?
DOWTON: I'm afraid not.

In the boys' study, Rod prepares for departure as Tim agonizes, torn between guilt derived from remaining silent and fear of losing his scholarship if the truth were known (21). He worries that either course could put his "pater"—previously identified as a poorly-paid clergyman and father of five (8)—into a desperate pass (21). Rod reassures Tim and light-heartedly anticipates considerable free time for himself (22-23). He expresses concern only for his school cap with its institutional insignia, which he speculates should now be covered over. In a melodramatic move, he says he does not want to be like the infamous Derek Vane, who, having taken the rap for a classmate's indiscretions, had his school insignia ripped from his trousers by the headmaster, whose daughter had stitched it there (24-25). The Freudian connotations of that story would not be lost on subsequent adapters of this play. Neither would the allusion to the Old Boys.

The scene shifts (with no hint of the protagonist's transitional descent down an empty stairway or crossing of a lonely courtyard) to the Berwick home in Kingston, a *nouveau-riche* suburb of London. There Roddy playfully jokes with his ''Mummy darling'' and teases his sister Sylvia, who admits embarrassment at friends' discussions of his ''getting a girl into trouble'' and bluntly suggests he should be sent to Canada (29-31). When his mother learns he is spending his meager allowance on theater tickets, she slips him money (33), concluding ''You were foolish, Roddy, not wicked'' (34). Intent upon teaching him a lesson, his father volubly upbraids Roddy for irresponsibility and lack of discipline resulting in expulsion (38-40). Roddy protests his innocence and attempts to explain the situation, but his father castigates him for ''bringing this appalling disgrace on me—on all of us'' and accuses Roddy of lying (40-41). When a servant brings a telegram from Doctor Dowton explaining that Mabel has married and exonerated Rod, the incensed youngster blows up at his father for doubting him, hugs his mother, and storms out.

Act II opens at the New Folly Theatre where Roddy is a chorus boy working in a musical revue starring Julia Blue. Roddy is infatuated with the actress, who admits to being ''expensive and entirely mercenary,'' then tantalizingly ''kisses him a long kiss'' (58-59). The Stage Manager, Manton, tells her that Roddy is a nice enough fellow who will never amount to much as a chorus boy (62). Roddy's main rival for Julia's attentions is Captain H. ''Toggs'' Hunter, who wants to take Julia to Epsom for the derby (62). It becomes apparent, through a reference to the ''Old Boys,'' that he knows the school Roddy attended: Lambton (68). Julia prefers Roddy's company and dismisses the Captain. Roddy presses the idea of marriage upon her. She is flippant, claiming to have several beaux and a husband who refuses to divorce her (74-75). Insisting that there is ''no good resisting,'' Roddy kisses Julia passionately (80). She acquiesces as the curtain falls on this scene.

When it rises Roddy has conveniently won the Calcutta Sweepstakes and invested in an expensive flat in St. James Street, where he supports Julia in high fashion (81-89). Julia is watching Roddy's money dwindle when Tim Wakeley arrives. Roddy tells Tim of his trips with Julia to Paris, Monte Carlo, Egypt, Budapest (95). Now engaged to marry, Tim encourages Roddy to accompany him and his fiancée to Vancouver, where Tim plans to take over his uncle's school and Roddy could head the athletic program (96). Roddy mentions that his mother had died the day he won the sweepstakes and admits to Tim that since they parted ways his life has seemed to go "down hill" (97). Tim leaves without his friend. Roddy's financial situation worsens and he discovers that Julia has been unfaithful (101-03). Distressed to learn that Roddy is now penniless, Julia reminds him that the flat is in her name and throws him out (104).

An alternate version of Act II appended to the typescript rearranges some scenes while reinforcing the stressful nature of Roddy's relationship with Julia.[5] In this variant, Roddy is fired from his chorus boy job at Julia's insistence, then promptly wins the sweepstakes and supports her luxurious lifestyle for a while (186-88). Several new characters are introduced in order to establish Julia's passion for extravagant spending within the context of her coterie of party-loving lushes (189-97). At a high-spirited gathering Manton proposes that Roddy should finance his next stage production (191). After Tim's visit, when funds are exhausted, Julia kicks Roddy out, as in the other version (225).

Act III opens at the Café Boule in Paris where Rod dances for pay (105). He is "immaculately dressed," yet appears "dead white with an almost green look to his skin . . . listless, bored, indifferent" (106). Monsieur Charles, the cafe's "Maître d'Hôtel," confronts Roddy concerning the boy's drug habit (111-13). Roddy admits addiction to cocaine, stating "I need it badly" (113). An American girl, Vivian Dexter, arrives and is sympathetic to Roddy's plight (114). She tries to encourage him and pays for him to take dance lessons (124-26). The scene ends as a waiter surreptitiously presents Roddy with a white packet, a "nice fat packet . . . full of lovely dreams" (129), which Roddy accepts.

The next scene is set in Marseilles in a garret above the Rue Cytheria, a "sordid room looking out onto a sordid street" (132). A mixed-race, "Eurasian" woman named Malia is discussing the troubling case of Rodingo—i.e., Roddy—with a Swede named Jensen (134). Malia has been giving Roddy "coca" for four days and he remembers nothing. Stage directions indicate that "privation and drugs have turned him into some half-witted animal" (135). The Swede agrees to hypnotize Roddy. Under hypnosis, Roddy gradually recalls everything, through a mental fog in which his rantings link together schoolmates, family members, Mabel, Vivian, and Julia (136-38). As he gradually comes to himself, he moralizes summarily: "Down hill. . . . You just roll and roll and down you go" (138). Jensen reads a letter found on Roddy, indicating that Tim will soon be returning from Vancouver to the U.K. (140). Malia states that she was in America once, and arranges for Jensen to take Roddy to meet Tim (140-43). As Jensen picks up Roddy and carries him out, Malia sobs uncontrollably (144-45).

The final scene takes place on the Embankment near Waterloo Bridge on a frosty night (146). Jensen is sitting on a bench with Tim waiting for Roddy, who has slipped away. Tim tells Jensen that Roddy has inherited his late father's fortune. Roddy appears from the shadows, "faint with hunger" (149), and in despair tries to throw himself into the river (152). Tim prevents him and delivers an impassioned discourse on picking oneself up from the muck (153-54). As the final curtain falls, they are making plans to travel to Vancouver via New York, where Roddy hopes to see the Statue of Liberty (155).

A Cinematic Treatment: "Down Hill"

As the Novello-Collier play was adapted for the screen, much of its form and some of its dialogue remained, despite significant alterations of characters and events. Numerous modifications surfaced in a preliminary treatment, apparently the work of Ivor Montagu, who collaborated as creative consultant and associate editor on this film as he had on *The Lodger*. This ''proposed scheme for screen adaptation of the play *Down Hill*'' comprises a twenty-page double-spaced typescript preserved in the Montagu Collection at the British Film Institute.[6] A cover letter addressed to producer-distributor Charles M. Woolf of W. & F. Film Service begins ''I enclose (after a struggle) my revised version for screen purpose, of the play *Down Hill*'' to be considered neither ''a final version, nor . . . a basis of the working continuity'' (i). The letter communicates the adapter's discomfort with the play's implausible plot and dearth of physical action. It also conveys a marked concern for Roddy's character: ''If he is to marry a clean girl, we must keep him as clean as possible'' (i). Consequently the play's rambling structure and its ''extravagant and occasionally erotic emotion'' should give way to ''logical sequence'' and a ''constructive story'' (i). The letter ends with a strong suggestion that the film should incorporate, through ''the Phonofilms process,'' a recording of a ''flowing melody, in a minor key''—to be ''provided by Mr. Novello, on the lines of Lemaire's 'Andantino' ''—at various points in the story as both a means of establishing continuity and a ''useful publicity stunt'' (ii).[7]

In this ''proposed scheme,'' several characters are eliminated, while four new ones are introduced: Vivien Dowton, the headmaster's daughter; Sam Horton, Mabel's so-called ''brother''; the Marquis de la Vallière, ''a French aristocrat''; and Madame Beaupré, ''a Marseilles cafe proprietress.'' A note beneath the cast listing explains that twelve of the characters from the play have been ''dropped or changed into other characters,'' among them Rod's sister, the proprietor of the Paris dance hall, Vivian, Malia, and Jensen (''Down Hill,'' 1). A second note proposes that Mabel should be rechristened Minnie, and the name Minnie appears consistently throughout this treatment.[8]

The protagonist's name is now standardized to Rod, although he is referred to as Roddy Berwick in the listing of

Dramatis Personae. The expressed interest in sonorization leads to an emphasis on piano playing, rather than dancing. The headmaster's daughter mentioned in Rod's passing allusion to the Derek Vane story comes to life here and subsumes the role of the American girl from the play. There is no reference to the school cap, although that will resurface in the film. Characterization of family members and associates is radically reduced, and we are now privy to the schoolboys' contacts with Minnie in the back room at the shop where she works. Significantly Rod is portrayed as less of a slacker and complainer, and his parents are allowed to survive to welcome him home. Despite an ostensible desire to "keep him as clean as possible," the doping angle is accentuated. Positive references to the United States as a locus of hope are omitted in this treatment, as in the film.

In this adaptation the French segments receive special emphasis. Here the London theater scenes are missing entirely, and with them Julia and Manton, Rod's proposal of marriage, and his life with Julia. In her place is Vivien Dowton, refined and "persistently faithful" (9), who will follow Rod to Paris and eventually to Marseilles. The role of the shop girl is much expanded. Her departure for Paris now coincides with Rod's movements toward France as, simultaneously, her boyfriend Sam sets sail for Marseilles. As a result, the French scenes that dominate the second half of the story are reconfigured to facilitate the eventual conjunction of the principals' trajectories.

From the outset Tim and Rod's characters are amply developed. They are depicted as "school chums who fancy themselves to be men" and who together sneak out at night, drink beer, smoke, play cards with Sam Horton, and flirt with his "sister" in the "back parlour of a little tuck-shop" (2) in the seaport of Carfax. Minnie is actually Sam's mistress, and he is merely posing as her brother when in port between sea voyages. She is depicted as a "clever, non-moral sort of girl" who loves to dance, and Rod is a "consummately good musician" who enjoys playing the piano in the private quarters off the shop (a cue for the "flowing melody" indicated in the cover letter).

Sam plots with Minnie to compromise both boys. "An expert tatooist," he tattoos the initials of each boy on the right arm of the other as a sign of mutual devotion. During a thunderstorm Sam slips "something strong" into the two chums' beers, then cuts off the electrical power (3). Minnie can be seen first approaching Rod and being repulsed by him, then moving over to kiss Tim. When the lights come on, Sam accuses the boys of molesting Minnie and says this will cost them dearly.

The scene shifts to Rod's scoring a winning point in a soccer match. He is congratulated by headmaster Dowton and his daughter Vivien, then confronted by a sneering Sam, his menacing unnamed friend, and Minnie. In their dormitory room the boys debate what to do about this awkward situation and discuss Rod's special relationship, "rather more than friendship," with Vivien Dowton (4). Rod wants to "come clean" but Tim is worried about his scholarship; Tim's father is identified as "a clergyman in modest circumstances" (4). When they hear that Sam and Minnie are in Dr. Dowton's office, Tim offers to make a clean breast of matters but Rod insists they will stand or fall together.

In the headmaster's office Vivien and Minnie exchange hostile glances as Vivien leaves. When the boys arrive, Sam joins Minnie in accusing Rod of molestation and threatens blackmail (4-5). Tim attempts to intervene, but Dr. Dowton dismisses Tim's comments as representative of "chivalrous," but misdirected friendship (4). The headmaster decrees that Rod must take the next train home and names another boy to replace him as school head. As his schoolmates learn of Rod's expulsion there is general consternation and "affecting leave taking" (5). Ever supportive of Rod, Vivien suspects what is afoot. Rod leaves for the railroad station, driving Dr. Dowton's car (in anticipation, as the treatment notes, of subsequent scenes in which Rod is an accomplished driver). At the school's main gate, Rod is stopped by Minnie, who apologizes. She and Sam fight as Rod drives away (6).

In his "city office" Rod's father pays Sam five hundred pounds. Then, in their Kingston home and within earshot of servants, he expresses distrust at his son's protestations of innocence (7). Rod (in this version an only child and sole inheritor) breaks with his father and mother. She presses money into his hand as he departs. The scenario proposes that images of Rod on a cross-Channel steamer should be intercut with shots of Sam setting sail on the high seas and of Minnie boarding a boat train for the Continent to find work as a dancer. It specifies that a timetable of departures for France should dissolve into "Parisian views" concluding with images of Minnie being engaged in a dance troupe.

The scene then shifts to Marseilles to a dockside cafe run by Mme. Beaupré, a "stout, good-natured soul." There Sam's conscience gets the best of him and he sends a letter to Dr. Dowton explaining that "the whole thing was a frame-up" (8). Tim, who has won a scholarship to Cambridge, comes forward to confirm the facts of the case. Dr. Dowton and Vivien visit Rod's grief-stricken parents (9). Vivien admits that she loves Rod, who is now viewed as a hero for saving Tim's career, and she vows to search for him.

We learn that, under an assumed name, Rod has become a driving ace employed by an auto manufacturer to race on their behalf in the Grand Prix. Before a trial spin at a racetrack near Paris, he takes "a pinch of dope in order to keep up his nerves," even though a mechanic warns against it (10). The head of the motorcar firm personally reinforces the importance of winning this race.

We next see Minnie in her dressing room at the Theatre des Folies where, under the stage name "Miss Minnie," she has become the "première danseuse" and is known for her daring dresses and "exotic" style (10). She attends the auto races, accompanied by the Marquis de la Vallière, "a lively flaneur, who is a notorious gambler" (10). There her attention is riveted on the "new English motor-racing champion, John Carfax, who is Rod, of course," Carfax being the name of the town where their adventure began (11). Doped, Rod loses the race because of misjudgment. He meets Minnie, who recognizes him and invites him to the theater. Believing that his fortunes are changing, he buys a lottery ticket.

On stage Minnie performs a dance number (11-12). In an aside (13), the scenarist notes that her "dancing turn in the theatre," is "not absolutely relevant to the story, but would make a good spectacle" (presumably reminiscent of theatrical scenes portrayed in *The Pleasure Garden* and suggested in *The Lodger*). In her dressing room, she and Rod discuss their changed situations. He asks, "Was there a child?" and she responds, "Of course not" (12). Rod sits at her piano and she asks him to "play that tune." He accedes, but ends the rendition with a discordant crash. She "paws him and he suffers her caresses"; then, as he breaks free of her clutches, she says "something rude" about Vivien (12). Rod tells Minnie that he loves Vivien, then leaves "with a mocking air." On his way out he "has a comedy touch with Minnie's dresser," whom he kisses (12). In dismay, Minnie attempts to play "a note or two of Rod's tune," then breaks down weeping. When soon thereafter the Marquis asks her to marry him, she reluctantly accepts.

Rod finds a job working at a dance hall in Montmartre, the Bal Populaire, as "a kind of M.C. or manager, not a dancing partner," interpreting for the English-speaking clientele (13). The scenarist suggests that the dope theme could be included here and an American girl smitten with Rod might be introduced, as in the play: "The main point is to work in the entire background of a Parisian dance-hall (not a tough joint but a middle-class place), without degrading the character of the hero" (14).

Having seen Rod's picture in a motoring magazine, Vivien searches for him in Paris. There she interviews the head of the motorcar company who explains that he had to dismiss Rod, and directs her to Minnie, who is getting married that very day. Vivien contacts Minnie at her wedding reception. This is presented as a "boisterous scene" during which it becomes clear that the honeymoon will be in Monte Carlo and that Minnie is quite concerned by the gambling propensities of the Marquis. After a stressful private interview with Minnie and a consultation with the police, Vivien tracks Rod to his hotel attached to the Bal

Populaire (15), where Rod, who has won the lottery, buys drinks for all. Rod talks with Vivien in a room off the main dance floor (16). When he learns he has been exonerated and realizes the extent of her devotion, he kisses her hand and she strokes his head. He promises to accompany her home to England.

He insists on escorting her to her hotel on foot. His lottery winnings are still in his pocket. The couple are tailed by a big car containing three hoodlums. Rod sees Vivien to her hotel, promising to call for her the next morning. When he is alone, the men jump him and stun him "with a jemmy or something of that kind" (16-17). They take his money and drug him, then haul him off to Marseilles with a view to continuing to Algiers. When Vivien discovers Rod has gone missing, she contacts the proprietor of the Bal Populaire and the police before returning to England to update Rod's parents.

Rod is discovered on the Marseilles docks by Mme. Beaupré. "Attracted by his looks," she takes him in and cares for him (17). Sam learns that Minnie and the Marquis are nearby at Monte Carlo (18). When Mme. Beaupré takes Sam to see "her Englishman," Sam recognizes Rod's tattoo and realizes that Rod is unable to recall who he is or what has happened to him (19). Sam sends a telegram which Dr. Dowton shows to Tim, who immediately leaves for Marseilles. In Monte Carlo, the Marquis loses heavily at gambling. Sam and Minnie watch as the Marquis commits suicide with a revolver. Minnie leaves with Sam.

Back in Marseilles, Madame Beaupré explains to her customers that Rod has lost all memory (20). They are sympathetic in a rough way and encourage him to console himself at the piano. As Minnie and Sam enter, Rod plays the distinctive "Down Hill" motif and his memory is instantly restored. When he spots Sam, Rod lunges toward him with a raised chair. Tim arrives, takes the chair, and explains that it is thanks to Sam that he is here. There is a teary leave-taking between Rod and Mme. Beaupré, and "the final scene, at the Berwicks' home, follows conventional lines" (20).

This cinematic treatment emphasizes action and setting more than characters' motivation or development. Thematically and structurally, it posits France as a locus for exploration and experimentation, for risk taking, for reunions, and ultimately for righting wrongs. It establishes geographic and societal patterns that allow characters' paths to intersect across France throughout the second half of the narrative while proposing a simple, if arbitrary, way of restoring order in the end.

In this context, the scenarist is insistent about portraying drug-related issues: "We want to plant very strongly the temptation of a racing motorist to take dope to keep up his nerves. . . . The fact that Rod dopes may even be suggested in the dressing-room scene" (11) and also, "if desired," in the Bal Populaire sequence (13). This emphasis is countered in the Marseilles segments, where Rod snaps out of his amnesiac state through the influence of music and the ministrations of Madame Beaupré, who, unlike Malia in the play, does not feed his habit.

It appears that, probably during an early stage of the film's development, this "proposed scheme" was perceived as problematic and discarded in favor of a screenplay that was in many respects closer to the original stage version. The name Minnie disappeared along with several of the treatment's other innovations, including the tattoos, overt references to drugs, reunions in France, the suicide, Carfax, auto racing, and the attempt at musical sonorization. However, the idea of "good spectacle" (13) remained and was expertly developed in the filmed version.

A Pre-Release Narration: "Downhill"

Although the preproduction schedule for *Downhill* was tight (from December 1926 through mid-January 1927), multiple preliminary versions of the script may well lie behind this film, as for others. In the case of *Downhill*, the issue of authorship is made more than usually ambiguous by the film's opening credits, which emphasize both its direct connections to its source play and its distinctive screen adaptation: the main title card reads with deceptive simplicity "DOWNHILL by David L'Estrange," while a subsequent card credits the "Scenario" to Eliot Stannard.

Downhill was the fourth of eight Hitchcock films in which Stannard received screen credit as writer.[9] Although no copy of his "scenario" for *Downhill* has resurfaced—it may well have been lost in the catastrophic fire at Gainsborough in January 1929—the film itself suggests that Stannard's text was much closer to the original play than to the preliminary treatment. The extent to which Hitchcock and Stannard may have been aware of the treatment is unclear. Yet the filmed version is so distant from it as to suggest a lack of connection and perhaps even determination on the part of the Gainsborough management, if not the writer and director, to move beyond it. One can imagine reasons that might have been invoked: fidelity to the successful Novello-Collier original, especially since the co-author/star of that stage production would be recreating the role of Roddy for the film; technical problems involving, among others, the musical components emphasized in that treatment; its numerous improbabilities of plot and characterization; financial considerations for its exotic settings; and so forth. Although the story as filmed undoubtedly owes much to the richly creative Stannard-Hitchcock collaboration, in the absence of Stannard's screenplay, considerations of this phase of the project's development are necessarily limited.[10]

One can deduce certain facts about the missing screenplay and its evolution into finished film from a narrative recreation, in digest form, apparently derived from it and published to coincide with the film's release in late October 1927. A four-page "narration" entitled "Downhill" appeared under the byline of John Fleming in that month's issue of *The Picturegoer*.[11] "Narrated by permission from the W. & F. film of the same name" ("Downhill," 39), this summary of *Downhill* was intended to stimulate broad-based interest in the movie. The narrative was accompanied by a listing of the principal actors and their roles and also by five photographs with captions that solidified identification: Novello as Roddy, Isabel Jeans as Julia, Ben Webster as Dr. Dowson, Annette Benson as Mabel, and Robin Irvine as Tim. Hitchcock was not pictured, and his name was not mentioned.

Much closer to the stage play than to the proposed cinematic treatment, Fleming's condensation attempts to streamline the narrative, to provide continuity, to introduce lively dialogue, and to clarify motivation and causality. Its style is crisp and emphatic. This digest version telescopes events but also indulges in occasional saucy commentary, and even offers some peculiar twists not reflected in extant prints. Its succinct format allows the author to eliminate problematic or suggestive scenes or merely to hint at them, while giving the narrative a degree of consistency and focus, as well as a measure of spice.

As in the film, Dr. Dowton is now Dr. Dowson, and daughterless. Sam and the gambling Marquis are nowhere to be seen. The spendthrift Julia is back, in top form, as is her boorish male companion, now renamed Archie. Like Julia (and unlike the vagabond Minnie of the prose treatment), Mabel, her name from the play restored, never leaves England. In this version, as in the film, the protagonist is consistently called Roddy and the Old Boys prefer rugby. However, as in the play, Roddy has little direct contact with Mabel, his role being limited to that of a caring observer of a roommate's dalliances.

The defining features of the relationship between the two schoolboys are delineated in the opening phrases: "For Roddy life would always be a game; for Tim a task" (39). Mabel is identified as "the daughter of the proprietor of the tuck shop," who—in premonitions of *Waltzes from Vienna*—"played waitress" on special occasions, including the day of the school rugby match. Roddy's misapprehensions concerning his roommate's distracted state leave little room for doubt as to her condition (39-40). Her motives are made clear in the headmaster's office when, pointing at Roddy, she cries, "It was him! And his father's rolling in money—he's got to see me through!'' (40). And ''what could he say?'' except, ''Does this mean that I won't be able to play for the Old Boys, sir?'' (40). In this account, Roddy's departure from the school involves his descending a ''familiar . . . staircase'' but makes no mention of his crossing an empty courtyard, the film's dramatic overhead shot apparently being a Hitchcockian innovation not recounted in this synopsis.

In this version of events at home, Roddy's wealthy father awaits him alone, in his town house ''near the Park,'' telegram from Dr. Dowson in hand. Here there is no reference to a servant, a male visitor, or the mother, all of whom are prominent in the film. An irate Sir Thomas reminds Roddy that his ''grandfather's grandfather went to that school,'' and, as soon as his son mentions the waitress, exclaims ''That servant girl!'' (40). When Roddy pleads ''Hear my version,'' his father shouts ''Liar! . . . You have sinned!'' and peremptorily dismisses him (40). Pelting rain in the ''friendless street'' drives Roddy into a nearby Underground station, where he descends the advertisement-lined escalator murmuring ''Downhill! Always down!'' (40).

Fleming provides glimpses of several scenes that may have been scripted but omitted from the film, or incorporated in different ways. His account specifies that as Roddy moves about London he recognizes that he has no trade, that his ''marketable stock'' is low, and that occupations normally open to someone of his background are closed to him (40). Since he has a ''pleasing presence, a passable voice, a talent (of a kind) for dancing,'' he tries the stage and becomes a hoofer in a musical comedy called ''Kick High'' (40-41). There he encounters Julia and experiences ''pangs of jealousy'' as Archie calls for her and escorts her away each night. In this version Roddy keeps silent for weeks, until his godfather, Sir Roderick Kemper, dies unexpectedly, leaving him thirty thousand pounds.

Now Roddy dares to ask Julia out. Aware of the inheritance, she accepts. Since Julia is ''a particularly expensive friend,'' Archie agrees to this arrangement and hands Roddy Julia's bills to pay (41). She is shocked when

Roddy asks her to marry him. "Of men she had had many," Fleming explains, then adds, in sharp contrast to the play, "but never before had any of them said this to her" (41). Being ready to try "anything once," she accepts, and Sir Thomas sees the wedding notice in the newspapers. Roddy takes a sumptuous flat and furnishes it to Julia's tastes, which are "not necessarily his own" (41). Bills accumulate and he takes the matter up with Julia—proposing less expensive lodging and getting a job—but she is unsympathetic. He notices a man's hat and discovers Archie in the wardrobe. They fight. After the fracas, Julia kicks Roddy out. Entering the elevator he mutters bitterly "Always down, down, down" (42).

He remembers having visited, during a stay in Paris with Julia, Madame Michet's Dancing Saloon. He returns there and "for weary weeks" allows himself to be "rented out to foolish Parisiennes" (42). Without mentioning drugs or sex explicitly, Fleming cautiously suggests the unsavory side of this lifestyle: "At night there was forgetfulness—drink. . . . Other things . . ." (42). The film's episode with the faded poetess, apparently another Hitchcock invention, is passed over in discreet silence, and Roddy's departure from Paris is presented as through a mental haze: "How? Why? Well—why worry about it?" (42).

Fleming's description of events in Marseilles diverges significantly from the film, recounting several scenes absent from extant prints while ignoring altogether the dominant female character from the Marseilles sequences. Roddy is in a large port city three days before he knows it is Marseilles. He does not find it strange to sleep with dock rats (a nod at Novello's stage and screen appearances as "The Rat"). A "rough, vile voice" penetrates his stupor. It belongs to a "giant Swede," who is accompanied by a black man called Hibbert (42). They spend the night by the docks, eventually find work, and take up quarters in a "common lodging house in the vilest of the slums" (42). Listening to a delirious Roddy speak of his father, the two companions determine to return him to London, where "his friends will pay" (42). They manage to get Roddy aboard an "abominable" tramp steamer and eventually to his welcoming father who tells him "Tim Wakeley has cleared your name" (42). Fleming's account concludes with a short epilogue indicating that a month later Roddy was back at school "playing for the Old Boys" (42).

The Film: Downhill

The Gainsborough movie transforms a fairly static, verbose stage play into a kinetically oriented motion picture that differs significantly from previous versions of the story. Several action sequences are added at the beginning to establish background and mood. The opening shots, which depict Roddy's struggle to score in a hard-fought rugby game, accentuate the physical activity and corporal intimacy of the match and its aftermath. When tackled, Roddy hits the ground, tackler in tow, setting up a game-deciding play. Youthful spectators become frenetic, gesticulating wildly and waving their caps. In the victory celebration, Roddy is pawed by adoring fans as they lift him to their shoulders. Later in a changing room, a partially unclothed Roddy, framed by an opened door, grabs a towel to shield himself from Tim's sister's gaze. None of these scenes appear in earlier versions.[12]

Unlike its antecedents, the film offers substantial sequences in the school refectory and assembly hall, where bodies are tightly packed and physical contacts are underscored through shots amalgamating activities on several planes. These include exchanged glances, an assignation note, spit wads finding their targets, an awkward bump connecting Roddy with Mabel, and the madding throng at the assembly where Roddy is named school captain. There he is presented a special cap bearing the word "honour" on which Hitchcock's camera focuses ironically to underscore breaches of institutional and personal honor. Other scenes also feature distinctively Hitchcockian humor. The striking contrast between vivacious students and staid adults is reinforced through a running gag involving appearances of the spitball kid: exuberant in early scenes, where he is twice seen with a juvenile female pal, he reappears in the film's finale as a mustachioed "Old Boy" with the maturer young lady at his side.

Chief among the film's ironic, motion-oriented innovations is the memorable episode at the candy store, suggestively named Ye Olde Bunne Shoppe, where events leading to Tim's troubles and Roddy's expulsion are visualized cinematically. Hitchcock's film goes further than any of its prototypes in depicting physical contact, at once playful, sensual, and risky. His camera highlights the seductive dancing that occurs first in front of, then through, and finally behind a beaded curtain bearing an exotic floral motif. The film dwells on the candy shop scenes, depicting in considerable detail the touching hinted at in previous versions. In the film, both boys dance with Mabel. First it is the sure-footed Roddy, then the awkward Tim, who steps on her toe before eventually disappearing with her behind the beaded curtain. In striking counterpoint, scenes showing Tim and Mabel passionately kissing are punctuated by closeups of urchins' dirty faces in the shop's sales area and by extended coverage of Roddy's errors at the cash register, played broadly for laughs.[13]

Another major departure involves Tim Wakeley's role, which is substantially developed and then dropped. The film presents Tim in the context of a well-delineated family including his highly visible father, a parson, and also his sister, Sybil, who subsumes aspects of Vivien and Sylvia.[14] It depicts Tim's difficulties as unfolding reality rather than as past events recalled. Although his family ties receive considerable attention in the opening reels, after Roddy takes the rap for him, all the Wakeleys disappear, never to resurface. This constitutes a marked change from the stage play and also from the "conventional" finale suggested in the cinematic treatment, which presumably could have united Roddy with an appropriate love interest. Here his homecoming is limited to encounters with his parents and an elderly manservant.

Throughout the film, dialogue-heavy scenes from the play are enlivened with activity—in the dormitory and headmaster's office, at Roddy's home, with Julia and her associates, in the Parisian dance hall, in Marseilles—while intertitles conveying dialogue are at a minimum. Hitchcock's mobile, subjective camera follows the boys on their long walk to the headmaster's office, then, during the tense accusation scene, advances with them as they approach him. In the sequences involving Julia, the camera cunningly sweeps across a musical act in progress, lingers on evocative details in Julia's dressing room, perches overhead in a cab, and offers coolly distancing perspectives on the couple's cavernous apartment. A slapstick fight scene in their drawing room is heavily action-oriented. So are striking portrayals of Roddy's physical, financial, and spiritual descent, conveyed through nightmarish visualizations of events after he leaves Julia, culminating in a haunting montage of unsettling images of delirium.

On screen the hero's dancing skills are exploited more systematically than in the stage play or the treatment. *Downhill* builds on the appeal of another Novello-Collier play, *The Rat* (1924), which Graham Cutts turned into a successful Gainsborough feature in 1925. In that film Novello also played opposite Isabel Jeans in a story of his own concoction, where he assumed the role of a light-footed Parisian gang leader with a flair for apache dancing. Like the play, the film of *The Rat* featured flamboyant choreography.[15] Exploiting that background, *Downhill* presents a Roddy defined in part by his dancing. In addition to the Bunne Shoppe scenes where he is Mabel's favored dancing partner, that ability is featured in the carefully-staged musical production number with Julia and again, in a degraded mode, with paying clients in the Paris dance hall. However, in both public venues, Roddy's dancing is subdued and occasionally awkward. In *Downhill*, Hitchcock exercised a trait for which he would become famous: casting a well-known actor—in this case a musician-dancer-playwright renowned for his stunning dance routines—against type.

Audiences expecting to see Roddy gymnastically twirling Mabel or Julia or an aging poetess would encounter something much more sedate and manipulative. Here, as in *To Catch a Thief* and *Torn Curtain*, Hitchcock chose to emphasize the exploitative potential of dancing, rather than its artistry or liberating exuberance.

Hitchcock's filmed version also adds fanciful visual flourishes to other sequences involving shadowy stairwells, a nearly empty courtyard seen from above, an elevator and an escalator presented as mechanisms of degradation, and an open-topped double-decker bus exposed to drenching rain. The treatment's proposed incursions into sound are evoked by repeated shots of a spinning phonograph record, that, like the pulsing pistons of a ship's engine, are palpably suggestive. In Marseilles and thereafter, Roddy's delirium is dramatically visualized through roving camera movements, subjective dissolves, and the superimposition of disconcerting images. The disturbing effect is so strong that audiences may be left uncertain as to whether the final homecoming really occurs or is merely a part of Roddy's wild imaginings. Hitchcock's film offers a gripping depiction of mental anguish and alienation.

Another innovation is also intriguing. Two black characters are present in the Marseilles hovel. A young black man, played by an uncredited actor, now accompanies and abets the Swedish sailor. A nameless equivalent of the mulatto Malia from the play appears here in the form of a heavyset figure in blackface, also uncredited, whose physiognomy and movements are suggestive of Hitchcock himself.[16] No mention of this imposing personage is made in Fleming's narration. Although the face and gait resemble Hitchcock's, it is likely that we are seeing actress Barbara Gott, who was ''La Patronne,'' Mme. Michet, in *Downhill*'s dancehall and delirium sequences, and who claimed to have played two roles in this film, ''the parts of a Black and a White character.''[17] The issue of Hitchcock's portrayal of race, here and elsewhere, remains ripe for exploration.

Conclusion

Consultation of the the stage play, cinematic treatment, and descriptive narrative of *Downhill* underscores the extent to which earlier versions of the story served as narrative prototypes to which the film's director made noteworthy alterations. The school scenes were augmented to include depictions of sporting events, assemblies, and the extended sequence in the Bunne Shoppe. Added characters included Tim's sister in the opening reels, an aging habitué of the dance hall in the Paris section, and a black sailor in the Marseilles segment. The spitball kid was also introduced at beginning and end, and sporting and bathing scenes were altered for cinematic purposes. Julia's role was concentrated, her personality intensified, through the consolidation of secondary characters. The theme of drug usage was downplayed, while scenes in Marseilles received increased emphasis and memorable expressionistic settings.[18]

What matters in Hitchcock's adaptation is less whether the ''Old Boys'' fancied soccer or rugby, less whether the troublemaker is named Minnie or Mabel, than the transformation of a pedestrian accusation scene in a headmaster's office into a dynamically visualized ''lying flashback.''[19] Among other notable cinematic enhancements are mesmerizing shots of twirling school caps decorated with concentric circles and spinning phonograph records; haunting scenes of stairwells, corridors, and courtyards; dreamlike images of beaded curtains and kids' dirty faces, of sunlit Gothic windows and the cruel light of dawn penetrating an all-night cabaret or an eerily illuminated hovel. The theatrical and narrative versions are left behind as superimpositions communicate Roddy's contorted imaginings and as closeups convey his tortured mental state, Archie's callousness, Julia's insensitivity, the ardent longings of an urchin, the gorgonian avidity of the poetess.

Hitchcock's camera truly became his own when, during the filming of *Downhill*, cinematographer Claude McDonnell fell seriously ill and Hitchcock ''combin[ed] the roles of cameraman and director."[20] Whether in Hitchcock's hands or under his direction, that camera proves to be remarkably agile. It advances with the protagonists as they face their fate, hovers vertiginously above a courtyard, perches over a descending escalator or a jostling cab, turns upside down to register an inverted point of view, pans exhaustively to encompass the unsettling reality of a decadent dance hall, and effectively evokes the obsessive sights and seemingly the sounds of delirium. Such characteristic Hitchcockian touches distinguish the film from other versions of the story.

Considerations of these collateral sources highlight the effectiveness of this adaptation. Even the revisionist spelling of the film's title suggests the action-oriented adjustments that occurred as the stage play was reconceived cinematically. A small change in orthography, effectively transforming a substantive into a form that was more adjectival or even adverbial in thrust, is indicative of the kinetic transformation of *Down Hill* into *Downhill*.

Rhodes College

Notes

Research for this project was funded by Faculty Development Grants from Rhodes College in 1999, 2002, and 2004 that enabled me to consult primary documents in England and France, and to view archival prints at the Museum of Modern Art (MoMA) and the British Film Institute (BFI). I am indebted to the staffs at MoMA, BFI, the British Library, the Bibliothèque du Film, and the Centre Georges Pompidou, as well as to Darlene Brooks, Annette Cates, Roy and Muriel Gibbs, Janet Moat, Kenan Padgett, Joe Rees, Sue and David Sevier, William Short, Olwen Terris, and especially my patient, insightful research associate, Nancy F. Vest.

1. Noble's annotated filmography identifies *Downhill* as simply "a film of [Ivor] Novello's . . . play" ("An Index to the Work of Alfred Hitchcock," *Sight and Sound, Index Series*, no. 18 [London: British Film Institute, 1949], 9). John Russell Taylor is content to

note that *Downhill* is "based on" a play by Novello and Constance Collier (*Hitch: The Life and Times of Alfred Hitchcock* [1978; reprinted New York: Da Capo Press, 1996], 84). Maurice Yacowar refers to it as "the film of the play *Down Hill*" (*Hitchcock's British Films* [Hamden, CT: Archon Books, 1977], 42). Donald Spoto describes it as "a patchy melodrama based on a series of sketches by Novello and Constance Collier" (*The Dark Side of Genius: The Life of Alfred Hitchcock* [1983; reprinted New York: Da Capo Press, 1999], 96). McGilligan's *Alfred Hitchcock: A Life in Darkness and Light* (New York: HarperCollins, 2003) mistakenly calls the film "a straight-line adaptation" of the stage play (91).

2. Mogg writes teasingly that "Hitchcock and regular script-writer Eliot Stannard made cuts and other changes" to the play, but does not explore those alterations in detail (*The Alfred Hitchcock Story* [London: Titan, 1999], 16). In *English Hitchcock* (Moffat, Scotland: Cameron and Hollis, 1999), Barr considers *Downhill* as a "vehicle for experiment" (46) and, in a brief discussion of the stage play, points the way toward further investigation of its sources (220). Michael Williams' *Ivor Novello: Screen Idol* (London: BFI, 2003) emphasizes the value of long-overlooked primary documents, such as those central to the present essay; in his revisionist study of Novello's "charismatic persona" (165), Williams asserts that "the stage and film versions of the story are markedly different" (138).

3. Throughout this article, the appellation *Down Hill* will be reserved for the stage play, "Down Hill" for the cinematic treatment, "Downhill" for the narrative synopsis, and *Downhill* for the film as represented by prints viewed at MoMA and BFI. Several of these sources are referenced, to different ends, by Williams (*Ivor Novello*, see especially 137-48). I encountered Williams' work during the final stage of revising this essay.

4. This play remains unpublished. The official typescript submitted for purposes of registration and censorship (1925/41 in the Lord Chamberlain's Plays Collection at the British Library) includes contact addresses for both Novello and Collier, on the Strand and York Street respectively. The exact date of registry is a bit foggy: the cataloguing card for the typescript indicates that the play was first produced on November 26, 1925, whereas a handwritten annotation on its title page reads "Grand Theatre Blackpool, 21 Dec[ember 1925]." Williams refers to a run in December 1925 at the Palace Theatre, Manchester (*Ivor Novello*, 138). Barr reports that in London *Down Hill* had 94 performances, first at

the Queen's Theatre and then at the Prince's, beginning June 16, 1926 (*English Hitchcock*, 220). Novello starred in two Hitchcock films, *The Lodger* (1926) and *Downhill* (1927); Collier, who directed the original stage version of *Down Hill*, would play the role of Anita Atwater in *Rope* (1948).

5. There is no clear indication of the compositional or performance status of this alternate text. This version may have inspired a sequence planned for the film but absent from extant copies: a costume party documented in photographs in the BFI stills collection. The content of the play appears to have altered in various productions. A "new scene" set in a Marseilles garret was reported in the press in summer 1926 and discussed by Williams as an "extra" scene added when the stage play moved from the Queen's Theatre to the Prince's (*Ivor Novello*, 138 and 157, n. 19). This is probably a version of the garret scene in Act III of the typescript, perhaps deleted or abbreviated in the initial London production, then restored.

6. Item no. 21, catalogued as "DOWNHILL (Hitchcock) 1927: Ivor Montagu's comments on original play and suggested film treatment." In addition to the typescript, this packet contains a two-page unsigned cover letter (cited herein as i-ii) addressed to C.M. Woolf, who collaborated with Michael Balcon in producing and distributing *Downhill* and *Easy Virtue*. The top of the cover letter, which might have contained a date, has been sliced off. This adaptation almost certainly dates from 1926, since the play's London run occurred in late spring and summer of that year, and the movie version was announced soon thereafter and filmed in the first quarter of 1927; therefore, Williams' suggested date of April 1927 or shortly before (*Ivor Novello*, 40) appears unlikely. For details of Montagu's participation in the making of *The Lodger*, *Downhill*, and *Easy Virtue*, see Taylor, *Hitch*, 74-75, 85; Spoto, *The Dark Side of Genius*, 88-89, 98; McGilligan, *A Life in Darkness and Light*, 84-87, 92; and Ivor Montagu, "Working with Hitchcock," *Sight and Sound* 49, no. 3 (summer 1980): 189-93.

7. A similar musical number composed by Novello figured in an earlier Novello-Collier play, *The Rat*, made into a film in 1925. A prominent song writer, Novello would play a composer or musician in several movies, including *The Vortex* (1927) and *The Constant Nymph* (1928), the latter written by Alma Reville Hitchcock. On Novello as composer, see *Picture Show* (June 4, 1927): 18; *Bioscope* no. 1081 (June 23, 1927): 28; and Ivor Novello, "Inspiration," *The*

Picturegoer no. 71 (November 1926): 19. A signature musical leit-motif became an integral narrative feature in subsequent Hitchcock films including both versions of *The Man Who Knew Too Much*, *The 39 Steps*, *The Lady Vanishes*, *Rope*, *Stage Fright*, and *Rear Window*.

8. The cover letter accompanying this typescript specifies that the two women's roles have been expanded with specific actresses in mind: French-born Lili Damita, (1901-94; née Liliane-Marie-Madeleine Carré) as Minnie, and Montreal-born Frances Doble (1902-69) as Vivien (i). Neither actress actually appeared in the film.

9. *The Pleasure Garden*, *The Mountain Eagle*, *The Lodger*, *Downhill*, *Easy Virtue*, *The Manxman*, *The Farmer's Wife*, and *Champagne*. Barr (*English Hitchcock*, 22-26) and McGilligan (*A Life in Darkness and Light*, 77, 94) make a strong case for considering Stannard part of the writing team for *The Ring* as well, even though screen credit for writing goes to Hitchcock alone. When *Downhill* was in preproduction, *Bioscope* reported that Stannard was "collaborating with Alfred Hitchcock on the script of *Downhill*" and commented soon thereafter that the "scenario [for *Easy Virtue* was] being prepared, with the director's cooperation, by Eliot Stannard" (no. 1057 [January 13, 1927]: 51; no. 1064 [March 3, 1927]: 30). Recent scholarship has illuminated the extensive give and take that was common between Hitchcock and his scenarists, beginning with Stannard (e.g., Barr, *English Hitchcock*, 15-17, 21-26; and Steven DeRosa, *Writing with Hitchcock* [New York: Faber and Faber, 2001]).

10. The scope of the present essay is restricted to narrative antecedents of the Gainsborough film. My forthcoming study of *Downhill*'s preproduction, production, postproduction, and release will make use of contemporary accounts and other sources to document the evolution of the filmmaking project between autumn 1926 and autumn 1927.

11. Such prose condensations were a regular feature in this illustrated movie magazine that featured news about stars and directors. A similar condensation of *The Lodger*, also by Fleming, appeared in *The Picturegoer* in February 1927. Stylistically this condensation is quite distinctive from a press release such as the 800-word one for *Downhill* issued by Gainsborough (reprinted in *Cinema World* [October 1927]: 21-22) that offered a brief plot summary, sprinkled with bits of dialogue taken directly from the film's intertitles.

12. Mogg notes that this scene of "Novello naked from the waist up" corresponds to a post-game washing-up scene in the

stage play that "thrilled his fans" and exercised some drama critics (*The Alfred Hitchcock Story*, 16). The stage directions for that scene call for Roddy to take his muddied athletic "boots and stockings off" in order to soak his feet (*Down Hill*, 6). The *Observer*'s theater critic commented on the appeal for "maidens" of Novello's "knees, his shins, even his thighs, and his dear little wiggly toes" (cited in Paul Webb, *Ivor Novello: Portrait of a Star* [London: Stage Directions, 1999], 56). For a photograph of Novello on stage as Roddy in athletic garb, see Webb, illus. 7.

13. These Hitchcockian comic flourishes led Truffaut to misinterpret the offense against Mabel as theft (*Hitchcock*, rev. ed. [New York: Simon and Schuster, 1983], 51). The joke behind the name Ye Olde Bunne Shoppe, suggesting the colloquialism "to have a bun in the oven" (a euphemism for being "preggy"), is generally lost on non-British commentators. For a discussion of this and comparable Hitchcock jokes, see Yacowar, *Hitchcock's British Films*, 283, n. 1. For substantial interpretations of this film's themes and cinematic structures, see Yacowar, 42-53; Barr, *English Hitchcock*, 43-47; Williams, *Ivor Novello*, 137-44.

14. The two boys whom Sybil observes fighting in a stairwell are identified by Jane E. Sloan as Tim's younger brothers (*Alfred Hitchcock: A Filmography and Bibliography* [Berkeley and Los Angeles: University of California Press, 1993], 56); however, they are in fact the spitwad kid and a younger student, both wearing the distinctive jackets and caps associated with this school.

15. The Gainsborough film of *The Rat*, which, like *Downhill* was produced by Michael Balcon in conjunction with C.M. Woolf, was technically innovative with gliding camera movements and a color sequence for its main titles. Novello's vigorous "apache" dancing took audiences by storm, and sheet music of his composition, "The Rat Dance," sold well. On the importance of *The Rat* and its sequel, *The Triumph of the Rat* (1926), to Novello's screen image, see Williams, *Ivor Novello*, 91-93, 132-38, 148-53, and *passim*.

16. One might reasonably expect a directorial cameo in *Downhill*. Hitchcock made two appearances in his immediately preceding film, *The Lodger*, and could also be sighted in his next one, *Easy Virtue*, whose production schedule overlapped that of *Downhill* (see Sidney Gottlieb, "Alfred Hitchcock's *Easy Virtue* [1927]: A Descriptive Shot List," *Hitchcock Annual* [1993]: 59). Even if the actor in blackface in *Downhill* is merely a lookalike, the self-reflection is noteworthy.

17. Legend accompanying Gott's photograph in *Bioscope* no. 1080 (June 18, 1927): 114. For a reproduction of a BFI still of the black-faced figure in the film, see Paul Duncan, *Alfred Hitchcock: Filmographie complète* (Cologne: Taschen, 2003), 32.

18. Drug usage is central to Williams' discussion of Novello as embodying post-war trauma and angst (*Ivor Novello*, especially 14, 144-47). In light of the insistence on drugs in the play and cinematic treatment, it is significant that overt references to drug usage disappear in the film version.

19. Following Yacowar's lead (*Hitchcock's British Films*, 44), Barr posits "an element of 'lying flashback' in the images that accompany Mabel's accusation" (*English Hitchcock*, 47); however, neither pursues the distinctiveness of this feature in terms of the film's antecedents.

20. *Bioscope*, no. 1067 (March 24, 1927): 49. The report does not specify how long Hitchcock remained behind the camera, or for which shots.

R I C H A R D   A L L E N

Sir John and the Half-Caste: Identity and Representation in Hitchcock's Murder!

Murder! (1930) is the third in a trilogy of Hitchcock's early films, the others being *The Lodger* (1926) and *Blackmail* (1929), in which the character of a dandy plays a central role. The origins of the dandy lie in the early-nineteenth-century aristocratic man of leisure who exhibits an excessive attention to dress and self-comportment and who symbolized an effete, feckless, and sexually degenerate aristocracy in the eyes of the newly enfranchised middle-class.[1] From the standpoint of middle-class morality, the dandy was a sexually predatory degenerate. But the Byronic legend gave a different inflection to the dandy persona: the dandy as romantic who transcends the restrictive conventions of middle-class morality in the name of personal and social liberty. In the late nineteenth century, Oscar Wilde—emulating Byron—flaunted dandyism as a symbol of rebellion against stolid middle-class values in a manner that linked self-stylization to the creation of the work of art. While Wilde's trial for "sodomy" consolidated the association of dandyism not only with decadence in general but with homosexual "perversion" in particular, which was already a buried subtext of the Byron myth, his subsequent public humiliation also rendered the "dandy deviant" a figure of middle-class sympathy. In the spy fiction of John Buchan that was to have a central influence on Hitchcock in later years, the Byronic dandy is figured as a perverse, but not wholly unsympathetic, super-villain, who seeks to undermine civilization in the form of the British Empire.[2] English detective fiction, in contrast, squares the figure of the dandy with middle-class morality in the person of the aristocratic amateur sleuth or the dapper detective by attenuating the connotations of perversity attached to the dandy. In the figure of Conan Doyle's Sherlock Holmes the narcissism of the dandy is an index not of decadence or effeminacy but of bachelor discipline and restraint at the service of the social good. The amateur detective's powers of observation extend beyond conclusions based upon social conformity to truths that are obscured by ignorance or prejudice. Free from social conformity or conventional social ties, the aristocratic man of leisure restores rather than subverts the social order.

The significance of the dandy persona for Hitchcock's work, as I have explored elsewhere, is the manner in which it serves to articulate an essentially ambiguous and divided masculine (and sometimes feminine) identity in which the alluring surface of self-comportment harbors an incipiently perverse, and thereby enticing secret.[3] Is the dandy an authentic gentleman or a ''pervert'' and how are we to discriminate between them? In both *The Lodger* and *Blackmail*, the dandy is a seductive and alluring figure for the heroine but also demonized as a sexually licentious, incipiently murderous figure. In *Blackmail*, the dandy is an artist who invites the ingenuous heroine to his attic to view his etchings, but his surface charm masks rapacious intent. He is contrasted with the figure of the virtuous, anodyne cop according to the formula that Hitchcock was to repeat throughout his career. However, in *The Lodger* Hitchcock makes the dandy himself a figure of ambivalence: the dandy-hero and the dandy-villain are two sides of a Janus-face, and the possibility is seriously entertained that the dandy is a hero. The lodger may be a serial murderer of women in accordance with the cliché of the dandy as a rapacious, predatory, vampire figure consolidated in the popular imagination through the myth of Jack the Ripper. Yet, it is revealed near the end of the film that he may also be a gentleman-detective, a latter-day Arthurian knight seeking to rescue women from their fate at the hands of the killer. If contrasted, however, the two sides of this dual persona in *The Lodger* are also entwined in accordance with the logic of the double. The lodger-as-hero's project of preserving the virtue of innocent women from the fate that befalls his sister at her coming out ball has as its mirror-image the lodger as killer's project of rescuing women from their fallen or incipiently fallen condition as sexual beings by murdering them. In *The Lodger* it is impossible to discriminate the true gentlemen from the false, the straight and the perverted, on the basis of appearances and actions alone; indeed it is impossible, finally, to tell the difference between them at all.

In *Murder!* Hitchcock pries apart the two aspects of the dandy persona of *The Lodger* and creates two characters that are at once contrasted as detective and criminal according to the formula manifest in *Blackmail*, but also closely paralleled due to their complementary dandy personae. Sir John Menier (Herbert Marshall), debonair detective and romantic lead, and Handel Fane (Esme Percy), the dandy-deviant and killer, both display an elegant bearing, mannered speech, self-consciousness about the presentation of self, and hypersensitivity that suggests the narcissistic self-regard of the dandy. Furthermore, both Sir John and Handel Fane are cast as actors who are self-conscious of their performance of self both on and off the stage in a manner that suggests that the self in real life is as performed as the identity that is realized on stage. Ostensibly though, the parallel is drawn in order to dramatize the contrast between the characters.

Handel Fane is the closest Hitchcock comes to portraying the Wildean dandy as filtered through popular imagination. Fane displays a certain fayness or effeteness that connotes "perversity," manifest in the gesture of his wrist as he stubs out his cigarette, the roll of his eyes as he responds to a question, in his mannered step, and his heaving breast. Furthermore Fane's sartorial narcissism links that sense of perversity with the idea of an "inauthentic" or "fake" identity. His excessively flamboyant dress includes a tiepin, a prominent watch chain, a large gold ring on his pinky finger, and an ornate cane that goes with his Panama hat and leather gloves. He also enjoys female roles in the theater and dressing up in a female masquerade in the performance of his trapeze act.

Sir John, in contrast to the "queer" dandy Fane, is an establishment figure, a highly successful author-actor turned amateur sleuth whose narcissistic self-regard suggests not a fake self, but a form of self-perfection. Sir John combines sensitivity with a sense of emotional restraint and self-control in contrast to Fane's emotional insecurity. His narcissistic temperament is beautifully captured in a scene where he shaves himself in front of the mirror to the strains of Wagner's *Tristan and Isolde* as it dawns upon him that he is in love with Diana Baring and realizes that she has been wrongfully imprisoned. Sir John epitomizes the combination of reason and intuition informed by love, of rationality and romanticism that is the harbinger of redemption and social renewal in Hitchcock's films.

The contrast between Sir John and Fane is clear, yet the parallel between the characters draws that contrast into question. For while Fane's love of female masquerade suggests to Sir John a lying self or a false self that is ultimately the persona of a criminal, in fact his "female" persona appears as natural to Fane as his ostensibly real masculine identity. Conversely, Sir John's assumption of the role of Diana's redeemer and seeker-after-truth, although he inhabits it with aplomb, seems to be merely a conceit for a man who, like the aesthete, makes art out of life. The ostensibly inauthentic Fane commits the crime of murder in spontaneous response to vicious ridicule and in order to protect the women he loves, Diana from knowing the truth about his "half-caste" identity. Although Fane's love for Diana may be an impossible, unrequited love, perhaps even a love that for Fane can only be platonic, it is also a selfless love like the love of Alexander Sebastian (Claude Rains) for Alicia Huberman (Ingrid Bergman) in *Notorious* (1946). This love might seem more genuine than the love of Sir John, who so enjoys the idea of his own gallantry, and for whom rescuing Diana and bringing Fane to justice is something of a game. Hitchcock's villains are rarely simply psychotic: from the Lodger to Norman Bates, Hitchcock invites us to sympathize with the figure of the criminal deviant as a victim. However, the villain in *Murder!* is not psychotic at all and Hitchcock goes to unusual lengths to portray his victimized status and his affinity to Diana Baring, who is also a victim of social prejudice. Her aristocratic self-comportment betrays her to the jury who wrongly convict her of a crime she did not commit. The fact that Diana languishes in prison because she does not wish to betray her friend is itself evidence of the sympathy extended to Fane's character by the film. As Peter Swaab writes: "In Esme Percy's gently dignified performance, Hitchcock evokes a painful private predicament and he makes it harder for us to resolve the moral aspect of the doubled character in the innocent man's favor. Indeed, there is at times a persecuting complacence about Sir John, a sleuthing indifference to the distress that may have turned the victimized Fane into a murderer."[4]

Enter Sir John, the novel by Clemence Dane (pseudonym for Winifred Ashton) and Helen Simpson on which *Murder!* is based, is set in the world of the theater and thus allowed Hitchcock to exploit for thematic purposes the aesthetic possibilities available to the new medium of the sound film.[5] Sir John's authority is associated in both novel and film with his command over the spoken word. When the landlady of the murdered women insists that it was women she heard arguing before the murder, wrongly implicating Diana Baring in the crime, Sir John, applying the technique of art to the technique of life, moves "off-stage," and calls the landlady by using falsetto, thereby tricking her into thinking that a woman is calling her, and giving the lie to her conviction that she correctly identified a woman's voice before the murder. However, Hitchcock develops the significance of Sir John's command of the spoken word in a way that only the sound film made possible, by contrasting his mastery of speech and its power over life and death with the visual spectacle of

Fane's performance that culminates in suicide, and with the mute silence of the heroine Diana, who suffers in death row on Fane's behalf. Hitchcock's aesthetic in *Murder!* was undoubtedly influenced by Carl Dreyer's *Passion of Joan of Arc* (1928), which ranges all-powerful coercive male authority embodied in the word against a mute, suffering heroine. However *Murder!* also expresses a contrast between sound as an index of life and the mute deathly quality of silence associated with the aesthetics of the silent film.

The opposition between sound and silence, word and image in *Murder!* dramatizes the contrast between masculine authority embodied in the word and a feminine space of muteness, silence, and spectacle. Sir John is the male author who imposes sense, order, and purpose upon the incipient chaos of a life, restoring the virtue of the heroine and creating the possibility of romantic renewal. The authority of the male word is at once reparative in restoring justice and freedom for the innocent heroine, yet incipiently coercive in its insistent quest for truth irrespective of feelings. Sir John's self-authored romance, like Hitchcock's film, requires and produces a clear cut distinction between male and female as a precondition for the romantic narrative to be realized. But Fane's identity, as it is manifest in his different performance turns as theatrical cross-dresser and circus acrobat, is one that eludes this cut-and-dried distinction. If Fane's crime issues from a failure of society to accommodate who he is, that is, to accept someone with an undecidable and elusive identity, Sir John repeats this failure, even in the necessary and noble exercise of justice. As Tania Modleski argues, Fane occupies the feminine position in the narrative shared by Diana Baring. This space is defined by the ambiguity of silence and spectacle that resists the imposition of sense and is haunted by death.[6] In *Murder!* Hitchcock at once affirms the romance narrative and the normative gender hierarchies it typically reinforces and yet at the same time undermines the legitimacy of this narrative by exposing the incipiently coercive dimension of the masculine voice that seeks to impose a determinate sense upon the feminine image, and invites identification with a figure who defies the categorical identity that the male voice seeks to impose upon it.

In the remainder of this essay I want to focus on two central aspects of this complex sound film in more detail. First, I will examine how Hitchcock explores the relationship between word and image, silence and sound, in the new medium of the sound film in order both to articulate audience sympathy with each of the protagonists of the film and suggest the coercive authority of Sir John's word that seeks to pin down the mercurial identity of Fane. Second, I will explore the question of the nature of the identity of the criminal Fane, who is termed a "half-caste" in both the novel and the film. I will demonstrate how the identity of Fane is transposed in the adaptation from novel to film from a racial half-caste to an identity that is primarily defined through an ambiguous sexuality. Hitchcock turns the racially half-caste nature of the villain in the novel into a MacGuffin that is a pretext for exploring sexual deviance through the visual spectacle of film. While he may be accused of avoiding the question of racial difference and identity that lies at the heart of the novel, he also achieves, as a result, one of his most complex and humane portrayals of non-normative sexual identity in his work and his most articulate exploration of the oppressive nature of the gender system that labels deviation from the heterosexual norm degenerate. Furthermore, by at once transposing the novel into a cinematic idiom and transforming the meaning of half-casteness, Hitchcock transcends the authority of his source material and thereby secures his own claim for authorial originality.

Word and Image, Sound and Silence

In Hitchcock's *Murder!*, the romantic quest, the redemption of the heroine and the restoration of the social order are enabled and secured by the authority of the word as it is embodied in Sir John's command of language. As William Rothman has persuasively argued, Sir John seeks in effect to rewrite the story of the Baring case towards its redemptive conclusion that allows him to win the hand of Diana.[7] Hitchcock takes care to place the audience in sympathy with Sir John's ''authorial'' aspirations in the sense that there has been a flagrant miscarriage of justice that he seeks to reverse. The completion of the quest-romance is embodied in the triumphant authorship of the playwright-actor who proves able to hold death at bay and breath life back into the doomed Diana Baring. Baring is associated with the mute ''theatrical'' spectacle of the silent tableaux, which has an uncanny deathly quality, and is literally melodramatic in the original sense of the term of a drama without words.[8] Yet, at the same time, in Hitchcock's film, unlike the novel, the dandy Fane contests Sir John's attempt to script the ''happy ending'' and his resistance is portrayed as a rejection of Sir John's words. When Sir John tries to trick him into reading a script at the end of the film, which would implicate him as the murderer, he refuses to read his lines. Instead, soon afterwards, Fane embraces his own self-authored performance where he at once performs as a transvestite trapeze artist and stages his own death in front of Sir John in the circus ring in a spectacular, silent, melodramatic tableaux. Fane's staged suicide is act of defiance towards Sir John. Fane literally refuses Sir John's attempt to bring him to justice. More metaphorically, Fane denies Sir John's attempt to fix his place in the drama of the Baring case that he has been single-mindedly ''rewriting.'' Fane refuses the authority of the word, as it is embodied in the ''authorship'' of Sir John.

Counterpoised to the larger-than-life dramatis personae—the dandy detective; Baring, the wrong or wronged woman; and the dandy criminal—is the lower-class everyday world of the stage manager Markham and his actress wife, Doucie. These characters dramatize, in the ordinary, everyday world of the lower-middle-classes, the contrast between male authorship and the feminine space of spectacle and performance that finds a happy synthesis within their marriage. Markham is a morally upright, strictly conformist, lower-middle-class stage manager with lots of common sense and practical wisdom. He is not an actor

himself but admires actors, especially his wife, Doucie
Dearing, whom he praises affectionately to Sir John as "pure
Tallulah." Doucie in fact appears to be a caricature of flighty
femininity; the dumb blonde who always seems to be putting
on a show. The world inhabited by Markham and Doucie is
the realistic world of the ordinary, akin to the Bunting
household entered into by the Lodger. The "realistic"
touches in Hitchcock's English films have often been noted
by critics, but as *Murder!* makes clear, Hitchcock's realism has
a very particular function in rendering the world of the
ordinary that forms the field of action for his larger-than-life
protagonists. It is signified not simply by lower-class
character types but by a distinct aesthetic bred in part from
working with direct sound, the constraints of which
Hitchcock makes a virtue. The scenes involving the
Markhams are characterized by long takes in which
Hitchcock pans rather than cuts between the protagonists as
they speak in way that creates a unified sense of space where
characters are interconnected and defined by their shared
environment; by the use of off-screen sound that extends this
sense of unified space beyond the boundaries of the image,
often in a way that suggests the impact of the larger outside
word upon the life of the characters; and by overlapping
sound that evokes a sense of the hurly-burly, topsy-turvy
confusion of everyday life.

The opening scene of the film plunges us into the
everyday world as the theater manager and his wife awaken
in a comic state of undress to the off-screen sounds of
repeated knocking that resembles gunfire and the incessant
barking of a dog, and witness the coming and going of one
(or is it two?) policeman. Doucie bathed in light, puts on her
bloomers in a manner that underscores both her vitality and
her sexuality. In antithesis to this spectacle of femininity,
Markham off-screen is rendered abstractly in silhouette. This
figuration of gender difference is one that Hitchcock will
repeat almost exactly in the opening of *Notorious*. Hitchcock
may seem childishly prurient here but he also makes an
important point. Doucie's energy contrasts with the still

silence of death that follows which we witness in a silent melodramatic theatrical tableaux. The framing is closed and claustrophobic. Hitchcock's camera tilts and pans from the figure of the policeman down the seated body of Diana to the poker at her feet and then along the body, mimicking the pointing gesture of the poker and encouraging the spectator to make the false inference all-too-readily drawn by the policeman, Doucie, and Markham, and the subsequent jury. In this silent tableaux of death, the mute frozen figure of the heroine is linked to the prostrate female victim we do not wholly see; indeed, there is a sense in which appearing dead, though sitting up, she is placed in the position of the victim.

The contrast established here between the spectacle of life afforded by the sound film and the uncanny, deathly, melo-dramatic tableau of silent film is restated in the next sequence in the contrast between the mute heroine imprisoned in her cell and the noisy space of Fane's theatrical cross-dressing performance. The heroine is introduced by a rising curtain (as if in a staged tableaux) incarcerated in a prison cell, sitting in stillness, her head framed by pool of light against which Hitchcock's signature oblique parallel lines are reflected. The only sign of life is registered by a defiant gaze out toward the audience of the film that shows her resistance to the circumstances of her confinement. Subsequently, her resistance is given a realistic motivation as a backward tracking camera reveals that her look is directed towards a jailer who looks in at the window of her prison cell. It is a scene that recalls Joan of Arc's incarceration in Dreyer's *Passion of Joan of Arc*. Then, dramatically, Hitchcock cuts from the mute heroine incarcerated in her cell, to the noisy topsy-turvy world of the theater that is associated with a sense of freedom and being alive. This is a world of motivated chaos: characters come and go through the wings of the stage and identities are multiple and donned at will.

The entry of Sir John into the narrative brings a different dimension to the articulation of sound and image. While sound is associated with the "theater" of life as opposed to deathly silence, sound in the form of the spoken word also becomes a vehicle of coercion. I have already suggested that the coercive authority of the word is associated with the figure of Sir John. However, when Sir John himself is initially introduced, *he* is the mute victim of the coercive authority of the word in a manner that renders him a sympathetic hero. When Sir John is finally introduced as the last holdout of the jurors, Hitchcock takes great pains to establish our sympathy with him as the victim not only of inept authority embodied in the judge and the foreman of the jury, but of majority rule that is represented as a more civilized variant of the mob rule that victimizes and ensnares the Lodger in Hitchcock's earlier film. The coercive impact of the jury is framed as a verbal assault upon Sir John as he tries to introduce thoughtful reasoned objections to the verdict. A montage of voices builds up rhythmically and repetitiously in a "choric chant" that recalls the modernist poetry of W.H. Auden and T.S. Eliot, who were writing choric verse and plays at this time,[9] and evokes in its form the sense of the coercive force of language:

> SIR JOHN: Think of her personality. She's not the kind of girl to get drunk.
> JUROR: Brandy in the flask was there.
> JUROR: She doesn't deny it.
> JUROR: That's right.
> CHORUS OF JURORS: *Any answer to that, Sir John?*
> SIR JOHN: Not at the moment. Then there is a question of whether anyone else entered the house that night.
> JUROR: Landlady says not.
> JUROR: Girl says not.
> WOMAN JUROR: They were alone.
> JUROR: That's right.
> CHORUS OF JURORS: *Any answer to that, Sir John?*
> SIR JOHN: Not at the moment. But have we taken it too much for granted that no one else could have done the murder?
> JUROR: Said they were alone.

JUROR: Said they quarreled.
WOMAN JUROR: Admits it.
JUROR: That's right.
CHORUS OF JURORS: *Any answer to that, Sir John?*

Finally, we see Sir John alone in the frame, the "surrounding" voices now no longer occupying a physical but a mental space as the phrases repeat and resound in his head in a manner that recalls Hitchcock's "expressionistic" use of sound in *Blackmail*. Sir John's sense of isolation here under the weight of the verbal assault of the jury echoes the physical isolation of Diana Baring that we have already witnessed, and establishes at once Sir John's alignment with her and our sympathy with him. Again, Hitchcock's film evokes Dreyer's *Passion of Joan of Arc*, which though silent, evokes the coercive effects of the male voice upon the suffering heroine and her stoic resistance to it. But here, the hero, Sir John, is placed in the coerced, feminine position.

Sound is used here to represent an external source of coercion that insinuates itself into consciousness from the outside, but elsewhere Hitchcock uses sound to articulate the resistance of consciousness to external coercive forces. When Diana imagines the theatrical play from which she is excluded, she is negating through her imagination, identified with creativity, the sense of physical incarceration. Later, Sir John, in the solitude of his Mayfair apartment, is shown framed in his shaving mirror in a manner that echoes the framing of Diana's face in her prison door. In an inner soliloquy accompanied by the strains of Tristan and Isolde, he realizes his love for Diana and his faith in her innocence, in the face of all evidence to the contrary. His faith prompts him to intuit a telltale clue pointing to the presence of a third party at the scene of the crime. Creative imagination is here linked to love as a secular form of faith in overcoming the depredations of the external world, a faith that leads to the recognition of innocence and the identification of the guilty. The device of the internal soliloquy has the effect not simply of displaying Sir John's creative romantic imagination but also his command of language and the relationship that it bears to self-control, to the containment of his emotions, and to the enjoyment of solitude and to silence. Of course, the music is playing from the radio while Sir John shaves in the mirror, but although nominally external to his thoughts, it has the force of an internal accompaniment to them.

Sir John's romantic soliloquy stands in striking contrast to the subsequent scene in the crowded home of the theater manager Markham, where the daughter of the house plays the piano. She plays in a hesitant, faltering, discordant way, reflecting the impoverished circumstances of the newly unemployed Markham household. Art here is intimately bound with the practical exigencies of life. The daughter's diligent piano practice, like the Markham's engagement with the theater, articulates a petit bourgeois striving for respectability under conditions of economic scarcity and uncertainty. Reminded of this numbing reality in the form of the housekeepers' reluctant, yet ostentatious, display of a "For Rent" sign, they imagine redemption in the form of a call from Sir John. Fortune answers in the form of his summons that leads them to a frenzied preparation for their interview that is accompanied by a more confident, up-tempo etude.

In his role as detective, in the novel and the film, Sir John appears as both actor and impresario, carefully choosing his words in order to solicit the cooperation of his interlocutors and orchestrating and organizing the *mise-en-scène* to achieve his desired effect. In an interview with Markham that takes place in Sir John's apartment, Markham, who is seated, appears as a subordinate audience to Sir John's command performance—so subordinate indeed that he nearly falls off his chair—as Hitchcock tilts up from Markham to Sir John's towering, almost mesmerizing presence, and Sir John strategically entices Markham to his point of view of the case by offering him work and pandering to his vanity. However, Sir John's *tour de force* of strategic manipulation is reserved for a later scene, reproduced from the novel, where he interviews the landlady, with Markham, now wise to his ways, an appreciative audience within the film. Sir John steps out of the room and cries in a feminine voice "Miss Mitchum, Miss Mitchum, where are you Miss Mitchum. The Chimney's on fire." When he returns to the room, the landlady hastily brushes him aside: "Excuse me, sir, I can't stop just now. That Alice of mine has set the chimney on fire. Didn't you hear her calling?" "That was me, Miss Mitchum," Sir John responds, "Or is it 'I,' I can never remember." Sir John here mimics the position taken by the landlady when she eavesdropped upon the crime, and demonstrates at once the unreliability of sound (detached from the image), but also his own manipulation and mastery of the voice. It is inconceivable to the landlady to attach this voice to this body, and offended by his actions, she refuses for a time to stand corrected by Sir John. Though they register Sir John's controlling "authorial" agency, these scenes are essentially comic. While the lower-class characters are the butt of a joke, the consequences are essentially benign.[10]

When Sir John visits Diana in prison, he manages to extract from her the identity of the villain whom she is protecting from public exposure. Here, the manipulative nature of Sir John's actions is mitigated not by comedy but the way in which Hitchcock establishes his identification with the victim as Sir John enters into and seems to inhabit her mute space. Surveying in silence a long board table in the stark bare room that seems to resemble a coffin, he takes a place at the opposite end from her. They are separated not simply by the physical length of the table as revealed in long shot at the end of the film but by reverse-field cutting that, as Rothman observes, serves at once to separate the characters within the scene and parallel their condition as we see each of them framed by the table in the foreground in a manner that cuts them off at the waist and thereby metaphorically neuters them.[11] Yet Sir John is still obliged to interrogate her in order to solicit information that she plainly does not wish to volunteer about the identity of the culprit she is protecting, for fear that, as in the novel, Fane's "half-caste" status will be revealed. He finally tricks her into breaking her silence, by implying that Diana is in love with Fane.

The final confrontation between Sir John and Fane is the culmination of Sir John's attempt to rewrite the history of the Baring case as he invites Fane the actor to act the part of Fane the murderer. Fane, "framed" with his back to the closed curtains in two parallel shafts of light (as he is framed by Sir John's discourse), agrees to read Sir John's script, but his reading essentially involves acting the gestures supplied by Sir John's words, that is, supplying the image for Sir John's voice-over. As Sir John narrates how Fane came through the double-doors and approached the victim, poker in hand, he supplies the dialogue: "the other woman says, you fool don't you know that he's a half . . . ." A moment before Fane had asked to use a real poker for the part, threatening to place Sir John in the position of his previous victim, an appropriate place in the sense that Sir John is engaged in the same act of public humiliation as Fane's previous victim. However, Sir John offers him a pencil that at once suggests Fane's "castration" and serves as an ironic comment on his own castrating powers: Sir John's poker is his pencil. At the point of the utterance "he's a half . . ." Hitchcock cuts to an overhead shot of the two men positioned at opposite corners of an image that registers conflict in graphic organization of line and light, but evokes a sense of doubling in the opposition. A high-angle shot of the cowered Fane quickly follows, then a montage of accusatory glances from Sir John and the policemen who guard the door. The context in which Fane is placed here recalls the earlier position taken by Sir John in the face of the coercive jury. But Fane, unlike Sir John, refuses to be cowed and the sentence remains uncompleted.

In the novel, Sir John's final *tour de force* is his scripting of the story of the Baring case for Fane to perform. Fane breaks down before his eyes and confesses how fear of exposure forced him to commit murder. He is imprisoned but then escapes and is last seen "swimming for dear life" in the River Thames. However in Hitchcock's film, Fane rejects the authority of Sir John's word embodied in his attempt to script the conclusion to the story of the Baring case and assign Fane his role as villain, and he eludes capture not by escaping but by staging his own suicide. In the spectacular, carnivalesque, lowbrow space of the circus, we watch with Sir John and Markham as Fane emerges into the arena dressed up both as a woman and as a bird in an elaborate costume of feathers, which he flamboyantly discards to reveal a tight leotard that resembles peacock eyes. He ascends a rope ladder to his perch above the audience from where he will perform on the flying trapeze, accompanied by the lilting Spanish-gypsy circus melody played by a brass band.

This scene manifests a distinctive brand of Hitchcockian suspense whose focus lies in dramatizing the allure of a sexually charged secret. Hitchcock's characteristic approach to sexually charged suspense involves a playful ludic style that alludes to human perversity indirectly in the manner of the Freudian joke that at once refers to and disguises sexual content through word-play. In *The Lodger* this kind of suspense is manifest in the way that Hitchcock teases the audience with the thought that the Lodger might be a Jack the Ripper figure through punning visual ambiguity. In a similar playful vein, Hitchcock aestheticizes the most obvious moment of conventional suspense in *Murder!* when Sir John hunts down Fane for the final confrontation as Diana faces the hangman's noose. The conventional suspense situation is this: Will Fane be exposed before Diana hangs or will Sir John rescue her? Orchestrating this suspense, Hitchcock cuts with increasing intensity between Diana pacing her cell, shots of a weathervane that puns both on "Whether Fane?" and "Whither Fane?" as we hear voices searching for Fane, and shots of a hangman's noose on the prison wall. But as William Rothman points out, the noose is visually configured in such a way as to suggest the symbol of both male and female.[12] The audience is left "hanging" by Hitchcock about whether or not the person who will occupy the hangman's noose will be Diana or Fane. But what is also invoked in order to be denied in this complex gallows humor is the idea of imagining something hanging that is neither man nor woman, or both man and woman, that is, imagining seeing the perverse secret about Fane displayed—a secret that is at once entertained yet denied in a narrative of suspense that must insist on getting the relationship between men and women straight.

However, the suspense that characterizes Fane's final performance intimates the kind of aesthetic that Hitchcock was to fully realize only with *Rebecca* (1940), where the fascination with what is taboo is no longer contained by a ludic masculine detachment but is actually confronted and explored with affective intensity. Hitchcock seems to be inviting the audience of the film to ponder the relationship between aestheticism or idealization and abjection, to register not only the allure or fascination of the "perverse" body but to solicit our sympathy with it. Narcissism and perversion are linked together in the figure of the dandy-aesthete in Hitchcock in a manner that recalls both Freud and Wilde.[13] The surface of the narcissistic body is one whose idealized perfection intimates an abject "polymorphous" core that lies beneath; the body itself is like an artwork/fetish object. When Fane is initially presented he is hidden by a parade of elephants that exit the ring as he takes his place within it. As he discards his peacock feathers, Fane's body, including his genitalia, is revealed to be stuffed a little too tightly into his leotard. We view him from behind and below, looking up at his fleshy thighs in a shot that is echoed much later in Hitchcock's career when we view the swiveling buttocks of another cross-dresser, Norman Bates, as he ascends the stairs in the Bates mansion. What seems revealed by the manner in which Fane discards his plumage is the illusion of the narcissistic ideal of bodily perfection. Instead, Fane is an abject, vulnerable, to-be-stared-at body that is packed uneasily into his skin. Even as it is clad in the leotard, Fane's body is exposed, and while he is a source of voyeuristic fascination, he is also a figure of sympathy and identification. For here is a vulnerable body being exposed to the most difficult and dangerous challenges, where one's very life is at stake. The body of the deviant at this point stands for the human body itself in its vulnerability before death.

As Fane takes off on the trapeze, he is freed from the constraints of bodily space by the manner in which Hitchcock's camera depicts the background moving in a blur behind him, as if (as Rothman observes) he has become detached from a world that has cast him out and has entered into a trance-like state of sexual ecstasy that renders him momentarily omnipotent.[14] As he swings to and fro in a womb-like space, he sees before him with hallucinatory intensity and reality the faces of his persecutor and the woman they both love in the silent melodrama of a personal theater. Their images are bisected by a pattern of lights reflecting from behind his trapeze that evokes at once jaws of death that surround him, but also hearken back to a joke in opening scene of this sound film where Markham retrieves his false teeth from a glass in order to be heard. In other words, the jaws of death are also the jaws that have given voice to the persecution of Fane that are now in Fane's fantasy of omnipotence reduced to silence.

Once he concludes his swing on the trapeze he pauses, breathless, his body slumped, as if gathering himself for one last act. This act transforms his own death into a species of theater. He holds out his hand for the orchestra to stop. In dignified silence he carefully ties a noose and plunges off-screen. We do not see the body of the hanged man swinging on the rope but we do witness the shock and panic of the audience. These are undoubtedly realistic responses to the act of suicide, but given the sexualized body of Fane we have already witnessed, Hitchcock may also be evoking the myth, clearly unrepresentable, of the erection/ejaculation of the hanged man, wherein Fane's death becomes an auto-erotic *liebestod*.[15] Fane's staged suicide is the final unchallengeable reproof of Sir John's authority. Hitchcock makes tragically clear that the happy ending that secures the formation of the white, heterosexual couple, Sir John and Diana, is one that is achieved only by sacrificing the deviant who is neither white nor, simply, heterosexual.

In the final scene, whose only precedent in the novel is a hint in the last sentence of the book that Sir John perceives his engagement to Baring as a source of good publicity opportunities, Sir John and Diana unite in the kiss that cements their WASP union. But as Hitchcock's camera withdraws into long shot, the kiss itself is revealed to be a stage kiss, a fiction. Lesley Brill has suggested that the self-conscious artifice that underscores Hitchcock's staging of the kiss in his work is precisely what makes the kiss romantic, and this scene does indeed provide a fitting coda to Sir John's quest.[16] Yet Hitchcock's camera movement also self-consciously suggests, as Rothman argues, a separation of the point of view of the film from the depicted world of the theater in which is realized the conclusion of the romance that has been brought into being by Sir John's ''authorial'' actions.

This leads us to a conclusion that is opposite to the romantic happy ending that is explicitly affirmed. The kiss appears suddenly as *only* a performed kiss rather than the synthesis of art and life that Sir John aspires to.[17] Viewing the kiss as a performed kiss suggests that Sir John's scripting of the romance, has been just that, a script, and that Sir John's performance of the romantic lead is, after all, just a little too self-conscious and self-serving to finally carry conviction. Furthermore, it pales in comparison to the performance of Fane, where the synthesis of art and life is all too real.

This closing scene neatly captures not only the ambivalence of *Murder!* but the underlying ambivalence of Hitchcock's entire narrative universe. Is the triumph of heterosexual romantic love being asserted here or undercut? It is inadequate to interpret the scene either one way or another. The point is surely that the narrative *telos* of romantic love embodied in the happy end is at once being asserted, its self-evidently fictive character celebrated, and yet simultaneously ironically undercut, exposed as a mere fiction that is less authentic than the tragic performance of the dandy-deviant we have just witnessed. Hitchcock's narration is self-divided or romantic-ironic in character.

On Being a Half-Caste: Race and Sexuality

Murder! is a whodunit or mystery story that centers on the story of a woman wrongly accused of a crime that she did not commit and the efforts of the amateur sleuth to rescue her by discovering the identity of the villain. But as we have seen, *Murder!* is not a simple detective story. While Sir John spends a great deal of time and energy in the search for the identity of the culprit, the core whodunit question (''Who is the criminal?'') seems to ask not only *which* man, but also *what kind of man* committed the crime. Indeed, the secret of who the man is that has committed the crime is a one that covers the second much more interesting secret. Diana Baring (Martella in the novel) cannot remember what happened at the moment of the murder, for she has entered into a trance-like state (like the state of the female protagonist who unwittingly kills in *Blackmail*).[18] However, she also refuses to reveal the name of the third party at the scene of the crime, who is an obvious suspect, on the grounds that he has confided in her a secret. She believes that by revealing his identity, somehow his secret, which must be concealed at all costs, will also be revealed. In the novel *Enter Sir John*, the secret described is that Fane is a ''chi-chi,'' a term that Sir John clarifies as ''Half-caste—Eurasian.'' In the film, the secret is just that Fane is a ''Half-caste,'' the meaning of which is clarified by Sir John as ''black blood.'' This is a man whom Baring could not possibly love; indeed in the novel Martella says that Sir John must be ''completely lunatic to think such a thing.''

Before Clemence Dane's success on the stage with works such as *Bill of Divorcement* (1921), which exposed the gender inequities of the Divorce Law, she wrote a popular and influential novel, *Regiment of Women* (1917), about the powerful, if destructive influence of lesbian desire in a girl's boarding school. The lesbian heroine of *Regiment*, Clare Hartill, is a source of extraordinary power and allure, and the novel does not shrink from registering the full force of lesbian desire and the rewards of female companionship that the institution of the girl's school affords. Yet Clare Hartill is ultimately portrayed as a corrupt influence upon her charges, and in particular, Alywnne Durand, a young impressionable teacher. Physically barren, in a manner that literally realizes the early-twentieth-century sexologists' conception of the lesbian as a masculine woman, Clare is incapable of nurturing young people and forming psychologically healthy relationships. Alwynne is made to outgrow her romantic friendship (albeit with difficulty, for it is hard to escape the clutches of a vampire) and to form a "healthy" natural procreative relationship with a Lawrentian male, one Roger Lumsden, market gardener, who conveniently enough has a mixed gender school on his property. Roger succeeds in "uprooting all the weeds that were choking her" and plants "good seed in their stead." Although *Regiment of Women* displays the allure of lesbianism, it is ultimately phobic about same-sex desire. Clare Hartill (Heart-ill) is a dysgenic figure (to use the vocabulary of eugenic ideology), a degenerate whose influence will undermine the perpetuation of the race which it is the task of well-bred white women to uphold on both racial and sexual grounds. The novelist suggests that it is all right for a few women of money and exceptional intelligence to choose this path, but they must not be allowed to recruit weaker more impressionable women to their cause.[19] Indeed, we might conclude, it is all the more important for such masculine women (like Dane herself?) to uphold the values of race, procreativity, and empire.[20]

The issues raised by *Regiment of Women* are relevant to *Enter Sir John* and ultimately *Murder!* too, for *Regiment* is about how an institution fosters the break-up of normative patterns of sexual and social identity, even as it seeks to restore the natural order of heterosexual, procreative sexuality. In *Enter Sir John* and *Murder!*, the domain of the theater is a social institution that is accorded a similar role, as a place where social distinctions and class distinctions are conflated in the activity of performance, and a place where, due to the close physical and social proximity of the performers, norms of sexual decorum are transgressed off the stage as well as on. In both novel and film, Baring is a young ingenue who knew Sir John before the circumstances of the trial but was sent away by him to the provincial theater to learn her craft. He feels guilty, for it seems that her morality has been laid siege to by the circumstances in which she finds herself. First of all she is exposed to people of a lower class (and inferior moral sense), like the promiscuous Mrs. Druce, who seek to undermine her integrity and poise through gossip and innuendo. Second, and most critically, she is exposed to the advances of a man who is ''a half-caste.''

The threat posed by the half-caste is eloquently stated by feminist reformer Frances Swiney, who grew up in India, in her book *The Awakening of Women or Women's Part in Evolution* (1899):

> the half-caste . . . literally born of sin, inherits usually the vices of both parents, with the virtues of neither . . . it is to the influence of the white women in the future that we must look for the enforcement of that high and pure morality, which will restrain the conquering white man from becoming the progenitor of racial crossing with a lower and degraded type. Our modern civilization counts for little if the great Anglo-Saxon nation cannot keep its blood-royal pure and undefiled.[21]

According to Lucy Bland, Swiney was ''no aberrant exception; she spoke the language of maternalist Imperialism, held in common by many, if not most, English middle-class feminists of her time''[22] Her fears are echoed by the heroine of *Enter Sir John*, who also grew up in India. Fane explains to Sir John that he dared not risk the heroine discovering his secret ''because of a look I saw in her eyes once when a lascar [a native Indian] brushed against her in the street. She can't help the feeling. She was born in India. She was brought up to look at us—so! But I love her. And if ever she'd looked at me—so!—one of us would have died. And it was that poor meddling fool of a woman died instead. She'd

have let her know: and I'd rather she hanged than knew."[23]
Like Clare Hartill, then, the "half-caste" in Enter Sir John is
a threat to the purity and superiority of the race on both
racial and sexual grounds.

The novelists register the white woman's dread of a racial
and sexual contamination—the brush of a "degenerate" male
black body on her pure white skin—only to sympathize with
the victim of such prejudice. Indeed, it is finally in response
to racist insult that Fane murders Mrs. Druce: "Do you know
what she called me? She called me a black beast. She called
me a murdering nigger. I stopped her screaming then."[24] But
the sympathy with Fane is a product of the racial
assumptions of the novel rather than an antidote to them, for
this sympathy stems from assuming the racially
"degenerate" nature of Fane while objecting to his
prejudicial treatment on the grounds that he cannot help
being who he is. It turns out that Baring knew all along that
Fane was a half-caste, yet sustains her friendship with him
nonetheless and thereby risks notoriety, as Sir John makes
clear when he worries what will happen to her reputation
when her "semi-friendship" with Fane is made public. By
overcoming her "instinctive" responses of disgust in this
way, Baring manifests her sense of her racial superiority, her
capacity for self-control, that aligns her with Sir John. When
the hapless Fane finds out that she always knew his true
nature, he declaims: "Yes—she had control—she was white.
But I'm not white, and she knew it all the time." He then
proceeds to reveal his own absence of self-control:
"Suddenly he flung himself down in the low chair by the
window, and began to sob with . . . abandonment."[25] Fane
is thus a figure of sympathy precisely because through no
fault of his own he has been "handicapped," in the words
of Sir John, with the body and the passions of a half-caste
that would undermine the best will in the world.

Yet, if Fane is opposed to Baring and Sir John in terms of
race, he is also aligned with Baring and with the figure of Sir
John in terms of class (an alignment that is reiterated in the
film). We do not learn much about the way Fane looks, but

he is described as ''slim yet rounded, with his muscles lying close to the bone,'' and he is positively contrasted with the racist portrayal of the ''strong, but badly proportioned'' ''ape-like'' Jew who is his partner in an acrobatic turn. The theatrical agents who hire him to play the musical hall circuit describe him as being too ''la di da,'' and he appears for the reading of Sir John's play of the Baring case with a hat and cane. The suggestion is, I think, that one side of Fane's half-caste/Anglo-Indian status signals good breeding. Either way, Fane, like Diana, is a class apart from most of the company they keep in the provincial theater, because both of them exert self-control, in contrast to lower-middle-class theater people like Mrs. Druce. In the novel, it is precisely Baring's self-command that puts her under suspicion. Her control in the witness stand is taken as an index of her ability to pull the wool over people's eyes, but it also explains to one juror how it is that she committed the crime: ''Here's an excitable, vulgar woman letting herself go and an excitable well-bred woman holding herself back. I dare say the wretched girl's account of it was true enough; the quarrel really took her by surprise; and when she did lose control she really didn't know what she was doing, or what happened.''[26] Yet it is also on the same grounds that Sir John knows that Baring is innocent because a woman of her class and self-control could not possibly have drunk the glass of whisky she was accused of drinking after the crime. Sir John is at the apex of this hierarchy of self-discipline—discipline of the body. Sir John is a man who struggles with the passions of the body but has supremely mastered the art of self-control, a control that is epitomized in his mastery of language. It is for this reason that he identifies with Baring: he recognizes poise and breeding when he sees it.

In *Enter Sir John*, the metaphor of life as a stage and the idea of identity as a performance are linked to the idea of the attainment of bodily control and self-discipline. The performance of the self is about containing the beast within, and thereby about the necessary affirmation of normative identity of imperial, white, heterosexuality that is cemented by the union of Sir John and Baring. While Fane is a figure of sympathy and understanding in the novel and eludes capture at the end, the project of *Enter Sir John* is nonetheless to banish the threat of racial deviance and difference from the shores of Albion and assure the continuation of the race. But what exactly is the nature of the beast within, which this racial/racist discourse is at pains to neutralize? What kind of absence of self-control might threaten the formation of the couple? What might the name of Fane that condenses the idea of feigning, vanity, "faining" or wistfulness, and the derogatory adjective "fay," connote other than, and indeed more readily than, "racial degeneracy," especially when taken together with his "la di da" airs and feminine voice? How would this connotation affect our perception of the bachelor dandy hero as one who is best suited to preserve the race because he treats the passions with such disinterest and with such self-control? Are we not to find irony in the fact that the very straight theater manager, Markham, takes the first name Novello, after the homosexual theater impresario, matinee idol, and entertainer Ivor Novello? And could it be that Sir John is modeled upon Dane's homosexual actor-friend Noel Coward, of whom she sculpted a bust? Lurking in the novel, contained within its themes about identity, self-control, and race, is arguably an unstated preoccupation with homosexuality.[27]

Hitchcock and Alma were too keen observers of the wider theatrical and cultural milieu of which Dane was a part not to pick up on the connotations that are buried in the novel. They had, we should note, already collaborated on two films with Ivor Novello, *The Lodger* and *Downhill* (1927), and adapted Coward's *Easy Virtue* for the screen in 1927. Not only does Hitchcock invite us to sympathize with Fane's predicament, he suggests that Sir John's and Baring's understanding of Fane's identity, an understanding shared by the novel itself—namely, that Fane is a racial half-caste—is somehow an inadequate characterization of Fane's identity. In this way, Hitchcock and Alma at once distance themselves from the racial ideology of the novel (even as they do not wholly overcome it) and display its concealed subtext. For what we see in the film is that Fane is defined not by his racial half-caste status but by his ambiguous masculine-feminine identity, that is, by a queerness that is embodied in his *performances* of identity. For Hitchcock, though not for Sir John and Baring, this ''queerness'' is what Handel Fane's half-casteness seems to refer to.

The film furnishes essentially two sets of cues as to Fane's secret. The first set is given by facts that are reported about him by Diana, and more particularly by Sir John. These are culled more or less directly from the novel and pertain to his half-caste characteristics, although the identification of Fane as a half-caste in the film is severed from any explicit mention of his Anglo-Indian origins. The second set of cues whose significance entirely eludes Sir John is conveyed by the manner in which Fane acts and behaves, which I have already described. These cues suggest a feminine or effeminate quality to Fane's character explicit in the novel only through the conceit that it is Fane's feminine voice that leads Baring to be falsely implicated in the murder of Mrs. Druce. *Murder!* not only suggests that Fane's femininity is an essential part of his identity but also that it is self-consciously performed. Hitchcock is surely suggesting here that there is something to be shown about Fane that cannot be explicitly scripted by Sir John. Here he parts company with the point of view of his main protagonist, and it is through this split point of view that the audience is invited to take a critical standpoint upon the heroic male lead and to identify with Handel Fane.

The film completes the thought that Fane is a half-caste only twice, and in both cases Hitchcock sees fit to make a narrational comment that serves to render the apparent revelation ambiguous. It is as if the film is registering the thought, so buried in the novel, that, by naming Fane a half-caste and apparently revealing his secret, something is being hidden or disguised. While Diana begins to blurt out Fane's secret in the prison scene, she swallows the phrase on the word ''half'' and the camera swish-pans over to Sir John who is left to complete the sentence. The movement of the camera expresses the sense of emotional vertigo experienced by the character who struggles to say what she cannot easily state, but it also suggests a blankness of meaning at the heart of the film itself, that is, the sense in which Fane's identity as a half-something is unnameable. Sir John completes her sentence for her as "half-caste," and then, as if coming to an understanding of the full implications of this term, adds "Black blood." This is the dialogue in full:

> DIANA: There is something, something he daren't have known.
> SIR JOHN: But which you knew?
> DIANA: Yes.
> SIR JOHN: What was it? [silence] You realize what you're admitting by your silence. You're shielding this man because you know you're in love with him.
> DIANA: Oh, but that's impossible.
> SIR JOHN: Impossible, why should it be impossible? I see no reason why it should be impossible.
> DIANA: Why the man's a half- [caste is audible but swallowed as she puts her hand to her mouth and the camera swish-pans to Sir John who rises to his feet and leans forward]
> SIR JOHN: What's that? What did you say? A half-caste! [and with a moment's reflection] Black blood!

Later, in the final scene of the film, Fane's suicide note, which completes the script that Sir John composes in order to trap the perpetrator of the crime, repeats the idea that it was a secret he dared not have known that caused him to murder. He concludes by explaining how the man "walks home a murderer, a murderer on an impulse, to silence the mouth of a woman who knew his secret, and was going to reveal it to the woman he dared to love." What is noteworthy here is first that Fane clearly does not name his own secret, and second that Sir John reads this note in a context that renders it barely audible, given the hubbub created by the shock of Fane's suicide. Hitchcock is clearly making a pointed joke about a story that, through the expedient of a suicide note, attempts to tie up all the loose ends; he is also certainly presenting a telling indictment of the racial "half-caste" explanation of Fane's identity as it is confidently espoused by Sir John: "Well, Markham, you have it all. Poor devil. And Diana Baring, she knew all along—he was a half-caste."

In the meantime what we see frames the discourse of half-casteness in a manner that completely undermines the authority of Sir John's final authoritative understanding. In the scene that Diana thinks while in her cell, Fane plays a central role. After Fane has delivered his lines on stage in a woman's voice, he emerges through the wings back stage, in drag, strutting menacingly towards the camera (and the audience of the film). What is the nature of Fane's menace here? Retrospectively, of course, we understand that Fane is in fact the criminal, but here the menace seems to lie in the defiant effrontery of Fane's drag performance, its proud in-your-face quality, that seems to assert the right of the character to have this female identity. The stage manager jokes to the policemen "This is Handel Fane, 100% he-woman." Then, as if to be serious, he notes that "Mr. Fane is our leading man." His comment might refer to the Fane of the stage (the he-woman) versus the Fane of real life (the man), but it could equally be taken to assert that the performed identity of Fane *is* his real identity, that Fane is a he-woman.

The second time we see Fane in this scene, he is dressed up as a policeman. Again Hitchcock takes his cue from a moment in the novel (also referred to in the film) when a policemen who is seen leaving the scene of the crime turns out to be Fane—he has handily donned the costume of the law to beat a hasty retreat in disguise. But this mildly ironic parody of the law is given a radical twist in the film, when Fane reemerges on screen sheathed not in the costume of a woman but in the costume of a policeman. Fane appears as a fay or feminine man donning, with self-conscious awareness of its utter absurdity, the costume of a policeman. He comments wryly "blood always makes me feel sick, even the mention of it," as he struggles in a singularly unmanful way to put on the policemen's hat that is perched precariously on his head and to reach the stage in what seems nothing less than a "straight jacket." (Whether or not Hitchcock, a relentless and outrageous punster, consciously had such a joke in mind, there are key examples throughout *Murder!* of Fane being restricted and discomfited by both male and female attire, and imprisonment in the film is enforced by gender roles as well as iron bars.) If his assumed feminine identity has previously been asserted as real, now his "natural" masculine identity appears artificial, fictional, part only of a stage performance and something imposed on a body that resists or defies its containment.

Hitchcock's presentation of Fane radically changes the status and significance of his character from the novel. A number of critics have argued that, for Hitchcock, half-casteness suggests the homosexual identity of Fane, where homosexuality is conceived as the idea of a woman's soul in a man's body or, in the case of lesbian desire, a man's soul in a women's body.[28] Clare Hartill in *Regiment of Women* embodies a man's soul in a woman's body, which is what makes her heart ill. And, as I have suggested, the reverse is hinted at in Dane and Simpson's novel, even as it is denied, for the character of Fane. Furthermore, the equation of homosexuality with the half-caste is entirely in keeping with late-nineteenth- and early-twentieth-century ideologies of race and sexuality. For eugenic theory connected the perpetuation of race, the white race, the English race with the sexual instinct itself as it was realized in procreative sex. Since the half-breed was a product of "dysgenic" procreation, his "mixed blood" could also be an index of sexual disorder. The nomination of the lesbian or homosexual as a half-breed simply reverses the logic of this argument, imputing these "sexual disorders" to an improper biological balance between masculinity and femininity. As Peter Swaab notes, this is precisely the way in which Daphne du Maurier describes herself in her letters to Ellen Doubleday, where she conceived her youthful identity as a ''half-breed,'' one in which a boy's soul was lodged in her woman's body.[29] However, this equation of masculine woman or feminine man with half-caste simply maps the logic of an essential racial identity and hierarchy upon gender identity. Men and women are essentially heterosexual, and homosexual desire is thus a deviant, degenerate expression of this.[30]

It seems to me, however, that *Murder!* does not *simply* equate half-casteness and masculine-femininity to produce the figure of the homosexual. First, by stripping the term ''half-caste'' of explicit reference to Anglo-Indian identity (though Esme Percy retains an ''olive-skin'' and slick black hair from the novel), and by suggesting that the half-caste explanation in fact falls short of being an accurate explanation, the film presents ambiguous gender identity as something that Fane's half-caste status at once alludes to yet disguises. As we have seen, the film nowhere explicitly uses the term ''half-caste'' to describe the gender ambiguity of Fane; rather, the term is explicitly reserved only as a racial designation. Yet this racial designation of Fane's secret fails to satisfactorily capture what it is that we see. Second, by linking the idea of ambiguous gender identity to the idea of the performance of self in art and life, the film transforms the way in which the relationship between identity and the body that bears identity is to be understood. For Fane's feminine identity is not an index of an essentially (degenerate) identity, it is a performed identity. Yet this performed identity is shown to be as real as the masculine identity the character is assumed to possess. The body of Fane in the film is thus a source of instability and ambiguity that defies the biological assumptions about the origins and nature of identity upon which the racial discourse of the novel is founded.

While *Murder!* does more than simply equate half-casteness with feminine masculinity in a manner that calls into question the assumptions about ''degenerate'' identity that the concept of the half-caste depends upon, Sir John fails to connect Fane's half-caste status with his performance of a feminine persona at all, and is therefore completely blind to the nature of Fane's identity. Having discovered Fane's secret from Diana that he is a "half-caste," Sir John goes to visit Fane in his new role as a circus acrobat in a scene I have already described. Observing that Fane is dressed as a woman, Sir John confidently asserts that this is an ideal form of disguise. Presumably Sir John's reasoning here is that Fane must perform in the public eye to live but in this context risks his identity being recognized or exposed—though this is scarcely a rational line of reasoning from Sir John, given the fact that this apparent "disguise" is so evidently legible. Sir John's comment also betrays his profound lack of understanding as to who Fane really is. Whereas Hitchcock has invited us to see Fane as a feminine man, which his performance of femininity helps to define, he portrays Sir John as one who is essentially blind to this aspect of Fane's identity. Sir John does not, of course, think of Fane's performance of femininity as his "true" identity, but neither does he take it to be an expression of Fane's sexually "half-caste" status. Instead, for Sir John this feminine identity is merely a shrewd disguise for Fane's real identity as a criminal man, because Sir John, after all, knows the difference between what is acted and what is real, what is false and what is true, and what is masculine and feminine. Sir John of course is correct in identifying Fane as a criminal, but his insight here coincides with an essential blindness to Fane's identity, a "sleuthing indifference" or insensitivity to Fane's true character.

I have described how the discourse of half-casteness is transformed from novel to film, from an essentialist racial category that signals degeneracy into what is a pretext for a complex meditation of the nature of sexual identity that dramatizes the coercive nature of the normative, heterosexual system of gender, even as the heterosexual romance is celebrated and affirmed. The racial category of half-casteness that Hitchcock takes from the novel thus functions in *Murder!* as a MacGuffin, a pretext to dramatize an aspect of identity—human sexuality—that Hitchcock is more interested in, indeed, obsessively interested in. But while Hitchcock's transformation of the racial/racist terms of the novel constitutes the achievement of the work, it also necessarily points to the limits of that achievement. For to instrumentalize the racial theme of the novel to say something else, however compelling, nonetheless leaves the casual racism of the "half-caste" moniker unresolved. The film adds nothing new to the racial/racist discourse of the novel, indeed the film's unsure treatment of the novel's racial themes serves to obscure their import. The novel, by contrast, at least has the virtue of seriously exploring its racial premise, however problematic its underlying assumptions ultimately prove to be. In England of 1930, it was possible for Hitchcock to present a complex, frank, and remarkably sympathetic portrait of human sexuality. Yet it seems that it was not possible for him to address with the same complexity and understanding the problem of racial identity. This failure is undoubtedly derived in part from the constraints of the time, in part from the constraints of an entertainment medium in which the portrayal of human sexuality holds such an allure, and in part from the limits of Hitchcock's authorship. By using cinema to show the sexual subtext that lies beneath the imperial, racial discourse of the novel, Hitchcock asserts the superiority of his own cinematic authorship over that of the novel. But in doing so, he also leaves the problems posed by the racial discourse of the novel unresolved.

Notes

My thanks to Sid Gottlieb and Ira Bhaskar for their comments on this paper. Thanks also to Rebecca Walkowitz who invited me to speak on the film at the Modernist Studies Association Conference, Madison, Wisconsin 2002.

1. Examples of the perverse super-villain in John Buchan include Moxon Ivery in *Mr. Standfast* (1919) and Dominick Medina in *The Three Hostages* (1924).

2. On the history of the dandy, see Ellen Moers, *The Dandy: Brummell to Beerbohm* (New York: Viking Press, 1960).

3. See Richard Allen, "Hitchcock, or the Pleasures of Metaskepticism," in Richard Allen and Sam Ishii-Gonzalès, eds., *Alfred Hitchcock: Centenary Essays* (London: BFI, 1999), 221-37, and "The Lodger and the Origins of Hitchcock's Aesthetic," *Hitchcock Annual* 11 (2001-02): 38-78. For a general discussion of the significance of the dandy in Hitchcock's films see Thomas Elsaesser "The Dandy in Hitchcock" in Allen and Gonzalès, eds., *Alfred Hitchcock: Centenary Essays*, 3-13.

4. Peter Swaab, "Hitchcock's Homophobia: The Case of *Murder!*," *Perversions* 4 (1995): 21-22.

5. Clemence Dane and Helen Simpson, *Enter Sir John* (New York: Cosmopolitan Book Corporation, 1928). See Charles Barr's discussion of the attraction of the novel to Hitchcock's studio in *English Hitchcock* (Moffat: Cameron and Hollis, 1999), 109.

6. See Tania Modleski, *The Women Who Knew Too Much: Hitchcock and Feminist Theory* (New York: Routledge, 1988), 31-42.

7. William Rothman, *Hitchcock: The Murderous Gaze* (Cambridge: Harvard University Press, 1982), 64. The chapter on *Murder!* is a pivotal chapter in this book.

8. Thanks to Sid Gottlieb for this suggestion.

9. Particularly relevant here is Eliot's *Sweeney Agonistes*, parts of which were published in 1926 and 1927, which had roots in jazz and music hall rhythms and interplay of voices, and was also a key part of Eliot's experiments with shifting points of view and audience involvement in a dramatic work. I am indebted to Sid Gottlieb for this reference.

10. Later, in *Vertigo*, the power of this figure of control and authority that Rothman calls the "gamesman-aesthete" takes on much darker, demonic tones as the smooth, eloquent, and debonair Gavin Elster ensnares the gullible Scottie Ferguson in his tale of the possessed Madeleine as Scottie, seated, looks up at his "performance."

11. Rothman, *Hitchcock: The Murderous Gaze*, 75.

12. Rothman, *Hitchcock: The Murderous Gaze*, 84.

13. See Allen, "*The Lodger* and the Origin of Hitchcock's Aesthetic," 41-45.

14. Rothman, *Hitchcock: The Murderous Gaze*, 89. Rothman spends six more interesting pages discussing this scene.

15. Hitchcock hints at the ribald corpse in *Jamaica Inn*, where a bawdy smuggler vows that his public hanging "with the women

watching'' will ''make 'em sit up,'' and again in *Rope*, where the strangled victim of a murder that is staged in a way that connotes the act of sex lies prostrate in a caisson. See Peter Conrad, *The Hitchcock Murders* (London: Faber and Faber, 2000), 261.

16. Lesley Brill, *The Hitchcock Romance* (Princeton: Princeton University Press, 1998).

17. Rothman, *Hitchcock: The Murderous Gaze*, 99.

18. Throughout *English Hitchcock*, Barr gives examples of the recurrent figure of the ''tranced woman'' in Hitchcock's films. There are ''tranced men'' as well, like Jonathan in *Stage Fright* and Scottie in *Vertigo*. Handel Fane is a particularly intriguing example of a tranced character, coded as both male and female.

19. For further discussion of *Regiment of Women*, see Gay Wachman, *Lesbian Empire: Radical Crosswriting in the Twenties* (New Brunswick: Rutgers University Press, 2001), 54-63.

20. There are echoes of this ideology in the writings of Daphne du Maurier, whose novel *Rebecca* Hitchcock was to faithfully adapt. See Richard Allen, ''Daphne du Maurier and Alfred Hitchcock,'' in Robert Stam and Alessandra Raengo, eds., *A Companion to Film and Literature* (Malden, MA: Blackwell, 2004), 298-325.

21. Frances Swiney, *The Awakening of Women or, Woman's Part in Evolution* (London: William Reeves, 1899), 121.

22. Lucy Bland, *Banishing the Beast: English Feminism and Sexual Morality 1885-1914* (London: Penguin Books, 1995), 231.

23. Dane and Simpson, *Enter Sir John*, 252.

24. Dane and Simpson, *Enter Sir John*, 254.

25. Dane and Simpson, *Enter Sir John*, 253.

26. Dane and Simpson, *Enter Sir John*, 112.

27. According to Rothman the murderer's secret in the novel is that he is ''a homosexual'' (*The Murderous Gaze*, 82). This is plainly wrong and reflects Rothman's failure to confront the role of the racial theme in the film.

28. Eric Rohmer and Claude Chabrol note that ''there is no doubt that the assassin's true secret is not that he is a half-breed in the ordinary sense but a sexual half-breed, a homosexual'' (*Hitchcock: The First Forty-Four Films* [New York: Ungar, 1979], 27). François Truffaut says that *Murder!* is ''a thinly disguised story about homosexuality'' (*Hitchcock* [New York: Simon and Schuster, 1967], 53). Raymond Durgnat writes that the film ''leaves us, sophisticates of 1970, in little doubt that 'half-caste' means 'left-handed,' which means bisexual or homosexual'' (*The*

Strange Case of Alfred Hitchcock [Cambridge: MIT Press, 1974], 112-13).

29. Swaab, "Hitchcock's Homophobia?," 16. Daphne du Maurier's diary entry is quoted in Margaret Forster, *Daphne du Maurier* (New York: Doubleday, 1993), 222.

30. On the relationship between racial and sexual "degeneracy," see Bland, *Banishing the Beast*, 288-96.

M ICHAEL   W ALKER

Topaz *and* Cold War *Politics*

Topaz (1969) has consistently been one of Hitchcock's least
appreciated films. The main problem, as Robin Wood has
pointed out, is that it is so uneven: a film ''in which
something approaching Hitchcock's best rubs shoulders with
his very worst.'' In his comments on the film, Wood
discusses what he refers to as the ''three superb
sequences''—the opening defection in Copenhagen, the Hotel
Theresa sequence, and the sequence culminating with Rico
Parra (John Vernon) shooting Juanita de Cordoba (Karin
Dor)—but is dismissive of the rest of the film.[1] My position
in this essay is that there is much in *Topaz* that is of interest,
but it would be useful to begin by looking at the features of
the film which are, by Hitchcock's standards, mediocre.
There would seem to be four main problem areas, each of
which can be traced back to production difficulties.

First, Hitchcock lacked his usual tight control over the
project. Donald Spoto details the film's troubled history:
Hitchcock went into production with a script from the novel's
author, Leon Uris, which he disliked; in desperation, he
summoned Samuel Taylor, co-scriptwriter of *Vertigo* (1958),
to London to do a complete rewrite, and some scenes were
only scripted just before filming; some of the actors—notably
Karin Dor and Claude Jade (Truffaut's suggestion)—were
only cast at the last moment; André Malraux, the French
Minister for culture, initially blocked any filming in France
because the script was adjudged anti-French.[2] All this created
considerable tension for the sixty-nine-year-old director, and
he was most unhappy throughout much of the European

128 MICHAEL WALKER

location work. The studio work back in Hollywood went altogether better, and one can see this in the finished film.[3]

Second, the script failed to solve the foreign language issue. In Hitchcock's earlier films set in non-Anglophone countries—notably *To Catch a Thief* (1954) and *Torn Curtain* (1966)—the scripts were written so that it was possible for indigenous characters to speak their native language to one another without a mainstream audience losing understanding. But in *Topaz* everyone simply speaks English. In Hitchcock's words: "All those Frenchmen and Cubans and Russians speaking *English*—it just didn't work."[4] There was, in fact, a solution: subtitles. *Operation Crossbow* (Michael Anderson, 1965) demonstrates that it was indeed possible for a mainstream film of the period to use this option. The film is set during the Second World War, and not only do the German characters speak German to one another, but when the Allied heroes (played by George Peppard, Tom Courtenay, and Jeremy Kemp) go undercover in German-occupied Holland, they, too, speak German. All these scenes are necessarily subtitled and the overall effect is a massive gain in authenticity. Whether it was lack of time or a failure of nerve on Hitchcock's part that prevented him from adopting the same solution, one can only concur with his retrospective judgment.

Third, the film's hero, André Devereaux, is played by an actor who is, for Hitchcock, unusually lightweight. Frederick Stafford's performance is at best adequate, and he conspicuously lacks charisma. It's as if Hitchcock's concern that Paul Newman was "too big" a star for *Torn Curtain* has resulted in his swinging too far the other way. Nor is Stafford the only actor who seems inadequate. With the magnificent exception of Philippe Noiret as Henri Jarre, all the French actors in the film give awkward, unconvincing performances, as if chafing under the imposition of having to speak English to one another. As a consequence, the film's final section, which is set in Paris, is markedly weaker than the rest of the film.

Fourth, the film was significantly shortened after Hitchcock had completed it. Bill Krohn records that

Hitchcock was sufficiently satisfied with the film to have the negative cut before it was previewed in San Francisco. It divided the preview audience . . . [resulting in] a four-month standoff during which Hitchcock tried to hold on to his cut, which was contractually his right, before finally agreeing to eliminate almost twenty minutes.[5]

Now that *Topaz* has finally been restored to its original length—on the Universal video released to celebrate Hitchcock's centenary in 1999 and on the more recent DVD—one can assess the film that Hitchcock actually made. The additional footage is approximately seventeen minutes, and although the film is still uneven, certain features are now more developed and the structural links between episodes are clearer. It is this longer version that I shall be discussing, together with the film's three alternative endings. There are several key areas, which I will treat under a series of subheadings.

Adaptation and Politics

Topaz is the only spy film from Hitchcock's Hollywood period adapted from a pre-existing source and based on a real-life political incident: the Cuban Missile Crisis. Although Leon Uris's novel *Topaz* develops a fictionalized story around it, the crisis itself was perhaps the most serious throughout the period of the Cold War, bringing the world to the brink of nuclear war.[6] This introduces certain constraints regarding the tone of the film; rather more is at stake than usual in a Hitchcock spy movie, so that, for example, it seems less appropriate to refer to the microfilm, here, as the MacGuffin. After all, the film's most sympathetic character, Juanita de Cordoba—and others—have died for it.

A major feature of Uris's novel is its virulent anti-communism. Indeed, its stream of anti-Castro rhetoric smacks heavily of CIA propaganda—Uris's sources, *Look* magazine tells us, included ''former members of various diplomatic and intelligence services'"[7]—which would not have appealed to Hitchcock. The rhetoric is supported by suitably negative characterizations. The novel's main representative of the Cuban communist regime, Rico Parra, is a savage brute, and Juanita loathes him. She sleeps with him purely so that French intelligence agent André Devereaux can make a safe escape from Cuba, and the act is presented as a noble sacrifice: to save the life of the man she loves. In the film, both through the script and John Vernon's admirable performance, Rico is utterly transformed. He is at least as sympathetic as André, and there is nothing to suggest that Juanita's long-standing affair with him is purely in order to extract information from him. Juanita evidently finds Rico an attractive man, and when he discovers that she has been spying against the communist regime, the balance of political positions is surprisingly fair. Her claim "You make my country a prison" and his response "No, you cannot judge" are given similar weight. Although this scene climaxes with him shooting her, he does so to spare her the pain of inevitable torture, and is in anguish as he carries out the act. Brilliantly filmed by Hitchcock like a love scene, this is in fact the most powerful sequence in the film, well described by Robin Wood.[8]

Uris's paranoia about a powerful and sinister communist conspiracy does not stop with the demonization of Cuba and the Soviet Union. In the novel, thanks to the clever anti-American disinformation of Topaz (a Soviet-run cell of highly-placed officials in the French government), it is only a matter of time before France falls to a communist take-over. Even François Picard, André's daughter's journalist boyfriend (husband, in the film) is sacrificed to further the message: he is killed for seeking to expose the power of the pro-communist elements. The film preserves the key stages of the novel's plot: the opening defection of a KGB official and his family; the American concern with the Soviet presence in Cuba; André's working with the CIA to uncover the meaning of this; his use of Juanita's spy network on Cuba; his unmasking of the Topaz leaders in Paris. But the way in which the political and personal material is inflected in the film is very different from the novel.

Whereas Uris sees communism as the source of all evil, Hitchcock sees Cold War politics itself as the source of corruption. Everyone working within the espionage framework, including André, is either exploitative, or ruthless, or both. The film emphasizes its critical position through a series of parallels between East and West that begin in the opening sequence: the defection of the Kusenovs (parents and daughter) in Copenhagen. As the daughter Tamara (Tina Hedstrom) is secretly on the phone to CIA official Mike Nordstrom (John Forsythe), he tells her to be in Den Permanente department store at closing time, finishing with "Be aware that we will be outside." As if on cue, Hitchcock cuts to a shot of a silent Soviet heavy, outside the room from which Tamara is phoning. He moves restlessly back and forth, like an animal waiting to pounce. Then, in the ensuing sequence at Den Permanente, Nordstrom is positioned outside the store and he, too, is moving restlessly. Both the Soviets and the Americans thus seem like hunters, waiting to trap their prey.

When the moment of defection arrives, CIA heavies move in to cut off their Soviet counterparts. A little dance ensues, which is choreographed to suggest on the one hand a game of American football, with defense strategically blocking offense; on the other, a game which is deadly serious: one Soviet heavy almost gets off a pot-shot at the Kusenovs in the fleeing car. Boris Kusenov (Per-Axel Arosenius) is not impressed: when he and his family are safely on board the plane that will fly them on the first leg of their journey to the U.S.A., he comments acidly, "It was very clumsy, this operation . . . it wasn't the way we would done it." As the plane takes off, it flies into the sunset: a cliché image that one can only see in context as ironic.

Also established in this opening sequence is the sense of surveillance as a threat. In the second shot after the credits, Hitchcock's camera cranes down to focus on a mirror fixed on the outside of the Soviet Embassy, a mirror that enables those inside to monitor arrivals and departures. In the mirror, we see a man watching intently as the Kusenov family leave the building. As soon as the family has left the compound, the man signals to one of the heavies to follow them. Outside, this heavy is joined by a woman and another man, and the three of them doggedly stalk the family through the downtown locations. It's as if the man's suspicious look is transmitted from the Soviet Embassy to pursue the Kusenovs wherever they go. It thus becomes the responsibility of the Americans to break this hostile chain of looks. However, in the "safe house" outside Washington D.C., where the Kusenovs are taken, they are similarly under surveillance, albeit—we trust—one which is less threatening.

Included within the film's parallels between East and West is a series of betrayals. Just as Kusenov, a deputy chief of the KGB, betrays the secrets of the Soviet Union, so Jacques Granville (Michel Piccoli) and Henri Jarre, the leading members of Topaz, betray the secrets of the West. Likewise, despite the "justification" of the real-life political situation—the Cuban Missile Crisis was hardly Cuba's finest hour—Juanita is betraying Cuba to the West. Her espionage network has been in operation against the communist regime for some time, and the film also encourages us to draw a connection between her and Granville. After André has been exposed in Cuba as an intelligence agent, Rico interrupts Juanita's dinner with him to denounce him. But Rico cannot believe that Juanita is involved: "She is a widow of a hero of the revolution; she is loved and honored in this country." Indeed, Juanita is herself identified with the revolution: when she is with Rico on the platform for Fidel Castro's speech, she, too, is in uniform. It is thus suggested that she and Rico share a common past linked to the revolution. But there is an equivalent common past between André, Granville and Nicole (Dany Robin), André's wife, as war-time Resistance fighters. In the shortened version, the only indication of this is a photograph of the three of them from this period, but in the restored version there are other references. When Nordstrom comes to dinner with André and Nicole, he asks about the carbine on the mantelpiece: Nicole tells him that it was the one she used in the Resistance. At a cocktail party in Paris, Granville mentions to a friend how close he, André, and Nicole have been "since our days in the war," and that Nicole might have married either of them. These references reinforce the links between Juanita and Granville. The film indicates that both are betraying not just a country, but an old and trusted bond of friendship, one which had been sealed in the struggles for their respective countries.

The film's pattern of betrayals begins with Kusenov. Early in the series of interrogations he experiences in the safe house at the hands of the CIA, he gives them the name of Luis Uribe (Don Randolph), Rico Parra's secretary, adding in a contemptuous voice, "He's a security risk . . . I have used him." Later, now pleased with the deal he has struck with the Americans, he is expansive—smoking a cigar and dispensing coffee—when he gives André the name of Jarre as the second-in-command of Topaz in Paris. He is identifying these men as traitors to their countries, but his information also serves, in effect, to consign each of them to death.

On the Western side, the Americans are at the top of the hierarchy of power, and, after the opening sequence, they function less as operators, more as people who get others to do their dirty work. When Nordstrom approaches André to ask him to find a way to photograph the contents of Rico Parra's briefcase, he passes off this highly dangerous task with a casual remark: "Just a taxi ride to Harlem, that's all we're asking." André, in turn, gives the job to one of his own agents, Dubois (Roscoe Lee Browne), who is the person who actually goes into the Hotel Theresa—where the Cuban delegation are staying—and makes contact with Uribe in order to complete the task. (The Hotel Theresa in Harlem is not from the novel, but from real life: it was where Fidel Castro stayed and where he met—to the irritation of the U.S. government—such figures as Gamal Abdel Nasser, Pandit Nehru, and Malcolm X.) Dubois and Uribe are caught in the act by Rico, and Dubois barely escapes with his life. In the meantime, André waits across the road, which both emphasizes his role as passive spectator and demonstrates his stupidity: he is well known to Rico, and if he's spotted his presence will inevitably seem suspicious. Here the surveillance theme is reinflected: because it is linked to espionage, and because those doing the spying are Western agents, the underlying fear is that they will themselves be observed. In fact, André is seen, but by Rico's assistant Hernandez (Carlos Rivas), who does not know him. However, in Cuba, he attends the Castro rally, is spotted again by Hernandez, and his cover is blown.

André's taxi-ride to Harlem in fact takes him to Dubois's flower shop, an iconographic gangster movie setting. As in a gangster movie, the shop is also a front, in this case for espionage work. The gangster overtones are not gratuitous. At several points in the film, the activities of the intelligence agents suggest gangsters without the flamboyance: the choreography of the opening defection is a good example. If the metaphor is extended to the whole film, we could say that the intelligence agents are like semi-official gangsters, the information they seek from one another is like the various rackets gangsters fight to control, and they are just as ready as gangsters to torture and execute "traitors." Spoto has commented on the film's use of flowers: "Every set is ablaze with floral arrangements, and the image suggests a ubiquitous and massive funeral, since each locale has the faint redolence of death."[9] It's as if the ubiquitous flowers carry the gangster overtones of the flower shop to the rest of the film. Hitchcock even includes a moment of typically black gangster humor. When Dubois escapes from his Cuban pursuers and returns safely to his flower shop, he adds a ribbon inscribed "Rest in Peace" to a cruciform arrangement of flowers. It's as if he's making ironic reference to the fate of Uribe.

The sense that André does not simply use other people, but does so rather recklessly, is enhanced when he goes to Cuba. Because of the Soviet presence, the island is under extremely tight security, but André persuades an initially reluctant Juanita to mobilize her spy network: her agents the Mendozas (Lewis Charles and Anna Navarro) are, as a consequence, captured, tortured, and—we assume—executed. Under torture, they reveal Juanita's name, which leads in turn to her death.

But the film strongly suggests that André's mission to Cuba is, in fact, too late and therefore unnecessary. In the novel, his presence in the country is sufficiently in advance of the crisis for the information he brings out to be useful to the Americans. But in the film, he does not fly in until October 22, 1962 (visible on the *New York Times* that he reads), the very day President Kennedy gave his alarming TV address to the nation, in which he stated that the Soviet Union had placed missiles in Cuba and he was going to instigate a ''quarantine'' of the island to stop further weapons arriving. That André's arrival on that date is intentional is confirmed by the newspaper's headline: ''Capital's Crisis Air Hints at Development on Cuba: Kennedy TV Talk is Likely.'' In other words, by this stage, the die was already cast: how much could André find out that was new? Now, this detail may well have been simply to give a sense of urgency to André's mission, but Lesley Brill picks up on another point that hints at the mission's redundancy:

> When Mike [Nordstrom] . . . gets the intelligence André Devereaux has obtained at the cost of at least four lives, he remarks that it ''confirms our information from other sources, including the U-2 photos.''. . . The combatants . . . have given their lives only to reinforce information already gained elsewhere.[10]

The film is clearly implying that André's trip to Cuba is an act of folly. On the one hand, he is keen to impress the Americans with his ability to penetrate the communist defenses on the island; on the other, he is very pleased to be able to visit his extremely attractive mistress. But the only significant outcome of his trip is that people are tortured and killed. There are many Hitchcock heroes who are viewed critically, but few are presented as harshly as André, who is so in thrall to the Cold War demands of his profession that he causes the death of the woman he loves.

The headline from the *New York Times* is one of several used in the film to chart the rise and fall of the missile crisis. Altogether, there are six newspaper headlines (this is the third), from the bizarre example on the *New York Herald Tribune* Nordstrom is reading outside Den Permanente ("Soviet Bomb, Biggest, 'Dirtiest,' Shocks World—The Whys of It") to the rather more precise one on the same newspaper discarded in the film's final shot: "Cuban Missile Crisis Over: Khrushchev Agrees To Scrap Bases." There is a definite sense of growing alarm, even suppressed hysteria, in some of these headlines—e.g., "Sea Showdown With Reds Near; Soviet Bloc Orders Combat Alert" and "Bombing of Missile Bases Held a Possibility"—and most of the newspapers are either being read by, or associated with (e.g., the *Washington Post* on André's doormat) the spies themselves. Collectively, the headlines thus serve to extend the paranoia of the spies out into the "real world." Historically, they are like a series of warnings about the seriousness of the crisis, but they also capture the sense of a U.S.A. in the grip of Cold War anti-communist paranoia.

André's French superiors are hostile to his involvement with the Americans, but they, too, are criticized. Just before André is first introduced, the French Ambassador in Washington, René D'Arcy (George Skaff) and a French General (Ben Wright) discuss him in order to establish the kind of man he is: the General resents his lack of respect and his closeness to the Americans; D'Arcy agrees, but praises his intelligence work. When André enters, he is quick to realize the implications of Paris knowing about a KGB defector, and he confuses the General with his incisive questions. The scene is familiar: the maverick hero is introduced by setting his intuitive grasp of the film's issues against the more lumbering understanding of his superiors.

But the hero is also being positioned for the audience in another way. It is unusual, in a Hollywood Cold War movie, for the hero to be French. *Topaz* covers this by aligning the hero with the Americans, and differentiating him from his superiors in emphasizing his freedom from the constraints of narrow nationalistic concerns. But this imputes to the French authorities a blinkered isolationism, which perhaps was part of the reason for André Malraux's displeasure.

The surveillance theme in the film refers above all to the activities of the spies: their wish to seek out secret information and to avoid detection in the process. But the film also refers to a linked but contrasting theme, that of exhibitionism, which it attributes above all to the communists. The credits occur over the bombastic annual parade of phallic weaponry and marching troops in Red Square on May Day; in Cuba all we get of Castro's speech are the celebrities displaying themselves on the platform. Che Guevara, too, is included in this part-documentary footage, jauntily adjusting his beret for the crowd. It is precisely this weakness for display that Dubois exploits when he gets Rico on to the balcony of the Hotel Theresa to wave to the crowds below. Rico's vanity is flattered, and this gives Uribe the opportunity to steal his briefcase.

The Hero and His Doubles

It has often been observed that, in a number of Hitchcock films, the villain is a far more charismatic figure than the hero: *Shadow of a Doubt* (1942), *Strangers on a Train* (1951), and *Psycho* (1960) are obvious examples. It's much the same in *Topaz*: Rico Parra has a presence and stature that makes André seem relatively ordinary. Moreover, the film possesses another powerful villain, Granville. Even though Michel Piccoli fails to establish an equivalent presence to John Vernon's Rico, the pattern is clear. André is in fact involved in two sexual triangles: one in Cuba, where Rico is a rival for Juanita; and one in Paris, where Granville is a rival for Nicole. Both triangles are political as well as sexual, and in both the other man has a political power which far outstrips that of the hero. In the novel, Granville's power is spelt out: he is both a Soviet agent and an adviser to the French President. In the film, no doubt to appease André Malraux, his exact position in the French government is never specified. But his power is still clearly registered. It is emphasized further in the restored version, where we see his almost palatial main Paris residence, and the information that he acquired this through marriage implies that his power is sexual as well as political. Hitchcock's gravitation to charismatic villains at the expense of undistinguished heroes is thus here doubly emphasized: André is in competition with two such figures.

Both Rico and Granville, in their different ways, are like ''doubles'' of the hero: the former representing the sort of open, direct, commanding figure André would (perhaps unconsciously) like to be; the latter the crafty, duplicitous, sneaky figure he feels—in part—he really is. But there are two more men who also function as doubles for André: Nordstrom and Kusenov. As Spoto has pointed out, Nordstrom is matched visually with André: ''the same coloring, haircut, features and clothing.''[11] Nordstrom personifies the faceless-ness of the professional intelligence agent: he looks boringly conventional because he needs to pass as an ordinary bureaucrat (or whatever). There is no sense that he has any life outside the CIA; he represents the absorption of the individual into the system. In the restored version, Tamara Kusenov's knees are seen to be badly grazed after she falls during the defection, and Nordstrom asks the plane's pilots to radio ahead and arrange for some new nylons to be waiting for her at the Wiesbaden base. The pilots smile at the request—the gift is, after all, another cliché—but we know perfectly well that there's nothing sexual about Nordstrom's concern. He is strictly a desexualized double, a rather depressing indication of what could happen to André.

The more flamboyant Kusenov suggests another possibility. Although the Devereaux family structure is the same as the Kusenovs, the two men are not otherwise connected until relatively late in the film, when André is finally taken by Nordstrom to meet Kusenov. It's at this point that Kusenov tells André about Topaz, and identifies NATO economist Jarre as its second-in-command. He only knows its leader by his code name, Columbine. Since André has already been summoned back to Paris to account for himself (for his activities in Cuba), he thus faces the problem that his inside knowledge of the U.S.A.'s intentions towards Cuba and the Soviet Union will ''get back to Moscow'' if he explains himself to his superiors. Kusenov, still expansive, offers advice: ''You are faced with the same problem I had: whether to obey your conscience or . . . your government. Let me give you a piece of advice: don't go home. These people will give you a new life, a new job, everything. Think it over.''

André's four doubles serve to identify the conflict of forces within him. In the past, as a young man fighting in the French Resistance, he was like Rico. But he has since opted for intelligence work, which requires him to be self-effacing, like Nordstrom, and duplicitous, like Granville. The duplicitousness extends to his sexual as well as his political activities: Rico is quite open about his affair with Juanita; André lies to Nicole about his own affair with her. André would differentiate himself from Granville in that the latter is betraying his own country, whereas André has remained a patriot. But his association with the Americans, which he has cultivated over the years, has placed him in a perilously divided position, as Kusenov points out. Finally, Kusenov represents a temptation: even though we cannot imagine that André would do as Kusenov advises, he is already in some respects like a double agent, working for both America and France.

A motif linking the three communist doubles is cigar smoking. In earlier films, Hitchcock tended to associate cigar smoking with the villain—e.g., Tracy (Donald Calthrop) in *Blackmail* (1929), Uncle Charlie (Joseph Cotten) in *Shadow of a Doubt*—but in *Torn Curtain* and *Topaz* he associates it with communism. The association is reinforced by the well-known connection between Cuba and cigars. In *Torn Curtain*,

Gerhard (Hansjoerg Felmy) offers Michael (Paul Newman) a cigar with the comment: ''Cuban: your loss, our gain.'' In the novel of *Topaz*, cigar smoking is widespread, but Uris informs us that André smokes Jamaican cigars, thus making it quite clear that his hero is uncontaminated by any of those nasty communist cigars from Cuba.

In the film of *Topaz*, only the communists smoke cigars, but Hitchcock develops the motif by establishing a series of links between the smokers and the hero. Rico is seen smoking a cigar twice: in his hotel room while his private papers are being photographed, and when he comes to Juanita's house to expose André—and to try to displace him from Juanita's bed. In these two scenes, Rico believes himself to be in control, but André triumphs. The next example marks a shift in the balance of power. When Kusenov smokes a cigar, he emphasizes his sense of his own superiority by only offering André a cigarette. In this scene, André is first shocked by the revelation of Topaz, then advised by Kusenov to follow his own example and betray his country. Here the hero is troubled rather than triumphant.

The third example goes further towards undermining the hero. When Jarre realizes that he is in danger of being exposed as a spy, he visits Granville at the latter's *pied-à-terre* to suggest that André be killed. This is the scene where it is revealed that Granville is Columbine, but more relevant to the personal story is that Granville, as he repeatedly says, is expecting a guest. The guest turns out to be Nicole, and Granville is already wearing a red dressing-gown in anticipation of the sexual encounter. And so, his lighting a massive cigar as he talks to Jarre is a sign of his phallic mastery over the hero, whom he is about to cuckold.

The purpose of Jarre's visit here, together with its timing—just before Nicole's arrival—echoes Rico's interruption of Juanita and André's dinner. What saves André's life in the earlier scene is Juanita: in Rico's words, ''If it were not for her . . . that it might involve her, you would disappear tonight—you would be with Uribe.'' Granville's response to Jarre's suggestion is more ambiguous. He also rejects the idea of killing the hero, but does so by mocking Jarre: "How bloodthirsty you are. What: Devereaux dead; a grieving widow; an official investigation?" Again, a woman—Nicole, the prospective grieving widow—is mentioned as part of his reason for not wishing André dead, but Granville's tone suggests that he is being ironic. After all, he is quite happy, later that same day, to order the murder of Jarre, which could equally, one feels, lead to an official investigation. In keeping with his character, Rico is direct in his declaration that he really wants André dead; in keeping with his, Granville is deceptive. The irony in his voice is double-edged: he may genuinely not wish André killed; he may just be affecting mockery to stall Jarre. The first of the film's endings would suggest the latter, but the second implies the former.

The Endings

The ending of Uris's novel is fairly bleak. The Missile Crisis is, of course, resolved, but Granville is too powerful—and the French President too pig-headed—for André to be allowed a happy ending: he and his family are forced to flee into exile, and the final chapter ends inconclusively, with his making contact with Nordstrom to seek the latter's help. The only hopeful sign for André is that he has told his story to an American writer (implicitly, Uris himself), so that "the truth" will eventually come out.

Hitchcock evidently did not want the film to end with such a lack of closure. The first ending he filmed was a duel between André and Granville in the deserted Charlety stadium. One can see why he was attracted to this idea: sharing a common nationality as well as a personal history with André, Granville is the most important of his doubles. A duel would thus satisfy the sense of the hero doing battle with his dark side, and the formal, anachronistic ritual would also comment on the old-fashioned sensibilities of those involved. This and the other two endings are included on the DVD (the video only has the second ending) of the restored *Topaz*. All the endings have the same final shot: the *Herald*

Tribune ("Cuban Missile Crisis Over") discarded on an avenue leading to the Arc de Triomphe; the cast list coming up over a "life goes on" shot of people walking on the avenue. It is in the scenes immediately preceding this that the differences lie.

The duel ending is introduced by another scene between André, Nicole, their daughter Michèle (Claude Jade), and her husband François (Michel Subor). It's quite short—Andre tells the others that he felt he had no choice but to accept the duel—but, typically of the scenes with these four, it is awkwardly acted and unconvincing. The duel itself, with François as André's second, is slightly better, and the two duellists are dressed in identical black clothing, so that visually they mirror one another. As the men level their pistols at each other, Hitchcock inserts a point-of-view shot along the axis of one of the guns. We can deduce narratively that this is Granville's view of André, but it's hard to tell visually, which emphasizes the sense of the two men as doubles. But Granville is then shot by a sniper in the stands; André realizes that this is the work of the Russians, to whom Granville is now useless, and the sequence ends with André walking towards a tearful Nicole. It's not a terrible ending, just rather unsatisfactory. One can see why the preview audience rejected it.[12]

The second ending, which was shown in the West End in London in late 1969, also preserves the sense of André and Granville as doubles. As André and Nicole board a plane returning them to Washington, Granville boards an adjacent plane en route to Moscow, and waves a cheerful "Bon Voyage" to André. After a brief exchange between André and Nicole, in which they marvel that Granville has gotten away with it, André delivers the film's closing line: "Anyway, that's the end of Topaz." Yet André seems quite amused that Granville has escaped justice; reminding us that the men really are old friends, the tone is radically different from the duel ending. In Dan Auiler's *Hitchcock's Secret Notebooks*, there is a transcribed phone call between Hitchcock and the film's editor, Bill Ziegler, dated September 17, 1969, in which Hitchcock declares that this is ''the correct ending. In every case, whether it be Philby, Burgess [or] McLean, they've all gotten away with it and they've all gone back to Russia.''[13]

In the same conversation, Hitchcock refers to the third, ''suicide,'' ending as having been concocted purely to satisfy the French government, which was unhappy about Granville getting away with it. In this version, Granville's (implied) suicide is followed by a montage of shots taken from earlier in the film, superimposed over a freeze of the *Herald Tribune's* front page. Hitchcock declares that, even if they are forced to use this ending in France, he wants the second ending used elsewhere.[14] But, after its West End screening, *Topaz* went out on general release in the UK with the third ending, and this was the only ending seen in North America. Nevertheless, even though it is apparent that this ending was a last-minute effort—even the suicide is a mock-up, combining an out-take with process work and superimposing the sound of a gunshot—the montage, focusing on the pain and deaths of various characters, has at least an appropriate sense of bleakness. Krohn states that this is in fact the ending that Samuel Taylor wanted, and that it was he who talked Hitchcock into substituting it for the second ending, which he maintained was ''too light, too comedic, and in essence a betrayal of the very story you have told.''[15]

Spying and Sexuality

Hitchcock's tendency to sexualize even his spy narratives is well-known.[16] The beautiful female spy who is in some sense between the hero and an enemy agent is found, for example, in *Secret Agent* (1936), *Notorious* (1946), and *North by Northwest* (1959). The André/Juanita/Rico triangle in *Topaz* is another version of this; the (regrettably underdeveloped) André/Nicole/Granville triangle is a domestic variation (Nicole is not a spy). The combination of sex and spying enables Hitchcock—and others working in the genre—to link the deceptiveness of sexual relationships to the duplicity of the spy, and to introduce into the bedroom the plotting (the business with the key in Notorious) and paraphernalia (André's electronic gifts to Juanita) of the intelligence agent. The implicit eroticization of the spy's mission is encapsulated in Topaz in the farewell gift Juanita presents to André: a book, inscribed with her love, which also contains the microfilm.

The sexual triangles in Notorious and North by Northwest are both implicitly Oedipal, in that the heroine is involved with an older (Notorious) or more powerful (North by Northwest) man who is the hero's rival. This also applies to the first triangle in Topaz: as André first arrives at Juanita's hacienda, she comes out to greet him accompanied by Rico, who places a proprietorial arm around her shoulders. The ensuing scene on the doorstep combines elements from the party sequence in Notorious (the duping of the man who has possession of the heroine, which will culminate with the discovery of his secret weapon), and the first part of the auction room scene in North by Northwest (the hero's first sight of the heroine with the political villain, with the heroine's loyalties as yet unclear). In front of Rico, André hands Juanita a boxed gift, declaring that it's "nylon things from the United States." Again, Hitchcock ironizes the cliché: what else would André have brought from capitalist U.S.A. to communist Cuba? But this is also the equivalent of the pre-Columbian statuette Vandamm (James Mason) buys at the auction: the box in fact contains electronic espionage equipment; the statuette, the microfilm. In other words, the MacGuffin (North by Northwest) and the tools that will help reveal the MacGuffin (Topaz) are both introduced at a point of Oedipal tension for the hero. Since one can also extend this observation to the scene after the discovery of the MacGuffin in Notorious—when Sebastian (Claude Rains) catches his wife Alicia (Ingrid Bergman) and Devlin (Cary Grant) in a kiss—we can see that the MacGuffin is not necessarily as innocent a device as Hitchcock has always maintained. Although the scene in Topaz is undoubtedly lightweight in comparison with its predecessors, in all three examples—and one feels sure they are not alone—the MacGuffin is linked to psychosexual tensions between hero, heroine, and villain.

But in *Topaz*, there is an earlier scene in which the hero succeeds in discovering the secrets of his sexual rival: the Hotel Theresa sequence. This introduces further complications, since the sequence is charged with homosexual overtones. The furtive way Dubois approaches Uribe in the hotel lobby and takes him outside to proposition him, finally tempting him with money; the men's rendezvous in Uribe's bathroom; the way they are caught by Rico doing something illicit (taking the photographs) on the bed; Dubois's hasty escape through the window; the irate Rico firing a gun after the fleeing Dubois—the sequence of events is exactly like a forbidden sexual encounter that is rudely interrupted. (None of this is in the novel.) For the first stage of this series of encounters, André is a voyeur, watching Dubois pursue and win over the reluctant Uribe. This scene is particularly gripping: the camera films Dubois and Uribe from André's position across the road, using point-of-view editing, with the point-of-view shots filmed through a telephoto lens. The acting of the two men is slightly exaggerated, as they mime what's going on for our benefit, but it is striking how much physical contact occurs between them: not only does Dubois repeatedly touch Uribe, but, after the deal has been struck, Uribe reciprocates. Then, at the end of the sequence, André himself is incorporated into the gay subtext. Fleeing from the Cubans, Dubois gives André the camera by falling on top of him, a little charade which is like an echo of the sexual overtones of the illicit hotel encounter.

In *Hitchcock and Homosexuality*, Theodore Price maintains that there are homosexual overtones in many, if not most, of Hitchcock's films, but says that he could find none in *Topaz*.[17] Given the cavalier way in which Price attributes gayness to the most unlikely candidates—from Crewe (Cyril Ritchard) in *Blackmail* to Michael in *Torn Curtain*—this is surprising. However, if the Hotel Theresa sequence does have gay overtones, how are we to read them? It seems too facile to suggest that DuBois and/or Uribe could themselves be gay, and that the former is cleverly winning the latter over with a polished technique. The polished routine is certainly there, but there is a much stronger sense that Dubois is being presented as transgressive, able to cross the boundaries (sexual, racial, political) which otherwise hem in Hitchcock's characters. Dubois is, after all, one of the very few black characters in Hitchcock's work, and the location is Harlem. It's as if we are in a "zone of license," in which otherwise transgressive activities can occur. The corridor linking Rico's and Uribe's second floor rooms is a hive of feverish activity: uniformed Cubans talking and moving around, prostitutes, cleaners, cops, plainclothesmen, journalists, photographers, and anarchists wanting to bomb the Statue of Liberty. With its overtones of violence and licentiousness, we could see this as a representation of the Hitchcock "chaos world," but Dubois weaves his way through it with assurance and aplomb.

Another possible reading of the first part of the sequence is that the gay overtones could apply to André as voyeur, with Dubois's "flirtation with" Uribe standing in for André's own unconscious sexual fantasies. After all, Uribe is structurally in the same position as Juanita later: Rico's trusted partner who is "seduced"—in this case, by André's agent—in order to persuade him/her to give up Rico's secrets. But I think, rather, that the overtones arise out of the way in which Hitchcock sexualizes espionage, as if to say that spying inevitably carries an erotic charge, and that this applies to men looking at other men just as, in other contexts, it applies to men looking at women. Because of the use of the telephoto lens, the effect is particularly pronounced when André watches Dubois and Uribe. In *Rear Window* (1954), the telephoto lens point-of-view shots are all diegetically motivated, i.e., they only occur when we are seeing someone's (usually Jeff/James Stewart's) point of view through an optical device. Here it is Hitchcock-as-director who has introduced the mediating lens, the main effect of which is to draw us closer to the observed action. This suggests that it is Hitchcock's engagement with the voyeurism, and with the little play he has created between the two men, that creates the sexual charge.

Uribe's bathroom, which he and Dubois pass through en route to the fulfillment of their mission, is echoed in Juanita's darkroom at the back of her pantry. Both rooms are illuminated by a naked light bulb and associated with espionage: planning it, in the former; processing the results of it, in the latter. When, on the plane out of Cuba, André goes into a toilet to discover the microfilm hidden in the book Juanita gave him, he is uncovering the end result of this processing, which Hitchcock has set in another room that echoes the earlier examples. This, in turn, points to a curious motif in Hitchcock's spy films: the linkage of bathrooms/toilets to espionage. In *Secret Agent*, there is a relatively long scene between Ashenden (John Gielgud) and Elsa (Madeleine Carroll) in their hotel bathroom, in which Ashenden reads to her the details of a message he has just decoded, which concern their mission. Both *North by Northwest* and *Torn Curtain* include washroom and shower scenes in which the rooms are linked, in different ways, with espionage. It would seem that Hitchcock's penchant for setting scenes concerning the activities of his spies in bathrooms and toilets extends the familiar voyeurism/espionage connection. It's as if, at some—perhaps quite unconscious—level he associates the rooms themselves with voyeurism, and so tends to keep placing his professional voyeurs in them.

When André unpacks for Juanita the boxed gift he displayed in front of Rico on the doorstep, he demonstrates the workings of its contents, thus behaving, ironically, exactly like the salesman (''commercial attaché'') he is supposed to be. But the gift is also linked to its Russian equivalents. When Kusenov is questioned about Cuba, he is asked what the Russian technicians are doing there. His response is pointedly evasive: ''They came bearing gifts from Russia to Cuba''—exactly as André brings his own (Cold War) gift from the United States to Cuba. However, a more suggestive link is between André's gift and Rico's briefcase:

both are closely guarded secrets referring to or associated with exposing the Soviet missiles. In that André's demonstration ends with him and Juanita in bed together, DuBois and Uribe's investigation of the contents of the briefcase is once more, by association, sexualized.

Towards the end of *Topaz*, André again gets someone else to do the dangerous job of finding out politically sensitive information: François, a journalist, is sent to interview Jarre in order to expose him as a traitor. It is possible to deduce that this scene was intended as a darker version of the Hotel Theresa sequence, with the climactic fall from an upstairs window leading here to death. A small detail that explicitly connects the two sequences is an ''Out of Order'' lift sign in each of the lobbies. However, although the actual scene between François and Jarre is one of the better ones in the French section of the film—above all, because of Noiret's performance—the scenes around it, which should have given it substance, are poor. As a consequence, the implicit tensions have to be extrapolated from the material: one can see what Hitchcock was moving towards, but he has failed to dramatize this sufficiently.

For example, the father-daughter relationship. Abandoned by his wife and with his mistress dead, André is ''left with'' Michèle, but the father-daughter Oedipal overtones that Hitchcock seems to have wanted to imply never really materialize. In the restored version, André is driven from the Paris Airport by François and Michèle, and François then leaves André and Michèle together on Granville's doorstep. There seems little doubt that Hitchcock intended this doorstep scene to echo the one with André, Juanita, and Rico in Cuba. François, like Rico, leaves; just as Juanita wore a red dress, so Michèle is wearing a red coat, which, we discover once inside, is covering a red dress. But, inside the house, where Granville has set up a cocktail party for André, Michèle fades quickly into the background, as first Nicole and then Granville come over to talk to André. Although the scene ends with father and daughter back together, nothing then happens.

There is a similar sense of insufficient dramatization after François has exposed Jarre. As François phones André from Jarre's apartment, he is cut off, prompting André and Michèle to rush round to see what has happened. The apartment is empty, but Michèle looks out the window and sees a body on top of a car in the street below: her reaction tells us that she fears it is her husband's. Just as André's use of François to take on the dangerous task of exposing Jarre should have been seen as calculated, so this moment should have been readable as satisfying André's unconscious wish. (Jarre toys with the idea of shooting François before deciding to give himself up.) There are traces of this scenario: that it is André to whom François is speaking when he's knocked out and kidnapped; that, when he escapes from his kidnappers, he is shot in the arm, like Mrs. Mendoza (another victim of André's espionage demands). But, lost in the overall feebleness of the French section of the movie, such overtones barely register.

Narrative Structure and the Restored Version

To clarify the differences between the original release version of *Topaz* and the restored version, I would like to employ Kristin Thompson's model of narrative analysis, in which she challenges the traditional three-act division of films in which the lengths of the acts are in a 1:2:1 ratio. She argues, rather, that most feature films may be divided into acts of roughly equal length, and that the number of acts—three, four, or five—usually depends on the length of the film.[18] At 136 minutes on video,[19] the restored *Topaz* may indeed be divided into four acts of roughly equal length: 1) Copenhagen and Washington, D.C. (30 mins.); 2) New York plus a brief scene back in Washington (26 mins.); 3) Cuba, including the plane flights there and back (36 mins.) 4) Paris (34 mins.). The two minute credit sequence—which ends with a statement on the screen that a Soviet official present at the May Day parade is about to defect—may then be seen as the prologue; the final shot on the Paris avenue the epilogue. There is only one segment of the film that does not fit this neat structure: two scenes (8 mins.) in Washington between Acts 3 and 4. But this section (André being summoned back to Paris to account for himself, then learning from Kusenov about Topaz) is merely an extended example of what Thompson calls a "turning point," setting up the last act.[20] It is longer than usual because *Topaz* is, in effect, two distinct narratives that have been yoked together, and this is the point at which the first (the Cuban Missile Crisis) is put on pause and the second (unmasking Topaz) takes over.

In shortening the film, Hitchcock cut material mostly from Act 1 (roughly 5 minutes, mainly concerning the Kusenovs) and Act 4 (6 minutes, mainly by deleting the two scenes on the day André arrives in Paris: the car ride into Paris; Granville's cocktail party). The conversation during the car ride merely fills in what André is up to, but the cocktail party, already mentioned, is also important in establishing André and Granville's friendship, which in the shortened version has to be taken for granted. The Kusenov material in Act 1 is significant in that it sets up a tension between Kusenov on the one hand and his wife and daughter on the other. A brief early scene in the safe house outside Washington shows Mrs. Kusenov (Sonja Kolthoff) being fitted with a dress she had seen in a magazine. In a later scene, Nordstrom then lays out the proposed deal: the CIA is prepared to provide all of them with new identities (visualized as three busts of their new faces), provided Kusenov tells them what they want to know. Declaring "I will not betray my country!" Kusenov sweeps the busts to the floor. But Tamara rushes to pick hers up and, when Nordstrom mentions the "scholarship to . . . music school" they propose for her, says "Papa, I want this." It is thus implied that it is primarily on her account that Kusenov decides to cooperate: he goes downstairs and answers the questions about Cuba.

The color of the lavender dress Tamara is wearing in this scene is then matched very closely by the lavender dressing-gown Nicole wears as André packs to go to Cuba. Given that

André, here, is following the trail Kusenov opened up, we are invited to contrast the two men. Each is doing the bidding of the Americans, but Kusenov puts his family first, André his role as secret agent.

Another restored section that has a bearing on the film's patterns of meaning is in Cuba. The first scene in which André and Juanita are alone together is longer, and one of the things he tells her is that he knows about the Soviet missiles: he had Rico Parra's papers photographed in New York. Spontaneously, Juanita bursts into laughter. It's as if she is seeing the absurd side to this—one of her lovers surreptitiously photographing the papers of another—but also delighting in André's superior tactics: she obviously knows just how closely Rico guards his papers. In the next scene, André unpacks the boxed gift, which is to be used to demonstrate that his "magical agent" (the espionage equipment) is more potent than Rico's secret papers. The longer version makes the parallels—and sexual rivalry— between the two men that much sharper.

A final point about the longer version is more elusive. The implicit parallels between Juanita and Michèle through their red clothing are not the end of the story. As André and Nicole board the plane at the end, Hitchcock visually stresses a woman in a red suit who is boarding at the same time. It's as if the "woman in red" has become an icon, a symbol of André's unfaithfulness, and her presence here suggests that this will follow him back to the U.S.A. But then, in the credits shot, there is another woman in red casually walking her dog towards the Arc de Triomphe; as the newspaper is discarded, she is in fact unveiled by its movement, so that she is the first person whom we see on the avenue. Recently, it has come to light that Claude Chabrol filmed this ending at Hitchcock's request.[21] But did Hitchcock ask for a woman in red to be included in the shot? And if so, what might have been his thinking? (The woman in red boarding the plane is at least suggestive; this one is mysterious.) Since Chabrol must have been filming *Le Boucher* (1969)—in which red is a recurring visual motif—around this time, is this a Chabrol in-joke which "just happened" to intersect with Hitchcock's use of the figure? Or was red fashionable at the time, and the woman's presence just a coincidence? When I wrote on the film about a year after its release,[22] I stressed its melancholy: although it records the positive outcome to the political crisis, it also registers the suffering and deaths of a number of sympathetic characters. Thirty-odd years later, with the film finally available in the form that Hitchcock intended, I would speak, rather, of bleakness. And so, although it was a compromise at the time, the third ending now really does seem, in terms of tone, the most appropriate. The real events of this particular Cold War crisis seem to have brought out a much harsher view of international politics than Hitchcock had hitherto felt able to present.

Notes

Thanks to Richard Allen and Sid Gottlieb for very helpful feedback during the drafting of this article. This essay will appear in *Unexplored Hitchcock*, forthcoming from Cameron and Hollis.

1. Robin Wood, *Hitchcock's Films Revisited* (New York: Columbia University Press, 1989), 223-25.

2. Donald Spoto, *The Dark Side of Genius: The Life of Alfred Hitchcock* (London: Frederick Muller, 1988), 499-503.

3. A more detailed account of the film's production difficulties has since been supplied by Bill Krohn, in "A Venomous Flower: Alfred Hitchcock's *Topaz*," *Video Watchdog* 74 (August 2001): 28-35. Krohn discusses the restored version of *Topaz*, and his account is a key source for Patrick McGilligan in his more recent Hitchcock biography, *Alfred Hitchcock: A Life in Darkness and Light* (Chichester: Wiley, 2003), 683-95.

4. Spoto, *The Dark Side of Genius*, 503.

5. Bill Krohn, *Hitchcock at Work* (London: Phaidon Press, 2000), 270.

6. Leon Uris, *Topaz* (New York: Bantam, 1968), first published in two issues of *Look* magazine, September 1967.

7. Quoted on the opening page of the Bantam edition of *Topaz*.

8. Wood, *Hitchcock's Films Revisited*, 223-24.

9. Donald Spoto, *The Art of Alfred Hitchcock* (New York: Doubleday and Company, 1976), 430.

10. Lesley Brill, *The Hitchcock Romance: Love and Irony in Hitchcock's Films* (Princeton: Princeton University Press, 1988), 186-87.

11. Spoto, *The Art of Alfred Hitchcock*, 430.

12. Krohn, ''A Venomous Flower,'' includes details on Hitchcock's re-shooting the duel ending, 30-31.

13. Dan Auiler, *Hitchcock's Secret Notebooks* (London: Bloomsbury, 1999), 538.

14. Auiler, *Secret Notebooks*, 538.

15. Krohn, *Hitchcock at Work*, 270.

16. Four elements in this section—''The MacGuffin,'' ''Spying and the Look,'' ''Homosexuality,'' and ''Bathrooms''—are dealt with across Hitchcock's work in my book *Hitchcock's Motifs*, forthcoming from Amsterdam University Press in fall, 2005.

17. Theodore Price, *Hitchcock and Homosexuality* (Metuchen: Scarecrow Press, 1992), 89.

18. Kristin Thompson, *Story Telling in the New Hollywood: Understanding Classical Narrative Technique* (Cambridge: Harvard University Press, 1999), 22-44.

19. For the benefit of North American readers, I should point out that films on European (and Australian) TV are projected at 25 rather than 24 fps, and that retail videos are recorded at the same speed; 136 minutes on video is thus the equivalent of a film length of 142 minutes.

20. Thompson, *Story Telling*, 30.

21. See, for example, Patrick Brion, *Hitchcock* (Paris: Éditions de la Martinère, 2000), 542. The matter has also been mentioned on The MacGuffin website at www.labyrinth.net.au/ ~ muffin.

22. Michael Walker, ''The Old Age of Alfred Hitchcock,'' *Movie* 18 (1970/71): 10-13. Some of my ideas from that article are recycled here.

M ARK M . H ENNELLY , J R .

Alfred Hitchcock's Carnival

One of the *objets d'art* which graced—in the present case greased—Alfred Hitchcock's dining room was Thomas Rowlandson's 1812 "social satire" *Fast Day*.[1] This drawing portrays four porcine clerics dining on gargantuan helpings of food and drink in comically graphic violation of a church vigil requiring fasting before feasting. Ironic details underscore the hypocrisy of the ecclesiastical feast, including an inset of *Susannah and the Elders* depicting rabbinical elders spying on Susannah bathing.[2] *Psycho*'s (1960) viewers see this same frame-within-a-frame subject covering Master Bates's notorious glory hole after Marion's last supper and before Norman previews her carnal and his own coming attractions in the shower. Hitchcock called *Psycho* a "game with the audience"; here his pun plays a bawdy "carnivalesque game of names" with viewers.[3]

In *Carnivalesque*, Timothy Hyman and Roger Malbert find Rowlandson's drawings riddled with "a carnival sense of the world," especially the "exaggeration and degradation" characterizing the carnival's "grotesque humour."[4] In this "carnival sense," *Fast Day* features tropes apparently poised between a utopian celebration of carnal values and a dystopian or lenten caution against those values. Such poise between praise and abuse may be considered ambiguous, but carnivalesque rhetoric "abuses while praising and praises while abusing," that is, it invariably seems "ironic and ambivalent" (Bakhtin 165). Thus *Fast Day* may even advocate cyclically accommodating *both* carnal and lenten options. As the aptly named Sir Toby Belch queries the Clown in *Twelfth*

Night, ''Dost thou think, because thou art virtuous, there shall be no more cakes and ale?''[5] *Fast Day*'s presence in Hitchcock's dining room also supports Patrick McGilligan's point that from his boyhood onward, Hitchcock ''took special delight in carnivals and circuses,'' one of his favorite symphonies being Schumann's ''Carnaval.''[6] It is this life-long ''delight''—together with the wealth of extremely significant carnivalesque material in his films—that inspires my examination of Alfred Hitchcock's Carnival.

Indeed, it is arguable that more than any other major filmmaker except Federico Fellini, Hitchcock invokes carnivalesque motifs, reinforced with carnivalized visuals and acoustics, to entertain, enlighten, and entrap his audiences in a sideshow hall of self-distorting, self-developing, and ultimately self-defining mirror images. As M.M. Bakhtin emphasizes, carnival ''belongs to the borderline between art and life. In reality, it is life itself, but shaped according to a certain pattern of play. In fact, carnival does not know footlights,'' since, much like Hitchcock's famed audience identification and transfer techniques, carnival ''does not acknowledge any distinction between actors and spectators'' (Bakhtin 7). Thus his often spectacular pleasure-park sequences efface critical distinctions between spectatorial and participational pleasures, provoking viewers to see and sympathize differently or otherwise than usual, that is, according to the traditional wisdom of carnival alterity

Fellini's debt to carnival is obvious in films like *Fellini-Satyricon* (1969) and *The Clowns* (1970), and in repeated statements like ''The cinema is also circus, carnival, funfair, a game for acrobats.''[7] Conversely, Hitchcock's popular reputation as ''master of suspense'' tends to overlook his carnivalism—even though *The Ring* (1927) features a grotesque fairground underscoring underworld values; *Murder!* (1930) a climactic circus sequence identifying the bisexual murderer; *Rich and Strange* (1932) carnival costuming to contextualize conjugal exchanges; *The 39 Steps* (1935) opening and closing music-hall sequences emphasizing the political and personal values of an ''agent'' over a mere ''spy''; *The Lady Vanishes* (1938) a midway magic act to detect life's illusions and deploy female power; *Mr. and Mrs. Smith* (1941) a comically interrupted ferris-wheel ride cautioning against sexual indulgence; *Saboteur* (1942) a circus-troupe whose compassion ironically celebrates democratic ideals; *Stage Fright* (1949) a cellar climax in a carnival car staging its final fright; *Strangers on a Train* (1951) dark carnival alterity contrasting with lighter lenten orthodoxy; and *To Catch a Thief* (1954) a masquerade ball of mummers to deceive both the police and film viewers, leading to the ultimate unmasking and catching of the real thief.

To be sure, one does find sporadic references to the carnivalesque in Hitchcock criticism, like Brigitte Peucker's insight on the harlequin painting in *Blackmail* (1929): ''Mocking and accusatory, the jester with his pointing finger seems the representative of a carnivalesque inversion of the law.''[8] Still, the only sustained discussion of Hitchcock's carnivalism is David Sterritt's very pertinent essay ''The Diabolic Imagination: Hitchcock, Bakhtin, and the Carnivalization of Cinema.'' Sterritt perceptively argues that Hitchcock ''excels as a carnivalizer, primarily in the attitude he shows toward classical cinema itself, which he subverts and denormalizes with surprising frequency.'' More particularly, Hitchcock's ''deliberate carnivalizing gestures [are] aimed at reveling in grotesquerie, inverting social conventions, assembling 'improper' combinations of image, activity, and word, fetishizing'' the grotesque body, and ''gleefully undermining decorum.''[9] Sterritt focuses on *Rope*, *Psycho*, and *Frenzy*, especially their various carnivalesque decrownings of Hollywood cinema, but neglects Hitchcock's biographical ties to carnivalesque material and the Rabelaisian function of specific carnivals in his films.

Past readings of such films that feature carnivals, like *Strangers on a Train*, rarely go beyond Robin Wood's formalist caution against carnivalism: ''The fairground and amusement park is a symbolic projection of . . . a world of disorder, of the pursuit of fun and cheap glamour as the aim of life, of futility represented by the circular motion of roundabout and

Great Wheel that receive such strong visual emphasis in almost every shot," or Robert Corber's new historicist allegation "that the term 'merry-go-round' was used in the 1950s to refer to the gay male subculture."[10] My goal here is to correct this relative critical neglect and thereby address Terry Castle's lament over inattention to "all the philosophical and artistic transformations of the carnivalesque in nineteenth- and twentieth-century" art.[11]

Specifically, this essay explores Hitchcock's central carnivalesque vision as the concept is exemplified by Rabelais's bawdy epic *Gargantua and Pantagruel* (1532-64); defined (and theorized) by Bakhtin's *Rabelais and His World* (1968) as "the second life of the people, who for a time entered the utopian realm of community, freedom, equality, and abundance"; and re-envisioned by Michael André Bernstein's *Bitter Carnival* (1992) as a dystopian "carnival of rage" and abjection.[12] It does so by rehearsing the central carnivalesque motifs in Hitchcock's life and by seeing them coalesce in his early film *The Ring*, his middle-period *Strangers on a Train*, and late-period *Frenzy*. One could argue that Hitchcock's carnival vision develops from the relatively benevolent circus in *The Ring* to the more vicious and violent carnivalesque appetites in *Strangers on a Train* and *Frenzy*. Such a summary, however, seems too pat because it neglects the concurrent, growing tension between a (sometimes cautionary) "carnival of rage" and the possibility of a carnival of redemption in Hitchcock's films.

Bakhtin's relevant carnivalesque motifs include prandial and pantagruelian tropes, the carnal body with its attendant sexuality, carnival costuming and cross-dressing, heteroglossic debates, and the pivotal episteme of pregnant death. The only motif that Hitchcock may seem to neglect is Bakhtin's defecation series, though his carnival tropes do turn excremental as his *oeuvre* develops. But bathrooms and sewers plumb more than the anal tendencies Sterritt stresses, positing a deeply mythic stance toward "the waste products of our society" in *Frenzy*.[13] Such motifs are significantly supported by Hitchcock's favorite carnivalesque visuals and acoustics, which generally reflect Rabelais's "folklore method of contrast" (Bakhtin 403). In fact, just as Bernstein credits Dostoyevsky with achieving "not the dialogization of the novel, but rather the novelization of the dialogue," so too Hitchcock develops beyond Sterritt's "carnivalization of cinema." The cut-up director further creates a cinematic representation of life's carnival with, among other techniques, what he playfully called his "goddamm jigsaw method of cutting"[14]—especially in carnival films like *The Ring*.

Hitchcock's Carnival Life

The value of exploring Hitchcock's carnivalesque background, motifs, techniques, and themes is considerable. Most important, such an undertaking discovers that Hitchcock works consistently in the carnival (pan)genre of *grotesque realism*, with its harlequin motley of heteroglossic elements. Whether these ultimately contribute to an optimistic utopian or a nihilistic dystopian world view again poses a pivotal problem, one related to what Susan Smith calls the crucial "study of tonality in Hitchcock's cinema."[15] Although there is no easy answer to this central problem, the carnivalesque places the question of Hitchcock's prevalent world view(s) in a clearer context. Even his theme song from the *Alfred Hitchcock Presents* television series, Charles Gounod's "Funeral March of a Marionette," replays the *danse macabre* motif, which reflects a carnivalesque hybrid of Grand Guignol humor and horror (Bakhtin 50-51). Similarly, Hitchcock's signature cameo appearances not only darken the footlights in Bakhtin's figurative sense, but their comically sinister undertones are often carnivalesque, as in his portly appearance before the starving derelicts in the "Reduco" advertisement in *Lifeboat* (1944). Bernstein suggestively views such histrionic abjection as a carnivalesque theater of cruelty, which Hitchcock-the-actor performs in joining the crowd scapegoating *The Lodger*'s (1926) hero: "The very theatricality that condemns abjection to display itself as an aggressive *public* spectacle is what makes it so entirely and essentially carnivalesque. But it is a carnival of rage in which every position and each pronouncement seems, even to its speakers, fissured by artifice.''[16]

Further, a carnivalesque reading often serves to ground and coordinate the subversive reversals in Hitchcock's films, what Rusk in *Frenzy* calls turning ''everything ass-about-face.'' Such ''revolutions'' typify the somersaulting clown's heels-over-head overthrow of normative values, like the cross-dressing, ''half-caste'' acrobat and ''she-man'' actor Handel Fane, who defies monologic categories in *Murder!*:

> The entire logic of the grotesque movements of the body (still to be seen in shows and circus performances) is of a topographical nature. The system of these movements is oriented in relation to the upper and lower stratum; it is a system of flights and descents into the lower depths. Their simplest expression is the primeval phenomenon of popular humor, the cartwheel, ... the buttocks persistently trying to take the place of the head and the head that of the buttocks. (Bakhtin 353)

As Bakhtin posits, the clown's *cheeky* revolutions herald the central carnivalesque ''theme of birth-giving death'' (Bakhtin 352), itself a central reversal motif in films from *The Lodger* through *Family Plot* (1976). Hitchcock so routinely clowned-around on his sets that McGilligan labels his repertoire of practical jokes, sexual puns, gargantuan feasts, and pantagruelian excess ''Hitchcockery.''[17] These creative outbursts of carnival *libertas* seem, at the very least, to compensate for the analytical control the auteur (''who-knew-too-much'') meticulously exercised over his material, but which that same material often satirizes and overrides. Like the former underground freedom fighter Robie in *To Catch a Thief*, playing a circus acrobat-turned-thief-turned-underworld detective who out-sleuths the police, Hitchcock's clowning ultimately resists official authority within—and authoritative viewings of—his films. In this sense, Julia Kristeva's remarks on carnival's effacement of "*the author*" seem but half-true of Hitchcock *the auteur*, who cyclically dies only to be reborn as antic "court jester" on screen: "Within the carnival, the subject is reduced to nothingness, while the structure of *the author* emerges as anonymity that creates and sees itself created as self and other, as man and mask."[18] "Man and mask" not only suggest Hitchcock's comic cameo appearances as actor before the scenes as well as the auteur behind the scenes, like Rabelais reappearing as Master Alcofribas in *Gargantua and Pantagruel*. They also imply his recurrent device of comparative doubling, where representation again resembles a carnival hall of distorting mirrors, as in *Strangers on a Train*. Just as *Fast Day* memorably links Church and carnival traditions through its banquet imagery, so too such carnivalesque tropes give fresh, often synthesizing perspectives on Hitchcock dyads like food and memory (quite literally food for thought). When the ex-acrobat Robie faces a kitchen full of former French underground collaborators, he begins to remember and finally relive his own past.

Hitchcock, however, did more than just take "special delight in carnivals and circuses." He initially saw movies, "Animated Photographs" in "traveling bioscopes," at "fairgrounds [and] church bazaars."[19] And these early film festivals fostered a significant link between carnivalesque and cinematic performativity for Hitchcock, which reinforces Peter Wollen's historical linking of circuses with early cinema through the work of Eisenstein.[20] Patrice Petro contends that the "Vanishing Lady" magic act in *The Lady Vanishes* provides Hitchcock's "self-conscious reference to the Méliès 1896 substitution-trick film, *The Lady Vanishes*"[21]; and one could also argue that the Arab "storyteller" performing in the Marrakesh bazaar, complete with director's orchestrating baton, dramatizes a similar portrait-of-the-director and carnival-cinema link in *The Man Who Knew Too Much* (1955).

Hitchcock's bourgeois father's greengrocer and fishmonger shops paradoxically also rooted his young son in lower-class carnivalesque soil (he was even teased by classmates because he "stank of fish").[22] More important,

Hitchcock's intimate association with marketplace values, especially those in the billingsgate tradition, further links his art with what Bakhtin calls heteroglossic, "abusive language as . . . a special genre of billingsgate" (the landmark London fish market where such a creative idiom flourished): "The familiar language of the marketplace became a reservoir in which various speech patterns excluded from official intercourse could freely accumulate" (Bakhtin 16-17). The point here is not just that Hitchcock's private "conversation" (and racy film dialogue) frequently "took a very Rabelaisian turn," as actor Henry Kendall put it, or even that "Hitchcock's love of Rabelaisian humor was a key component of his work," as Sterritt notes.[23] The point is that his billingsgate values were also frequently devoted to "lower-middle-class Londoners"[24] (as subjects and as representatives of democracy)—and even extended, again paradoxically, to market-bound, middle-class Americans—"the people" of popular carnivalesque culture whose important leveling role Bakhtin emphasizes.

In *Saboteur*, for example, the circus troupe (Fat Lady, Midget, Bearded Lady, Siamese Twins, and Bones the Human Skeleton) provides an apt carnivalesque analogy "to the present world situation," one celebrating heteroglossic democracy over unilateral "fascism." As Barry Kane argues, "good people from all countries who will fight for life and truth" must ultimately become international allies (just as he and Pat finally become interpersonal allies). After the Bearded Lady puns on the meaning of "normal" while duping the policeman, the officer mistakes Pat for a circus "snake charmer." Carnivalized, she then establishes carnival difference as the moral norm: "[the freaks] made me feel ashamed. . . . they're wonderful people," suggesting that sideshow values need to be mainstreamed into society's central attractions. Invoking Rabelais's "comic etymology" (Bakhtin 461), we might even say that just as the original diabolist assembly or Sabbat subverts the latter-day Sabbath, *Saboteur* sabotages contemporary social values which exclude carnival's originary "people." Put differently, Hitchcock's marketplace carnivalism, centering on what he called "the man in the street," also reinforces his "mild brand of socialism"[25] personified by a "normal," but not-so-innocent "bystander" like Hannay in *The 39 Steps*, who is often carnivalized. And this initially spectatorial figure again implicates the film spectator as well as the director behind the viewfinder whose carnivalesque antics flout and counter studio control as much as his carnivalized "people" flout and counter state control.

Hitchcock figuratively suggested that he consumed marketplace foodstuffs to produce an "armor of fat" as protection for his private psyche; collaborator Michael Powell further alleges that Hitchcock's inveterate "love" of "talk[ing] bawdy" billingsgate "made up for his gross, clumsy body."[26] Nevertheless, Hitchcock's related banquet imagery also frequently approaches the philosophical status of "Plato's dialogue *The Banquet*" or *Symposium* featured on the first page of *Gargantua and Pantagruel*. And the Holy Eucharist feast of Hitchcock's Catholic faith, celebrating the union of God and man, reinforces, if ironically, this Platonic Love Feast celebrating the androgynes' union of love, and thereby creates a kind of "carnivalized Catholicism."[27]

It's not only that Hitchcock believed in the real value of androgyny, reflected in his recurrent motif of cross-dressing—he even "had men's suits made for [his wife] by a famous tailor" and similarly dressed himself as a flaming drag queen in publicity photos.[28] It's also that self-sacrificing characters like Jeff and Lisa in *Rear Window*, who ultimately learn to eat, talk, and love together, create carnivalesque symposia that counter the monologism of characters like detective Doyle, just as Aristophanes' myth of spiritually erotic love counters Eryximachus's turgidly technical treatise in Plato. More important, these love feasts visually counter Jeff and Lisa's earlier loveless banquet catered by the swank restaurant, "21," as much as they do the disturbing food fight between Thorwald and his wife, and the delusive dinner of Miss Lonely Hearts and her imaginary companion. And each of these table-talk sequences relevantly involves (per)versions of the carnivalesque *querelle des femmes* or arguments over the value and "nature of women and wedlock" (Bakhtin 239) so typical in Hitchcock films.

Other banqueting couples like Scottie and Madeleine in *Vertigo*, Norman and Marion in *Psycho*, Francie and Robie in *To Catch a Thief*, and Blanche and George in *Family Plot*, to name just a few, indicate how Hitchcock's table talk can significantly vary from holy communion to black eucharist rites. And the director himself has observed that "after five or six years, in most married couples, 'that old feeling' begins to dissipate. Food oftentimes takes the place of sex in a relationship."[29] Such comments suggest adding *Frenzy*'s Inspector Oxford and his gloriously gourmet wife to this carnivalesque list. Even Hitchcock's daughter Pat, ever careful to deny her father's dark side, readily acknowledges, "One thing that my father certainly knew well was food and, therefore, he used it at length to substitute for images that the censors of the time would not allow him to show."[30]

Further, food production/consumption and film production/consumption seem invariably linked in Hitchcock as his often "gargantuan lunches" between film work and his "four-hour dinners" before the next day's filming suggest.[31] Hitchcock's signature silhouette marketed this carnivalesque production/consumption code since it reproduces the traditional Gros Guillaume or Fat William "incarnation of the people's utopia and feasting," who "symboliz[es] bread and wine" and "typif[ies] the usual tendency of the popular carnival figure to efface the confines between the body and surrounding objects" (Bakhtin 292, 354). Hitchcock emphasized this carnivalesque relaxing of boundaries between consumer and consumed, calling audience discussions of his movies "icebox talk scenes."[32] These film symposia occur when viewers return home to digest both snacks (reenacting food scenes) and Hitchcock's delicious visuals. Speaking of his brand of "realism," Hitchcock even famously joked that "Some films are slices of life. Mine are slices of cake."[33]

Boxing, Wedding, and Circus Rings

We begin to appreciate Hitchcock's carnival vision by examining *The Ring* (1927), since this silent film provides a clear version of that vision. It tells the story of "One Round Jack" Sander, a fairground boxer who defeats all challengers until Bob Corby, the (initially unidentified) Australian champion, knocks him out and seems to win the affections of his fiancée Nelly. Jack becomes Bob's sparring partner in order to earn enough money to marry Nelly, but ultimately must best Bob in the ring to secure her heart.

The Ring is the only Hitchcock film for which he received sole script credit. This suggests an integrated auteur vision, especially as it appears in the "various Fun Fair sideshows" Hitchcock created on the British International lot, which revive his childhood's carnival "world of popular market-place forms."[34] He explores these sideshows in the opening montage sequence, which reinforces carnivalesque motley with heteroglossic visuals as he quite literally represents the carnival as a kind of cinema. For example, the swinging camera gives viewers the same vertical joyride as the fairgoers swinging on the merry-go-round, while the gigantic faces with cavernous mouths (like Rabelais's "Great Gullet" Grangousier) of the carnival barker and shooting-gallery tent visually circumscribe the paired close-up of the open-mouthed policeman laughing at the proceedings. Unlike the more lenten police in *Strangers on a Train*, the agency of potential surveillance here contributes to the carnival drama, perversely joining its polymorphous celebration of carnal pleasures. Indeed, Bakhtin's description of Rabelais's Prologue seems a fair account of Hitchcock's prologue, which features the leveling of social categories and thus the humanizing of the lonely crowd: "It is written from beginning to end in the style and tone of the marketplace. . . . The entire prologue is built like the announcement of a barker speaking to the crowd gathered in front of his booth."[35]

Relevant to this carnivalized camera work, Thomas Leitch calls *The Ring* "the most expressionistic of all [Hitchcock's] films,"[36] and the "drunken" visuals in the circus wedding scene seem clearly influenced by the similarly dizzy camera work during the wedding in F.W. Murnau's *The Last Laugh* (1924). In fact, Hitchcock's training in German Expressionism recalls notable carnivalesque sequences in films like Robert Wiene's *The Cabinet of Doctor Caligari* (1919), Paul Leni's *Waxworks* (1924), and E.A. Dupont's *Variety* (1925). This German influence undoubtedly helped generate Hitchcock's grotesque realism, which rotates viewers between upper-category values and subversive *grotto* or lower-category values. For example, Nelly's snake bracelet slithers up and down her arm as she alternately responds to Jack's lower-class and Bob's *haute-bourgeoisie* appeals, suggesting Persephone's alternations between lower and upper kingdoms. Leslie Brill finds Persephone's cycles "foreshadow[ing] five decades of variations on its central themes" in Hitchcock (though he neglects *The Ring*'s "variations"),[37] and Panurge likewise celebrates Pluto's bride-theft of Persephone (620) during Rabelais's giants' descent to the Subterranean Palace. John Russell Taylor relevantly sees such grotesque realism providing one more analogy between cinematic and carnivalesque subversion: "The tawdry side-shows . . . represented another aspect of that seamy underside of show business which had always fascinated Hitch."[38]

   The Ring's repeated superimposition of one image over another also visually expresses Hitchcock's grotesque realism, for instance, when champion Bob's head is superimposed on underdog Jack's punching-bag bladder, which Jack, desiring Bob's deflation, then knocks from its tether. Bob's actual fall from grace in the ring occurs in the concluding match where vertical geometries—low angles and overheads—repeat the opening swinging (and all the film's rising and falling actions) and so relevantly carnivalize the battle of life. More provocatively, the vertiginous superimpositions of dancers dissolving into piano keys dissolving into Nelly kissing Bob, which Jack projects on the spinning phonograph at Bob's party, dramatize life's carnival revolutions (both visually *and* "acoustically" in this silent film). The dissolves of Jack's name appearing progressively larger on the boxing poster as it ascends from lower undercard to featured Championship Match further capture every lower-class rube's—that is, non-carnivalized everyman's—rags-to-riches dream of climbing the social ladder. Conversely, Hitchcock's repeated dissolve transitions (and alternating high and low angles) suggest just how fleeting fame actually is in the fluid carnival world, which again approximates the real world. For example, the close-up of Jack's victory glass of bubbling champagne dissolving to its flat counterpart, as he waits for Nelly to help him celebrate, reflects Jack's vacillating fortunes in love.

The Ring's prevalent circular imagery, on the other hand, implies carnival's (seasonal) cyclicism: that is, what goes around in life and love comes around for One Round Jack, who must learn to suffer fortunate falls, go the distance, and become a man for all seasons. Thus, when Jack surveys the fortune teller's circle of cards, Hitchcock's visuals insist that he should not aspire to be the King of Diamonds or riches, but rather the King of Hearts who can win Nelly if he dethrones the pretender. And such a viewing supports Hitchcock's own account of being fascinated by all the "social rituals surrounding boxing."[39] In this sense, the fairground crowd or carnival people, repeatedly shot in the background, are ultimately foregrounded when their lower-class challenger Jack uncrowns the figuratively "aristocratic" Australian ring king (which also foregrounds and carnivalizes the crowd of film spectators). Jonathan Arac's reading of the pivotal "uncrowning of the king of carnival" captures the inherent cyclicism of its "primary performance": "In this cyclical process the pathos within the jollity becomes evident, the sadness of vicissitude and death as well as the promise of change and renewal. . . . [Carnival] is thus hostile to any final ending."[40]

After the opening fairground sequences, Hitchcock's most compelling carnivalesque scenes occur at Jack and Nelly's wedding, introduced by a dramatic parallel cut between the carnival and the church. Here several choric carnies appear, including the Showman, Fat Lady, Siamese Twins, Giant and

Dwarf, Fortune Teller, and Jack's boxing trainer. Maurice Yacowar claims that this motley crew represents "the simple and satisfying society that [Jack] leaves behind when he enters the larger world of [Bob's] circle."[41] A carnivalesque viewing further stresses their satyr play; for example, the carnies deflate and humanize the pompous solemnity of the occasion when they riotously applaud the deacon's demand for silence. A tribe of giants with gargantuan appetites is, of course, the nominal subject of Rabelais's epic. When matched with dwarves, as traditionally occurs at carnivals, they together personify the ambiguous duality of all reality—"the dual-bodied world of becoming" (Bakhtin 343, 420)—the same carnal underbelly of church solemnity that *Fast Day* undresses. (Nelly's outlawed desires—eye-balling Bob while she rubs-down Jack—constitute just one of *The Ring's* dual-bodied conflicts, representing what Samuel Kinser terms the traditional "Combat between Carnival and Lent," between carnal appetite and abstention.[42])

The Siamese twins who cannot agree where to sit reinforce such ambiguity (which is replayed in *Saboteur*) and prefigure the creative differences plaguing and blessing Bob's marriage. Indeed, as Rabelais's representation of Plato's androgynes suggests, such differences plague and bless all human relationships: "a two-headed human body, the heads turned to face each other, and four arms, four feet, and two pairs of buttocks—portraying exactly what Plato describes in the *Symposium* about human nature."[43] At the church service, the carnie trainer vies with the lenten minister for magisterial power, particularly when he places a button rather than wedding ring in the cleric's hand. This gesture toward what Hyman calls carnival's central "ideology of unbuttoning" also subtly links the master of revels with Hitchcock the creative auteur, since it is "emblematic of the liberty of the imagination."[44] Bernstein writes of "a certain kind of Saturnalian imagination" that its abject "longing for an all-engulfing carnival functions as a kind of call-to-arms, . . . in which the 'genius' is figured as a seer stung into visionary rage by the banalities and injustices of quotidian social existence."[45] Such sentiments clearly recall Hitchcockian carnival figures like Brandon in *Rope*, that homicidal, "sly little devil" with the "warped sense of humor" who, before the "sacrificial feast," ceremoniously intones, "Now the fun begins." Less of a visionary, the carnie trainer merely picks his nose, defying and deflating ecclesiastical codes again like *Fast Day*, but still prefiguring the bitter carnival that Jack's disturbing marriage embodies.

The outdoor wedding feast more anarchically reintroduces (fallen) human nature into the just solemnized marriage and thereby initiates *The Ring*'s bride-theft motif, the carnivalesque "theme of cuckoldry" or "uncrowning of the old husband," again like Pluto's theft of Persephone. And this uncrowning is commonly associated with a "ring [as] the sign of woman's sexual organ" (Bakhtin 241, 243). When the circular horseshoe falls, the fortune teller gives it to Bob, whispering "better luck next time," as if to stress life's aleatory quality. Bob's subsequent speech also emphasizes bride-theft, which the carnival traditionally tolerates if not promotes: "I think the prize at the [fair] booth should have been the charming bride." The subsequent wishbone pull between Bob and Nelly, which Bob ominously wins, reinforces this motif as its arching geometry visually reproduces the horseshoe shape[46]—the broken circle of a disrupted marriage. Festivities conclude with the carnie's drunkenly distorted view of the feast dissolving into a sparring session, where Bob again tries to steal Nelly. This pantagruelian dissolve suggests the way Hitchcock's camera work stresses the subjective or subliminal grotesque, which all the film's reflective "projections" on water and mirrors further imply.

In this sense, *The Ring* dramatizes a sideshow of self-disorienting mirror reflections subtly implicating both characters (as spectators) and spectators (as characters). Hitchcock confided to Truffaut about the opening fairground sequence: in "those days [I was] very keen on the little visual touches, sometimes so subtle that they weren't even noticed by the public."[47] Today's spectators still neglect subtle carnivalesque touches in *The Ring*. And no touch is more subtle than the talismanic snake bracelet, which Jack compares to a wedding ring and which is dropped, rediscovered, and thrown back-and-forth at the end of the film. Besides functioning as a "clear reference to the serpent in the Genesis account of the Garden of Eden," this transitional object or passport to the pleasure principle, like the equally slippery lighter in *Strangers on a Train* and tie-pin in *Frenzy*, also suggests grotto values or "slips" traditionally associated with the carnival.[48] Thus, it functions as a carnivalesque "curiosity," one of those "rare and unusual objects" that exert magical power in Rabelais (Bakhtin 445). Nelly's final dropping of it expresses her ultimate lenten rejection of Bob's temptation and thus may imply her discarding carnival values in general. Its resurfacing, on the other hand, might rather suggest the eternal return of carnival values. All such possibilities in *The Ring* must be courted, though they cannot be absolutely proven. What clearly should be evident, however, is that the titular transformative object refers to a carnival or circus ring as much as to a boxing and wedding ring.

Pluto and Plato at the Carnival

Strangers on a Train also features a carnival, but appears to stage a more bitter, existential, and oedipalized drama about underground life. Further, it may dramatize significantly different carnivals, or at least a medley of competing carnivalesque energies and heteroglossic values. And these range far beyond the "multiplicity of competing discourses" of sexual politics that Corber's provocative queer reading presents.[49] The plot of the film is familiar. Bruno Anthony, a psychotic playboy, and Guy Haines, a champion tennis player bent on divorcing his bourgeois wife Miriam and marrying his upper-class girlfriend Ann, accidentally meet on a train. Bruno thinks he convinces Guy to "swap murders"—Guy's wife for Bruno's father—and so strangles Miriam at a carnival. When the shocked Guy refuses to fulfill his end of this "bargain," Bruno decides to frame him by planting Guy's monogrammed lighter at the carnival crime scene. Guy follows Bruno to the carnival, and while police passively watch them battle on a runaway carousel, it wrecks, and the incriminating lighter reappears in the dead Bruno's hand. The crucial sequence here is the final return to the carnival, where the police mistakenly shoot a carnie, causing the carousel to revolve out of control. Afraid of its accelerating revolutions, they refuse to mend matters, prompting another cartoonish carnie to tunnel under the carousel to rescue its passengers by setting the emergency brake, which simultaneously destroys the merry-go-round. As we shall see, this sequence provides a perverse parable not only of competing carnival and lenten values, but also of various self-destructive and self-developing carnivalesque energies.

Although *Strangers on a Train* emphasizes carnival concerns and so clearly justifies a carnivalesque reading, its "non carnival" material also significantly previews Hitchcock's displacing such concerns in films like *Frenzy* that don't include carnivals. For example, Mrs. Anthony's grotesque painting of "St. Francis" recalls that Rabelais was himself a Franciscan, and "Franciscan degradations and profanation can be defined, with some exaggeration, as a carnivalized Catholicism" (Bakhtin 57). Since Bruno interprets this monstrous metatext as framing his father, film critics have been quick to typecast its Oedipal implications. When Bruno also insists, however, that he's "sick and tired of bowing and scraping to [this] King," it further suggests not only a cuckolded, rebellious son (and existential rebel), but also a rebellious court jester or "crazy fool" as Guy provocatively calls him. And the Tarot's "Fool" graces the title page of the first edition of *Gargantua*.[50] Pantagruel persuades Panurge to seek a similar histrionic "Fool" because he "is always played by the most talented and experienced actor in the troupe," just as Hitchcock and Truffaut agreed that Robert Walker's "poetic portrayal" of

Bruno the Fool was "undoubtedly more attractive" than Farley Granger's "[un]appealing" portrayal of Guy, the lenten rube Bruno fools.[51]

Well before the famous carnival sequences, in fact, *Strangers on a Train* visually grounds itself in grotesque realism with its focus on grotto-like tunnels. The film opens with an establishing long-shot of a huge, convex tunnel linking a bright exterior with the darkly concave, underground train station—and the perspective here significantly originates from within the underground. The Capitol's convex dome spectrally appears through the tunnel but also geometrically completes the concave grotto, previewing either the carnival's subversion of official culture or the possible compatibility between carnival and lent that Bakhtin finds in "towers and subterranean" tunnels (318). Cross-cut low angles on pairs of walking feet, examples of Bakhtin's "Bodily Lower Stratum" (368-436) immediately dominate the frame and are soon matched with ground-level shots of train tracks forming "X" and "Y" patterns. Given Hitchcock's love of bawdy billingsgate, training in graphic art design, and fascination with symbolic geometry like triangles in *The Lodger* and parallel lines in *Spellbound* (1945), this signature shot recalls Rabelais's emphasis on the "Y" sign of horny Priapus, the Greek letter upsilon.[52] The grotesque low angles (as if shot from a grotto) also preview the more clearly carnivalesque "low camera setups" of "the merry-go-round," which were so difficult to achieve, as Hitchcock tells Truffaut, and which, upon review, tend to carnivalize these early visuals even though they exist "outside" the actual carnival.[53] In doing so, the early low angles give promise of excavating and exploring the grotesque dimensions of life itself.

The grotto or tunnel motif thus foreshadows the carnival's Tunnel of Love, thereby previewing a homoerotic element before Bruno and Guy's suggestive symposium or love feast on the train. It also adumbrates other dark tunnels (again "outside" carnival) like those at the Forest Hills tennis courts and in the sewer where Bruno drops Guy's lighter.

And the parallel struggles within and between these two liminal sites are themselves visually matched by comparative montages and cross-cutting. The sewer grotesquely links cloacal and carnival "perversions," while the mysterious slogan above the tennis tunnel, "And treat those two imposters just the same," links straight, normal "hero" and gay, abnormal "psychopath." The unidentified source here is Kipling's poem "If—" where the "two imposters" are "Triumph and Disaster," which makes perfect sense for tennis players. It also, however, makes carnivalesque sense for viewers remembering references to "knaves" and "fools" in "If—" and applying the slogan equally to the knave Bruno and the fool Guy's shared attempt, in the poem's words, to "be a Man, my son!"[54]—whether as Oedipal sibling rivals, carnival Siamese twins, or closet gender-benders of male and female (im)posturing. "Imposters" further incriminates the film's other poseurs, Rabelais's targeted "sanctimonious hypocrites,"[55] particularly Ann's Senator father and his upper-class obsession with sanitized appearances, and terror of "orgies," which renders him a typical Rabelaisian *agelast*, "a man who does not know how to laugh and who is hostile to laughter" (Bakhtin 267). "Triumph and Disaster" finally implicate the viewers of *Strangers on a Train*'s roller coaster suspense plot who live vicariously through such vicissitudes. They may also learn, however, to submit to life's dangerous elements like the authentically courageous carnie and carnivalized Guy playing the pivotal tennis match in "a complete reversal of his watch-and-wait strategy."

Without referencing the carnivalesque, Brill sees the carnival in this film as "a subterranean world of anxiety and nightmare."[56] Spoto likewise views it as "the underworld of corruption, sin and death" in his first edition of *The Art of Alfred Hitchcock*. In the revised edition, he more reductively stresses "the tradition" of demonic "fairground[s]" where "the demented aspects of life are concentrated and expressed, where all the Dionysian riots and the repressions of the year are set free . . . until the whirling carousel [is] destroyed so that normality may be restored."[57] Spoto's last point echoes Umberto Eco's insistence on a relational separation between carnival and everyday life: "Without a valid law to break, carnival is impossible,"[58] but neglects other significant dialogic relationships between "carnival" and "reality." Hitchcock, conversely, would agree with Kristeva's more integrative reading of carnival's serious laughter as the discourse of the (political) Unconscious: "The laughter of the carnival is not simply parodic; it is no more comic than tragic; it is both at once, one might say that it is *serious*. This is the only way it can avoid becoming either the scene of law or the scene of its parody, in order to become the scene of its *other*"[59]—like Bruno standing under the carnival sign, "International Oddities." Thus, Hitchcock's ambiguous carnival sequences graphically recall Goethe's famous Roman Carnival simile: "life, taken as a whole, is like the Roman Carnival, unpredictable, unsatisfactory, and problematic."[60]

In the early carnival sequence, Bruno's talismanic lobster tie unpredictably transforms into a surreal, Daliesque image (reflected in a ground-level shot of the broken glasses) of his hybrid claws strangling Miriam like some misshapen sideshow monstrosity. This grotesque vision, as if from the ocean floor or carnival hall of distorting mirrors, seems later transferred—in a warped, tilted shot—to Bruno's Siamese twin, the (now) carnivalized Guy, about to enter his house after Miriam's murder. It is also uncannily doubled by Barbara's glasses at the Washington party when Bruno's repetition compulsion mimics strangling Mrs. Cunningham while he is visually entranced with bespectacled Barbara. For Bruno, then, the *revenant* Miriam reappears as Barbara in another carnival doubling as "The Band Played On" echoes the haunting merry-go-round music. In fact, pregnant Miriam herself projects a deceptive double image of the monstrous two-in-one, as does Hitchcock himself when he enters the Metcalf train with a detached Siamese-twin double bass. And just as Bruno leads the bespectacled blind man safely away from the carnival after the murder, Hitchcock parallel-cuts to Guy in his train's "observation" car, apparently safe from carnival contamination. This visual doubling (Bruno and Guy both check their watches) of the carnival and such a quarantined reality ironically rejects any possibility of a healthy observation of either life or time outside the carnival's lifeline. Indeed, the drunken math professor's suggestive speech on "integration" and ribald "song about a goat" imply that a life like Guy's, inoculated against carnival's *mundus inversus* energies, can have no possible alibis.

This first carnival sequence also compares traditional feast-of-fools and ship-of-fools motifs, besides playing with grotesque (and suppressed) puns on *Pluto* and *Plato*. In the carnival tradition, "festive fools" are usually "ambivalent" figures, and sometimes "each and every one [may] play the fool" (Bakhtin 382, 246), as the circus Fool *Il Matto*, Gelsomina, and Zampano all differently play fools in Fellini's *La Strada* (1954). In *Strangers on a Train*, both Bruno and Miriam play feasting fools at the carnival, though Bruno is soon associated more with Saturnalian violence than gluttony or lust. Still, while Miriam suggestively licks an ice cream cone and delights in hot dogs, Bruno similarly munches popcorn—in Patricia Highsmith's novel *Strangers on a Train*, the food choices are reversed, Bruno eating the sausage and Miriam the corn, suggesting their carnival interchangeability.[61] The phallic cone seems talismanic of horny fools like Guy whom Miriam cuckolds, while corn, though not etymologically linked to the horn of the foolish cuckold Oedipus Bruno, is phonetically linked to Latin *cornu* (horn)—both carnival phallus and carnivalesque cornucopia, Rabelais's "lovely horn of plenty." The priapic hot dog, like Rabelais's Fat Sausage People on Wildman's Isle, provides the traditional icon of carnivalesque license, "always two-faced and traitorous," which also describes Miriam and Bruno (especially on Magic Isle, Hitchcock's deceptive dystopia).[62]

The value of such correspondences within a clear carnival context is again characteristically ambiguous. I would say, however, that Hitchcock's carnival vision seems to condemn Miriam's sexual licentiousness as well as Bruno's violent license, since the one betrays and the other brutalizes the spirit of carnival *communitas*, though the carnival also promises a more liberating life for the whole community. At the same time, their shared laughter and song on the merry-go-round imply their momentary postures as "innocent" fools, a role that the guyed Guy (like Blaney in *Frenzy*) more successfully plays when he rescues the child on the merry-go-round. One can also see that Bruno's suit, tie, and hat, which make him appear so extraneously formal at the carnival (as he is visually out-of-place at the Jefferson Memorial), ironically invest him with carnival alterity (a carnie later calls Bruno "the other one"), especially since his pyramidal hat itself resembles a truncated cone.

When Bruno and Miriam voyage through the shadowy Tunnel of Love, they further participate in the *vanitas* tradition of *stultifera navis* or the ship of fools obliviously voyaging toward death, besides again recalling Pluto's bride-theft of Persephone and Plato's shadowy Allegory of the Cave. *Pluto* is the barely visible name of Bruno's boat, and Guy leaves Plato's *Dialogues*, not his lighter, with Bruno in Highsmith.[63] The medieval ship of fools tradition, like the ship of death (ferrying the dead to the underworld) and the dance of death (insouciant revelers being led to the graveyard), satirically punishes the inconsistently foolish vanity of human wishes for both carnal pleasures and celestial rewards. *Gargantua and Pantagruel* ironizes these traditions in Panurge's voyage to the Subterranean Palace, "the utopian land of death and regeneration," where he seeks the answer to his question of whether or not to marry (Bakhtin 452). The "magical Bottle" oracle ultimately belches the pantagruelian solution to this life-defining decision: Old French "*Trink!*"[64] that is, one must drink to the depths life's cocktail with all its dangerously mixed, intoxicating but also invigorating ingredients.

Like Rabelais's ambiguous Abbey of Thélème and its gospel of "Do What You Will,"[65] Hitchcock's take on carnival philosophy seems ambivalent here. Does he mean to satirize Bruno's comparable "theory that you should do everything before you die" because it is *merely* a "theory," or because it includes "harnessing the life-force"? Bruno's violent act of bride-theft, of murdering Miriam and her unborn child on Magic Isle, graphically violates Pluto's loving example of allowing Persephone to live alternately underground and above ground. In this sense, Bruno's elitist vanity (like Rupert's in *Rope*) in believing some people "deserve to die" seems an ironic carnivalesque caution against neglecting the democratic values of carnival *libertas*. On the other hand, *Strangers on a Train*'s vision of hell ultimately duplicates that in *Gargantua and Pantagruel*: "Hell is a banquet and a gay carnival" (Bakhtin 386). Hitchcock, then, alternately seems to condemn extreme forms of Saturnalian violence and celebrate carnivalesque vitality, liberty, and creativity.

The metatext of Plato's dialogues, suppressed in the film version of *Strangers on a Train*, spectrally reappears in the Tunnel of Love's carnival (per)version of the Allegory of the Cave, a shadow-play preview of Bruno strangling Miriam. Like *Susannah and the Elders* within *Fast Day*, Hitchcock's reconstruction of Plato's allegorical discourse in *The Republic* seems ironic within its carnival context. Shot from near water level, it significantly reverses, or at least dialogizes, Plato's privileging the "upper world" of Light, Goodness, and Truth over the grotesquely "cavernous chamber underground" of darkness, evil, and illusion.[66] Bruno's looming penumbra, overshadowing Miriam's shade, transforms into another carnival hybrid: a monster who demonstrates grotesque truth, a tormentor who mentors the viewer in seeing this truth, to which the film's official upper-world of police, senators, and churchmen are all blind.

Moreover, Hitchcock uses Plato's scenario again to represent the carnival cinematically, since the projected play of shadows appears filmic, originating from some occluded light source— ultimately the projector lamp.[67] Such an apparatus directed by the auteur as ludimagister also subverts Plato's dismissal of art as delusion, since the aesthetic "delusion" here foreshadows a future truth. And this reversal qualifies Francis Cornford's otherwise insightful note on the Cave Allegory: "A modern Plato would compare his Cave to an underground cinema, where the audience watch the play of shadows thrown by the film passing before a light at their backs. The film itself is only an image of 'real' things and events in the world outside the cinema.'"[68]

The audience of *Strangers on a Train*, therefore, seems maneuvered both like and unlike the "strange picture" of the "strange sort of prisoners"[69] bound by carnal appetites, viewing Plato's delusive shadow play. Somewhat like Plato's prisoners, Hitchcock's viewers must finally exit the dark theater, re-enter the "real" world, and drink deeply of (disillusioned) life. Conversely, the carnival themes in this film can liberate its viewers, but only if they preserve their individual "strangeness" or otherness, refusing to be cloned by Socrates' education of future rulers who must "bind . . . the community into one.'"[70] Such a reasonable republic would exist without "strangers" but also without shades of difference under the Sun's white mythology in Plato's monologue masquerading as dialogue.[71] The viewers of *Strangers on a Train* must further realize that the film's fools project haunting shadows of themselves on the screen's wall—authentic (not delusive) carnival shades which must be self-identified and then either assimilated or discarded for individual and cultural health. Put differently, what looks like Miriam's actual murder (complete with her "fearful" scream), only to be revealed as a shadowy illusion (with her pleasurable scream), turns out to be a grotesquely real foreshadowing of Miriam's represented murder by Bruno's monstrous lobster claws.

Hitchcock's second carnival sequence places such heteroglossia—and possible alternatives to them—in final focus. The police's irresponsible killing of the carnie dramatically dialogizes not only the official hostility to carnival, but also the result of such murderous monologism: carnival's (the carousel's) running amok. And yet Hitchcock also presents another, "deeper" carnival personified in the cartoonish carnie who tunnels under the carousel to arrest its violent revolutions and rescue its passengers, while the crowd of spectators, revealed in Hitchcock's stunning ground-level shot, likewise drops to the earth to view his carnival performance and imitate its grotesque antics. Like the histrionic death of the "actress" Annabella Smith in *The 39 Steps*, which reinforces its carnivalesque focus on performativity, the carnie's heroism in *Strangers on a Train* seems comically staged. Audiences invariably laugh at it, recalling both Bakhtin's point that "fear defeated by laughter" (394) is a primary goal of carnival and similar confrontations between induced fear and laughter throughout Hitchcock's canon.

Brill's emphasis on the film's ludic quality must also appreciate its bitter carnival to reach the ambivalent heart of Hitchcock's matter: "The final impression derives largely from its tall-tale exuberance, its artistic playfulness. Hitchcock's self-indulgent razzle-dazzle gives us the distance we need to laugh at what we might otherwise find painful or shocking."[72] As the focus on music-hall performances spills over into the performativity of everyday life in *The 39 Steps*, so too the focus on performed carnivalism repeatedly spills over into the playfully painful carnival of everyday life in *Strangers on a Train* as represented by Hitchcock's carnivalized camera work and sound track.

What could be viewed as carnival's comically sacrificing its own violence by derailing the carousel so that the forces of lent can again gain the upper hand (or head), may even be *Strangers on a Train*'s vision of a more comprehensive "Carnival" world view, one that underpins both carnival and lenten energies and that ultimately defines Hitchcock's grotesque realism. Hitchcock's audience would then participate in what Bernstein calls "probably the most arresting of all the textual developments of the Saturnalian dialogue": ambivalent "emotional identification with the voices of rage and thwarted rebellion . . . at the same time that the dangers of that role are ever more explicitly argued" so that viewers "find in each a welcome counterbalance to the demands of the other."[73]

The Carnival, the Wasteland, and the Grail Maidens

In closing, I'd like to pursue Hitchcock's ambivalent carnival vision by sketching a carnivalesque view of *Frenzy*, which certainly appears darker than the relatively benign carnival in *The Ring* and even the allegedly bitter carnival in *Strangers on a Train*. Rather, *Frenzy* seems Hitchcock's most excremental vision of the modern wasteland. My purpose is to suggest that a carnivalesque focus on *Frenzy* also reveals provocative ways of viewing Hitchcock's "non-carnival" films, for these frequently displace carnivalesque material. Indeed, he once planned a film depicting how cycles of food production and consumption constitute a very bitter carnival: "I'd like to try to do an anthology on food, showing its arrival in the city, its distribution, the selling, buying by people, the cooking, the various ways it's consumed. . . . So there's a cycle, beginning with the gleaming fresh vegetables and ending with the mess that's poured into the sewers. . . . Your theme might almost be the rottenness of humanity."[74] This perversely populist focus on "the rottenness of humanity" appears in the Covent Garden and potato truck sequences in *Frenzy*, which reprise Hitchcock's greengrocery origins and which his ribald trailer sardonically and self-referentially markets as Hitchcock performs the roles of both floating corpse and necktie-murderer, extolling Covent Garden's "fruits of evil" and "horror of vegetables."[75] Viewed in this manner, Hitchcock's "wrong man" film appears rather obviously carnivalesque, doubling a greengrocer, Bob Rusk, with a war-hero-turned-bartender, Richard Blaney. Rusk fools and frames Blaney for his own bride-thefts or "necktie murders," including Blaney's ex-wife Brenda and girlfriend Babs, until Inspector Oxford finally unmasks Rusk.

If the refrain "Ain't we got fun?" verbalizes audience disorientation in the surreal carnival world of *Strangers on a Train*, the potato-truck hearse where Rusk comically wrestles with Babs's corpse visualizes viewer entrapment in the more solid carnal world of *Frenzy*. Typically for Hitchcock, this entrapment begins with an ideal-to-real transition: a spectacular, wide-angle aerial approach (visual quest) above the Thames and to a final close-up of the bloated, naked backside of a female corpse, emphasizing grotesque realism and the lower-body substratum with a vengeance. Thereafter, displaced carnival motifs and techniques dominate *Frenzy*, perhaps the most telling being the close-up of another monstrous beauty/beast hybrid: pig's feet on blue Wedgewood china, bathed in Mrs. Oxford's triumphant "tripe" sauce, Rabelais's crowning carnival figure:

> In the image of tripe life and death, birth, excrement, and food are all drawn together and tied in one grotesque knot; this is the center of bodily topography in which the upper and lower stratum penetrate each other" (Bakhtin 163).

Inspector Oxford's attempts to cut apart this grotesque "*pied du porc*" even replay the comically macabre montage (Hitchcock's own "cutting") of Rusk attempting to pry apart Babs's fingers abjectly clenched on his monogrammed tie-pin.

Other carnival material in *Frenzy* include its sometimes cruel, sometimes comic concern with pantagruelian and prandial motifs (Blaney initially reveals his impotence by crushing both a bunch of grapes and a wine glass), and Sterritt stresses carnival cannibalism and doubles in the film. While Rusk's devouring "forbidden fruit" after his bride-theft murder of Brenda leaves a decidedly bitter taste, the pregnant-death potential of sliced and then replanted potatoes provides some vegetative hope for renewal. The matched Fat Lady and her dwarfish mate at Brenda's dating service not only personify typical carnival pairs, but like so many couples in Hitchcock, they again stage a comic *querelle des femmes* debate on the values of women and marriage. Name games and billingsgate puns repeatedly occur, for example, in Bob's touted racehorse "Coming In" and the name of the truck bearing his violation of Babs, "Commer." His "Bob's your uncle" slanging to Babs further suggests his family-romance pathology (the "Bob's" and "Babs" puns reinforce this incest motif, as does the shot of red-haired Bob with his red-haired "mum" matched and framed in the window).

While the camera tracks Bob leading Babs from the pub upstairs to his apartment, he assures her, "you have a long life ahead of you," and confides, "you're my kind of woman," his verbal cue for murder. The camera then appears to backtrack fluidly down the stairs and out the front door (this is actually a reconstructed process shot whose cutting is masked by a worker bearing a potato sack), leaving the helpless audience to await Babs's screams, which are never heard through the noise of the marketplace. The verticality, Saturnalian irony, foreshadowing of Babs's pregnant-death resurrection from the potato sack, and market-place motifs all identify this famous sequence as displaced carnivalism. That is, its carnivalesque elements appear detached from any specific carnival locale, but their sheer number and collective value establish a significant carnival context. *Frenzy*'s final close-up on the large trunk where Bob intends to conceal his latest victim (recalling *Rope*'s final frame on the trunk as sacrificial altar) recycles the opening far-to-near camera movement and close-up on a corpse. Here it's not just that the carnal, the charnel, and the cyclic characterize the carnivalesque, however; it's also that Rabelais's fascination with grotesque "objects in which depths (holes) . . . are emphasized"—*Frenzy*'s cells, cellars, potato sacks, trunks, bottles—reveals them to be versions of Heraclitus's "bottomless well in which . . . the truth is said to be hidden."[76] Still, what "truth" can lie behind the various fools: Rusk, Blaney, Oxford (too foolish to heed his wife's carnivalism), the corpse, and viewer, imprisoned in this arresting shot? Is it the corpse's promise of pregnant death and resurrection, affirmed in *Frenzy*'s final joke, "Mr. Rusk, you're not wearing your tie!" which predicts Blaney's "legal" innocence and acquittal?

Frenzy's central carnivalesque motif, its wasteland myth (which undercuts its Edenic plenitude), may fulfill that promise or dash it with bitter abjection, as Hitchcock ironically modernizes and integrates Parsifal's quest for the

Holy Grail with Panurge's voyage to the Holy Bottle. Bakhtin notes the carnival's role in "travest[ying] elements reflecting the King Arthur cycle," while Bernstein stresses "how often the carnivalesque is triggered not by any outpouring of abundance but, on the contrary, by the most pressing of [wasteland] wants."[77] Up to a point, both remarks are true of *Frenzy*, which clearly contrasts feast with famine and natural with artificial or hypocritical fools.[78] And awareness of Hitchcock's displaced double focus on the carnival and wasteland can critically integrate Brill's analysis of "the motif of food" with Gabriel Miller's (unfortunately) general discussion of *Frenzy*'s "modern wasteland."[79] Brenda insists that Blaney has "acted the fool," but like Parsifal he has also played "chivalrous knight" during the war, even though he currently seems one of "the waste products of our society." When Hetty Porter charges her husband Johnny with being "a bloody fool" for "getting yourself involved" with innocent Blaney, she implicates both "natural" fools with carnivalesque sympathies like Mrs. Oxford and "artificial" fools concerned with convention like Johnny (Blaney later calls the Porters "cowardly shits!").

Ironic verbal references to "kingfishers" and "Sir George," besides visual emphases on the Globe pub's stained-glass grail, another pub's medieval logo "Courage," and the Red(-haired) Knight Bob (Parsifal's carnal double), all seem as graphic and global wasteland motifs as those in Terry Gilliam's *The Fisher King* (1991). But given the "polluted" Thames, prevalent disease of men who "hate women [and] are mostly impotent," and final freeze frame, we must again ask if *Frenzy* dramatizes any forgiving compassion after such wasteland knowledge? Indeed, its examples of bride-theft and disturbing victories of flesh over spirit recall similarly bitter carnivalesque moments in Buñuel, particularly the virgin's near rape by her uncle in *Viridiana* (1961).

Certainly Hitchcock provides no compassion from Brenda's lenten secretary (ironically named Miss Barley) nor the Eliotesque *agelast* Mrs. Porter, nor from the relatively ineffectual male triplets—Blaney, Rusk, and Oxford, all of whom, Tania Modleski argues, create "a world from which women are altogether excluded."[80] Conversely, the figurative grail maidens or "handmaidens of the Salvation Army hostel," gourmet Mrs. Oxford, barmaid Babs, and matchmaker Brenda, may provide healing hope though their overlapping associations with the carnival values of food, drink, and love, and their telltale compassion for Blaney. Loopy Mrs. Oxford's dining room, like Hitchcock's, particularly promises more feast days than fast days, with its cornucopian abundance of tripe, margueritas, and *querelle* chatter: "I told you it wasn't Blaney. I told you you were on the wrong track. . . . Women's intuition is worth more than all those [police] laboratories." In this sense, Mrs. Oxford, the sole-surviving grail maiden, seems intimately connected to the carnival *caquet* tradition of "chattering females" (like Lisa and nurse Stella in *Rear Window*) who know so much more than the monologic males they nurture and challenge (Bakhtin 105-06). *Frenzy*'s final vision of Mrs. Oxford comically in her cups may make her seem foolish, but as Wallace Fowlie suggests in *The Clown's Grail*, the cup and fool can also redeem the wasteland.[81]

As we've seen, such carnivalesque possibilities are true of much of Hitchcock's work. In films that feature a carnival and even those that displace it, Hitchcock visually reimagines the carnival as a film festival of moving pictures that play ambivalently with utopian and dystopian visions, licentious-lenten conflicts, and subversive Saturnalian ironies. For Hitchcock, as for Bakhtin and Goethe, carnival "is life itself," and his grotesque realism repeatedly excavates and explores this world view. Ultimately, though, it carnivalizes Hitchcock's spectators, first by transfiguring them into participating performers and then by returning them to life's bittersweet banquet, humanized with appetites and thirsts to savor it more fully, if also more painfully.[82]

Notes

1. Patrick McGilligan, *Hitchcock: A Life in Darkness and Light* (New York: Regan, 2003), 477.

2. See Joseph Grego, *Rowlandson the Caricaturist* (London: Chatto and Windus, 1880), vol. 2, 226. For a discussion of the "Susannah theme" in art history, see Mary D. Garrard, "Susanna," *Artemisia Gentileschi: The Image of the Female Hero in Italian Baroque Art* (Princeton: Princeton University Press, 1989), 183-209.

3. The Hitchcock quotation on *Psycho* appears in François Truffaut, *Hitchcock* (New York: Simon and Schuster, 1983), 269; the "game of names" quotation appears in Mikhail Mikailovich Bakhtin, *Rabelais and His World*, trans. Hélène Iswolsky (Cambridge: MIT Press, 1968), 461. Further quotations from this book will be cited as "Bakhtin" with page numbers in the text of my essay.

4. See Timothy Hyman, "A Carnival Sense of the World," in Timothy Hyman and Roger Malpert, ed., *Carnivalesque* (London: Hayward Gallery, 2000), 48, and Roger Malpert, "Exaggeration and Degradation: Grotesque Humour in Contemporary Art" in Hyman and Malpert, *Carnivalesque*, 76-77.

5. William Shakespeare, *Twelfth Night*, in *The Complete Pelican Shakespeare*, ed. Stephen Orgel and A.R. Braunmuller (New York and London: Penguin, 2002), 454 (II.iii.106-07).

6. McGilligan, *Hitchcock: A Life in Darkness and Light*, 8-9.

7. Quoted in Helen Stoddart, "Subtle Wasted Traces: Fellini and the Circus," in *Federico Fellini: Contemporary Perspectives*, ed. Frank Burke and Marguerite R. Waller (Toronto: University of Toronto Press, 2002), 46.

8. Brigitte Peucker, "The Cut of Representation: Painting and Sculpture in Hitchcock," in *Alfred Hitchcock: Centenary Essays*, ed. Richard Allen and S. Ishii Gonzalès (London: BFI, 1999), 147.

9. David Sterritt, "The Diabolic Imagination: Hitchcock, Bakhtin, and the Carnivalization of Cinema," in *Framing Hitchcock: Selected Essays from* The Hitchcock Annual, ed. Sidney Gottlieb and Christopher Brookhouse (Detroit: Wayne State University Press, 2002), 94, 98.

10. See Robin Wood, *Hitchcock's Films Revisited* (New York: Columbia University Press, 1989), 88, and Robert J. Corber, "Hitchcock's Washington: Spectatorship, Ideology, and the 'Homosexual Menace' in *Strangers on a Train*," in *Hitchcock's America*, ed. Jonathan Freedman and Richard Millington (New York and Oxford: Oxford University Press, 1990), 121, n. 24.

11. Terry Castle, *Masquerade and Civilization: The Carnivalesque in Eighteenth-Century English Culture and Fiction* (Stanford: Stanford University Press, 1986), 333.

12. See Bakhtin, *Rabelais and His World*, 9, and Michael André Bernstein, *Bitter Carnival: Ressentiment and the Abject Hero* (Princeton: Princeton University Press, 1992), 101.

13. Sterritt, "The Diabolic Imagination," 101-03.

14. See Bernstein, *Bitter Carnival: Ressentiment and the Abject Hero*, 116, and McGilligan, *Hitchcock: A Life in Darkness and Light*, 252.

15. Susan Smith, *Hitchcock: Suspense, Humour and Tone* (London: British Film Institute, 2000), x.

16. Bernstein, *Bitter Carnival: Ressentiment and the Abject Hero*, 101.

17. McGilligan, *Hitchcock: A Life in Darkness and Light*, 100. Hitchcock delighted in carnivalesque name games involving his school nickname of "Cocky"; see Donald Spoto, *The Dark Side of Genius: The Life of Alfred Hitchcock* (New York: Ballantine, 1983), 32, for the origin of this name. In *Blackmail*, for example, "Cocky" becomes a visual pun in the thrusting neon cocktail shaker Alice sees after killing Crewe, which then morphs expressionistically into a knife and so concocts a telltale carnivalesque medley of drink, sex, death, and self-reflexive auteur cockiness.

18. Julia Kristeva, *Desire in Language: A Semiotic Approach to Literature and Art*, trans. Thomas Gora, Alice Jardine, and Leon S. Roudiez, ed. Leon S. Roudiez (New York: Columbia University Press, 1980), 78. For the "court jester" reference, see McGilligan, *Hitchcock: A Life in Darkness and Light*, 99.

19. McGilligan, *Hitchcock: A Life in Darkness and Light*, 15.

20. Peter Wollen, *Signs and Meaning in the Cinema* (London: Secker and Warburg, 1969), 21, 28-29.

21. Patrice Petro, "Rematerializing the Vanishing 'Lady': Feminism, Hitchcock, and Interpretation," in *A Hitchcock Reader*, ed. Marshall Deutelbaum and Leland Poague (Ames: Iowa State University Press, 1986), 129.

22. McGilligan, *Hitchcock: A Life in Darkness and Light*, 22.

23. For the Kendall quotation, see McGilligan, 121. See also David Sterritt, "Alfred Hitchcock: Registrar of Births and Deaths," in *Framing Hitchcock: Selected Essays from* The Hitchcock Annual, 315.

24. McGilligan, *Hitchcock: A Life in Darkness and Light*, 115.

25. McGilligan, *Hitchcock: A Life in Darkness and Light*, 253, 257.

26. See McGilligan, *Hitchcock: A Life in Darkness and Light*, 23, 115.

27. Bakhtin, *Rabelais and His World*, 57. For a book-length discussion of the role of Catholicism in Hitchcock's films, see Neil Hurley, *Soul in Suspense: Hitchcock's Fright and Delight* (Metuchen, New Jersey: Scarecrow Press, 1993).

28. For a discussion of Hitchcock's take on androgyny, see Spoto, *The Dark Side of Genius*, 96. For the "cross-dressing" quotation, see Pat Hitchcock O'Connell and Laurent Bouzereau, *Alma Hitchcock: The Woman Behind the Man* (New York: Berkley, 2003), 84, and for a drag-queen photo, see Truffaut, *Hitchcock*, 321.

29. Spoto, *The Dark Side of Genius*, 552.

30. O'Connell and Bouzereau, *Alma Hitchcock*, 226-27. For examples of the Hitchcocks' favorite recipes, see 233-54. For an example of Hitchcock's own dinner menus and management, complete with a name game, see Alfred Hitchcock, "Alfred hitchcock Cooks His Own Goose," *Harper's Bazaar* 109 (December 1975): 132.

31. See Spoto, *The Dark Side of Genius*, 527.

32. In Jane E. Sloan, *Alfred Hitchcock: A Filmography and Bibliography* (Berkeley: University of California Press, 1995), 38, n. 23.

33. Truffaut, *Hitchcock*, 102.

34. For the "sideshows" reference, see Dan Auiler, *Hitchcock's Notebooks: An Authorized and Illustrated Look Inside the Creative Mind of Alfred Hitchcock* (New York: Avon, 1999), 450; the "marketplace" reference is from Bakhtin, *Rabelais and His World*, 380.

35. François Rabelais, *Gargantua and Pantagruel*, trans. Burton Raffel (New York: Norton, 1990), 167-68.

36. Thomas Leitch, *The Encyclopedia of Alfred Hitchcock* (New York: Checkmark, 2002), 280.

37. Leslie Brill, *The Hitchcock Romance: Love and Irony in Hitchcock's Films* (Princeton: Princeton University Press, 1988), 86.

38. John Russell Taylor, *Hitch: The Life and Times of Alfred Hitchcock* (New York: Berkley, 1978), 75.

39. Thomas Leitch, *Find the Director and Other Hitchcock Games* (Athens: University of Georgia Press, 1991), 55.

40. Jonathan Arac, "The Form of Carnival in *Under the Volcano*," *PMLA* 92 (1977): 487.

41. Maurice Yacowar, *Hitchcock's British Films* (Hamden, Connecticut: Archon, 1977), 59.

42. Samuel Kinser, *Rabelais's Carnival: Text, Context, Metatext* (Berkeley and Los Angeles: University of California Press, 1990), 51.

43. Rabelais, *Gargantua and Pantagruel*, 25.

44. Hyman, "A Carnival Sense of the World," 10.

45. Bernstein, *Bitter Carnival Ressentiment and the Abject Hero*, 172.

46. See Yacowar, *Hitchcock's British Films*, 61.

47. Truffaut, *Hitchcock*, 52.

48. The "Garden of Eden" interpretation occurs in Hurley, *Soul*

in Suspense: Hitchcock's Fright and Delight, 96. For a relevant Lacanian reading of such "slipping" objects, see Mladen Dolar, "Hitchcock's Objects," in *Everything You Always Wanted to Know about Lacan (But Were Afraid to Ask Hitchcock)*, ed. Slavoj Žižek (New York: Verso, 1997), 44. Again, Hitchcock's deployment of such "ordinary household article[s,] as the murder weapon is called in *Rope*, often carnivalizes them, just as Gargantua carnivalizes hats, napkins, gloves, and many other "household articles" (Bakhtin 376) into "ass-wiper[s]." See Rabelais, *Gargantua and Pantagruel*, 35-37.

49. Corber, "Hitchcock's Washington: Spectatorship, Ideology, and the 'Homosexual Menace' in *Strangers on a Train*," 119.

50. See Fred Gettings, *Tarot: How to Read the Future* (Stamford, Connecticut: Longmeadow, 1993), 110.

51. Rabelais, *Gargantua and Pantagruel*, 338; Truffaut, *Hitchcock*, 199.

52. See Rabelais, *Gargantua and Pantagruel*, 313. For a discussion of Hitchcock's repeated use of a "pattern of parallel vertical lines," beyond *Spellbound*, see William Rothman, *Hitchcock: The Murderous Gaze* (Cambridge: Harvard University Press, 1982), 33.

53. Truffaut, *Hitchcock*, 197.

54. Rudyard Kipling, "If—," *Rewards and Fairies*, vol. 25 of *The Works of Rudyard Kipling* (New York: Scribners, 1911), 200-01.

55. See Rabelais, *Gargantua and Pantagruel*, 235.

56. Brill, *The Hitchcock Romance*, 76.

57. See Donald Spoto, *The Art of Alfred Hitchcock: Fifty Years of His Motion Pictures* (New York: Hopkinson and Blake, 1976), 213, and Spoto, *The Art of Alfred Hitchcock: Fifty Years of His Motion Pictures*, 2nd rev. ed. (New York: Anchor, 1992), 193.

58. Umberto Eco, "The Frames of Comic 'Freedom,' " in *Carnival*, Approaches to Semiotics 64, ed. Thomas A. Sebeok (Berlin: Mouton, 1984), 6.

59. Kristeva, *Desire in Language: A Semiotic Approach to Literature and Art*, 80.

60. Johann Wolfgang Goethe, "The Roman Carnival," *Italian Journey 1786-1788*, trans. W.H. Auden and Elizabeth Mayer (New York: Pantheon, 1962), 469.

61. See Patricia Highsmith, *Strangers on a Train* (New York: Norton, 2001), 77.

62. For the "horn of plenty," see Rabelais, *Gargantua and Pantagruel*, 24; for the Sausage People, 459.

63. Highsmith, *Strangers on a Train*, 36. Perhaps Hitchcock made this significant switch in order to exploit the visual potential of the

lighter: its telltale monogram "A to G" (Ann or Anthony to Guy?) and double-crossing tennis rackets as well as its darkly illuminating flame. Or perhaps the lighter is simply an early instance of product placement for Ronson.

64. Rabelais, *Gargantua and Pantagruel*, 617.

65. Rabelais, *Gargantua and Pantagruel*, 124.

66. See Plato, *The Republic of Plato*, trans. Francis MacDonald Cornford (New York: Oxford University Press, 1945), 231, 227.

67. The projected shadows are compared to a "screen at a puppet show." See Plato, *The Republic of Plato*, 228.

68. Cornford, "Notes," in Plato, *The Republic of Plato*, 228, n. 2.

69. Plato, *The Republic of Plato*, 228.

70. Plato, *The Republic of Plato*, 234.

71. In the novel, Bruno ironically confides that he "didn't know there was so much conversation in Plato" (47).

72. Brill, *The Hitchcock Romance*, 75.

73. Bernstein, *Bitter Carnival* Ressentiment *and the Abject Hero*, 160.

74. Truffaut, *Hitchcock*, 320.

75. See Hitchcock's *Frenzy* trailer on the *Rear Window* videocassette, MCA Home Video, 1983.

76. For the quotation on Rabelais's containers, see Bakhtin, *Rabelais and His World*, 318, n. 6; and for the Heraclitus citation, see Rabelais, *Gargantua and Pantagruel*, 192.

77. See Bakhtin, *Rabelais and His World*, 342, and Bernstein, *Bitter Carnival* Ressentiment *and the Abject Hero*, 149.

78. For a relevant discussion of "natural" and "artificial" fools, see Sandra Billington, " 'Suffer Fools Gladly': The Fool in Medieval England and the Play *Mankind*," in *The Fool and The Trickster: Studies in Honour of Enid Welsford*, ed. Paul V.A. Williams (Ipswich: D.S. Brewer, 1979), 36-54. Rabelais lists more than two hundred types of fools in *Gargantua and Pantagruel*, 340-42.

79. See Brill, *The Hitchcock Romance*, 137, and Gabriel Miller, "Hitchcock's Wasteland Vision: An Examination of *Frenzy*," *Film Heritage* 11 (1976): 1.

80. Tania Modleski, *The Women Who Knew Too Much: Hitchcock and Feminist Theory* (New York: Routledge, 1988), 110.

81. See Wallace Fowlie, *The Clown's Grail: A Study of Love in Its Literary Expression* (London: D. Dobson, 1948).

82. In closing, I'd like to thank Sidney Gottlieb for all his guidance with this essay. Sid's helpful suggestions are too numerous to credit individually.

Book Reviews

James M. Vest, *Hitchcock and France: The Forging of an Auteur.*
Westport, CT: Praeger, 2003. 222 pp. $69.95.

LELAND POAGUE

Few among the standard *topoi* of Hitchcock studies are
more familiar than the contrast between the British and
American films. A contemporary instance of this trope in
action is Peter Wollen's essay ''Hitch: A Tale of Two Cities
(London and Los Angeles).'' Though his purpose is to write
''against compartmentalization—specifically the national
compartmentalization of Hitchcock into 'English' and
'American' '' (66)—Wollen's method subtly maintains the
duality by saying that Hitchcock was always already both,
because he began his career working for the London office of
Famous Players-Lasky (eventually Paramount, the site of his
greatest 1950s accomplishments) and because he continued,
regardless of studio and national affiliations, to make movies
with British collaborators, from British sources, and with
British settings. Wollen's title, however, is prophetic: the two
cities in the Dickens novel alluded to are London and Paris,
and the Wollen book that includes the essay is entitled *Paris
Hollywood: Writings on Film.* It is a primary claim of James
Vest's *Hitchcock and France* that Paris is a city equally as vital
to the Hitchcock legacy as London and Los Angeles; hence
Hitchcock's ''La nouvelle vague, c'est moi'' (190)
proclamation—offered in reply to a question from a French
journalist during a promotional appearance for *North by
Northwest*—is something well beyond mere press-conference
Hitchcockery.

The possibility that Hitchcock was engaging in calculated
if not fabulous self-promotion, to be sure, is forecast from the
outset in Vest's subtitle: *The Forging of an Auteur.* Indeed, two
crucial moments in the process whereby Hitchcock the
commercial entertainer became Hitchcock the serious film
artist both center on the question of Hitchcock's turthfulness
and credibility. One of these involves a press conference in

the Hitchcock suite at the Hotel George V in Paris on June 28, 1954, which Vest, paraphrasing Truffaut, labels ''a major turning point in cinema history'' (74).

Côte d'Azur location shooting on *To Catch a Thief* had just finished, the principal cast members were en route to California from the Riviera, and Hitchcock had stopped briefly in Paris, where he asked the local Paramount office to organize a press conference to which Chabrol, Truffaut, and other important French film journalists were invited. Though André Bazin had scooped his *Cahiers du Cinéma* colleagues by interviewing Hitchcock on location two weeks earlier, this was Chabrol and Truffaut's first direct encounter with Hitchcock, their first opportunity to confront the director with critical theories of his work that had been developing in the pages of *Cahiers* and its predecessor, *La Revue du Cinéma*, since 1948. As first reported in *France-Soir* and *Le Figaro*, and subsequently in *Cahiers*, Hitchcock employed production anecdotes and self-effacing humor—at the expense of all American films, or just his own, depending on the account— to take his interlocutors ''for a ride'' (80). Chabrol labored mightily to inject a theological or metaphysical note into the proceedings, even phoning Hitchcock afterwards (at Truffaut's suggestion) to pose additional questions, which solicited an invitation to return to Hitchcock's hotel room, though according to Chabrol's report the pattern of dissembling answers to serious questions continued in the ensuing exchange.

The other crucial moment pertaining to Hitchcock's veracity is the publication of the famous ''numéro Hitchcock'' (October 1954) of *Cahiers*, where Chabrol's account of the Hotel George V encounter appears, along with several essays, most importantly Bazin's skeptical report of his earlier interviews with Hitchcock (''Hitchcock contre Hitchcock'') and Truffaut's ''Un Trousseau de fausses clés.'' Indeed, Truffaut quotes Bazin's interview directly—the passage where Bazin, for the only time, sees Hitchcock respond positively to a *Cahiers* axiom (''the transference of personality'') as if caught unawares—in order to assert that the appearance of illumination was just that much more dissimulation. ''I will not give it up: Hitchcock lied to you'' (62, per the *Cahiers du Cinéma in English* text). And Truffaut supports that contention by what Vest calls, after Rohmer, analogical criticism (''mode analogique''), which takes two forms in Truffaut's essay: an enumeration of the ''trans-ference of identity'' motif across Hitchcock's American films (*Rebecca, Suspicion, Under Capricorn, Strangers on a Train, I Confess, To Catch a Thief*) and a more extended formalist enumeration of ''doubling'' or ''twoness'' in *Shadow of a Doubt:* ''two Charlies, two church scenes, two murder attempts, two suspects'' (83), as Vest paraphrases Truffaut. Concludes Truffaut: ''It is not due to the machinations of the Holy Ghost that the films are so perfectly fitted together. One does not improvise the construction of a scenario such as that of *Shadow of a Doubt*'' (64).

Much of the value of *Hitchcock and France* is the encouragement Vest offers, by his own studious example, to revisit some of the documents in question. To reread Bazin's ''Hitchcock versus Hitchcock'' and ''How Could You Possibly Be a Hitchcocko-Hawksian?'' and Chabrol's ''Story of an Interview'' now—the latter two only lately available in English, thanks to Peter Wollen, Jim Hillier, and Sidney Gottlieb (and to Vest himself, who translated the Chabrol piece for inclusion in Gottlieb's *Alfred Hitchcock: Interviews*)—is to understand how deeply things have changed in the interim, and how they haven't. What's most obviously changed is the extent to which academic critics, at least, take Hitchcock's texts as primary, and as being artistically and ideologically serious. In describing Hitchcock's critical fortunes, Vest collects numerous comparisons of Hitchcock to artists of unquestioned stature: to Joyce, Faulkner, Kafka, Brecht, Sartre, and so on. While these comparisons might have been intended or taken as rhetorical firebrands, they now appear as altogether reasonable ways of charting Hitchcock's relationship to twentieth-century modernism. The weight of commentary is so enormous that no amount of Hitchcockian prevarication can undo it.

Then again, the concept of cinematic authorship remains an endlessly fascinating puzzlement—Truffaut's "Skeleton Keys" description of Hitchcock as a Hitchcockian character more than hints in that direction, as do Bazin's "Hitchcock versus Hitchcock" remarks about the difference between the "precritical, unrefined documentation" provided by interviews and criticism proper, which he calls, in "On the *politique des auteurs*," "criticism by beauty." Echoes of T.S. Eliot and Wimsatt and Beardsley sound between the lines here, as well they might for literary-minded Anglo-American readers. It's more than slightly interesting that film criticism's first serious and sustained confrontation with the gap between the language of production and the language of criticism—Eisenstein's writings being the chief exception— might well have happened in France, and chiefly around the figure of Alfred Hitchcock.

But not around the same Hitchcock that American audiences and critics had in mind when they finally began to take Hitchcock seriously under the mid-1960s influence of Robin Wood, though it bears saying that *Hitchcock's Films* began as a contribution to *Cahiers* on the subject of *Psycho* at the time of its U.K. release. One "thread" of Vest's *Hitchcock and France*—to which I must give short shrift—is the degree of "Alfred Hitchcock's long-standing interest in French culture" (ix). Given all the energy devoted to charting the relationship between British and American Hitchcock, it comes as something of a shock to realize, with Vest's encouragement, how intricately the "French" thread is woven into Hitchcock's carpet. Few film scholars or Hitchcock fans are likely unaware that *Vertigo* derives from a French novel by Pierre Boileau and Thomas Narcejac—though Vest disputes the oft-repeated claim that the novel was written with Hitchcock specifically in mind (167)—but the fact that "Over one-fourth of Hitchcock's films included substantial allusions to France or sequences in French" (3) may come as a surprise. Yet Paris is a setting for a significant portion of *Rich and Strange* (1932), and the Riviera serves a similar function in *Rebecca* (1940), not to mention the wartime Ministry of Information films, *Bon Voyage* and *Aventure Malgache,* both shot in French with largely French casts. The pattern is increasingly evident in Hitchcock's 1950s films, especially *Strangers on a Train, I Confess, To Catch a Thief,* and the second *The Man Who Knew Too Much.* (Though Vest's project is mainly historical along reception studies lines, he periodically discusses how ''Frenchness'' functions in Hitchcock's 1950s films—*Strangers on a Train* and *Rear Window* most notably—with considerable tact and critical insight.) That Hitchcock was so interested in France is likely a crucial reason why France was so interested in Hitchcock.

Numerous factors, according to Vest, contributed to the latter phenomenon, some of them familiar to film criticism from the history of *film noir.* Crucial here was the existence of an institutionalized cinephilia (or ''cinémanie'') in the form of film archives (preeminently the Cinémathèque Française) and film festivals, of Ciné-Clubs and film journals (especially *L'Ecran Français, La Revue du Cinéma,* and subsequently *Cahiers du Cinéma* and *Positif* among many others). Equally crucial was the post-Liberation flood of World War II-era Hollywood films that opened in France long after their initial releases in America; Hitchcock's *Lifeboat* (1944) did not open in Paris until 1956, for example. As a result, French (or at least Parisian) audiences were far more likely to see Hitchcock's films en masse, as a body of work allowing for ''analogical criticism,'' than audiences elsewhere.

In all, fourteen Hitchcock films were newly released in France during the 1950s. Moreover, revivals and museum showings meant that Hitchcock was always on the film-critical agenda. ''Some two dozen Hitchcock films were screened commercially in France during the decade following the Liberation''(12), Vest observes, and his almost year-by-year account of Hitchcock's critical and commercial reception in 1950s France repeatedly punctuated with reports of multiple Hitchcock films in simultaneous release: *Dial M for Murder* and *Rear Window* opened in successive months in early 1955, for example, and ''Reprises of *Notorious, Rope, Strangers, The Lady Vanishes,* and *The 39 Steps* from March through November fueled anticipation" of *To Catch a Thief* (99). Especially significant here was a retrospective of British films at the Cinémathèque Française, "consisting in large part of Hitchcock films," six of his British silents, and "twelve of the fifteen British talkies" (143), which followed the "five-month first run of *To Catch a Thief* and coincided with the unprecedented six-month run of *[The Trouble with] Harry* and with reprises of *Notorious, Dial M,* and *Rear Window* during the summer" of 1956 (144). Indeed, the Cinémathèque retrospective was crucial to the decision of Eric Rohmer and Claude Chabrol to write their 1957 *Hitchcock* book for the "Classiques du Cinéma" series.

Also important in Vest's account of Hitchcock in France is the fact that certain films proved central to the debate over Hitchcock's stature as an artist. Thus "The brouhaha surrounding Hitchcock in France in the 1950s," Vest notes, "was precipitated by three unlikely films released there in rapid succession": *Rope, Under Capricorn,* and *Stage Fright* (13). Though all were reviewed in newspaper venues, the two Transatlantic films were defended in the pages of *Gazette du Cinéma* (another forerunner of *Cahiers*) by Eric Rohmer and Jacques Rivette as early as May of 1950. (They defended Hitchcock against charges leveled by writers in another short-lived journal, *Raccords,* which paved the way for *Positif,* the journal most steadfast in its antagonism toward Hitchcock during this period.) In 1953, "*I Confess* competed head-to-head with Clouzot's *Salaire de la peur*" (37) at Cannes; Clouzot's victory in the competition was another challenge to the "Hitchcocko-Hawksians" and sparked a lengthy reply in *Cahiers* from Rohmer (whose "De Trois Films et d'une certaine école" discussed *Under Capricorn, Strangers on a Train,* and *I Confess* via his "mode analogique" [40]) and from Rivette, in an extended review of *I Confess.* More significantly, the only film given extended analysis (in an article by Jean Domarchi) in the first Hitchcock number of *Cahiers* was *Under Capricorn.*

In his concluding pages Vest lists as "touchstone" Hitchcock films—in addition to *Rope, Under Capricorn,* and *I*

Confess—Dial M for Murder, The Trouble with Harry, The Wrong Man, and *Vertigo.* Clearly, *Dial M* is on the list because it opened in direct competition with Clouzot's *Les Diaboliques,* and occasioned sustained comparisons between the two directors. *The Trouble with Harry* had been a resounding success in France, by contrast with its weak American receipts, and it also marked a critical ''turning point,'' in that ''Several critics who were generally resistant to the Hitchcock touch were captivated by *Harry*'' (139)—in part, Vest and others speculate, because its absurdist humor appealed to French viewers schooled in the absurdist theater of Ionesco and Giraudoux, and also because its pastoral idiosyncrasy proved that Hitchcock was a true auteur, marching to his own drummer rather than blindly following studio dictates.

The Wrong Man and *Vertigo* raise the complex issue of the extent to which Hitchcock was influenced—perhaps overly influenced—by his New Wave French acolytes, which in some quarters was taken as proof positive less of Hitchcock's cinematic genius than of his public relations instincts and his willingness to pander to prevailing standards of taste. That both films were seen by Hitchcock partisans as vindication is hardly surprising, at least in retrospect. I have always seen the intricate family melodrama of *The 400 Blows* as a homage to the restraint and *gravitas* of *The Wrong Man,* just as Truffaut saw the latter's combination of documentary reality and providential sublimity (in ''The miracle of Fonda's deliverance,'' per Vest [158]) as Hitchcock's acknowledgment, in advance, of the New Wave. But the writer who reviewed *The Wrong Man* for *Positif* lamented (in Vest's summary report) that ''someone told poor old Alfred that he was a serious director, even a metaphysician, and he believed them'' (161). Likewise, Michèle Firk, in a subsequent issue of *Positif,* describes *Vertigo* (again, in Vest's paraphrase) as ''nothing more than Hitchcock by the *Cahiers* book'' (185), as if Hitchcock had employed the ''lexicon of Hitchcockian motifs'' (145) that had appeared in the third ''Hitchcock number'' of *Cahiers* (August-September 1956) as his template.

Clearly "serious," used pejoratively à la *Positif*, is the key word here. Though the success of *The Trouble with Harry* with French audiences and critics indicates clearly enough that they were alive to Hitchcock's sardonic streak, the "Hitchcock" that was constructed in France between the Liberation and the end of the 1950s was decidedly different from the one that British and American critics were discovering in the middle and late 1960s, though both of them were "serious" in ways Georges Sadoul and Hitchcock's other French detractors could never abide. The "Paris" Hitchcock—the Hitchcock of *Rope, Under Capricorn, I Confess, The Wrong Man,* and *Vertigo*—is an independent filmmaker with a formalist experimental bent, a penchant for theological figures and parables, a decided disregard for plausibility, and an obsession akin to devotion for spiritual and sexual extremity, often correlated with something like celibacy.

By contrast, the "Los Angeles" (via London) Hitchcock on view in Robin Wood's *Hitchcock's Films*—in effect, the Hitchcock of *Strangers on a Train, North by Northwest, Psycho, The Birds,* and *Marnie*, given that *Rear Window* and *Vertigo* (to which Wood also devotes chapters) had been withdrawn from distribution by the time the book became a standard reference—is in many ways a more "public" or political figure. Wood's evocation of the Holocaust in the conclusion to his chapter on *Psycho* and the apocalyptic overtones in the cold-war intrigue of *North by Northwest* and in the revolt of nature in (by) *The Birds* all come to mind. And Wood's Hitchcock is a more "sexual" one as well—the carnality of *Psycho* and *Marnie* show Hitchcock taking full advantage of the progressive loosening of the Production Code, though there is astonishing tenderness in some of these films as well, which Wood glosses under the theme of "therapy," especially in reference to *Marnie*. This Hitchcock is also, if anything, an even stronger advocate of cinematic experimentalism, given his New-Wavish, semi-documentary approach to *Psycho*, the special sonic and visual effects in *The Birds,* and the expressionist (even painterly) use of color in *Marnie*. Strikingly, what's lacking in these sixties films is anything akin to the respectful treatment of Catholicism (or religion generally) that we find in *I Confess* or *The Wrong Man*.

I confess that these latter speculations, though inspired by Vest's *Hitchcock and France*, are entirely my own. I offer them in order to suggest the kind of difference that's at stake in the historical claims that Vest advances. To remark that Hitchcock had been engaged with French settings and themes from early in his career, for example, makes his increased interest in French culture—both as topic and audience—seem something other than mere opportunism. To say that French culture obviously needed Alfred Hitchcock (along with Howard Hawks and Nicholas Ray and *film noir*) to work out a new relationship to Hollywood and to cinema after the dark night of the occupation—an always "hybrid" Hollywood given the Hitchcockian mixture of London and Los Angeles and Paris too—also tempers the view that the *Cahiers* critics were merely using Hitchcock as a stalking horse for their own filmmaking ambitions. That he helped them define those ambitions is beyond question, but so too is the critical and cinematic productivity they helped to realize—and the ambitions were obviously shared. Though Vest hears Hitchcock's "La nouvelle vague, c'est moi" as questionably proprietary and preemptory, it can also be taken as an assertion of common cause or community, not least for being spoken (evidently) in French, and by reference to Flaubert.

Vest closes *Hitchcock and France: The Forging of an Auteur* with the claim that "'Le cas Hitchcock,' as it unfolded in France during the 1950s, provided a remarkably solid basis for the massive edifice of Hitchcock criticism to come" (201). In rereading the standard biographies of Hitchcock in preparation for this review, I was struck by how little attention was devoted to the rise of auteurism à la *Cahiers*, in which Hitchcock played an essential part, by contrast, say, with the ink devoted to the impact of Hitchcock's television series. John Russell Taylor, for instance, mentions Truffaut only five times, mostly in reference to his 1967 interview book. Both Donald Spoto and Patrick McGilligan briefly mention Bazin's 1954 interview with Hitchcock; both mention Truffaut's book as designed to establish "Hitchcock's status as the quintessential *auteur*" (Spoto, *The Dark Side of Genius*, 524) in the face of American critical skepticism. Moreover, Spoto acknowledges that Truffaut's book helped mark the moment "when movie reviewing was graduating to the status of film criticism and when 'Saturday night at the movies' was becoming 'Monday morning in the classroom' " (525).

However, McGilligan would likely see the latter phenomenon as infected by the "particular lunacy" of academic film study (*Alfred Hitchcock: A Life in Darkness and Light*, 749), and neither Spoto nor McGilligan attends to any of the debates that preceded Bazin's interview with Hitchcock, debates which on Vest's account established the specific "Cartesian-Existential" terms in which that interview was conducted. Given Bazin's misgivings about Hitchcock, which only gradually abated and were never entirely renounced, the implication that Bazin was pro-Hitchcock, or was preeminent among Hitchcock advocates, is obviously mistaken. (McGilligan repeatedly and inexplicably describes *Positif* as collaborating with *Cahiers* in promoting the pro-Hitch position, which amounts to a far more serious *faux pas*.)

In saying that the "Paris" Hitchcock is different from the "London" or "Los Angeles" Hitchcocks, however, I am effectively urging an "institutionalist" view that privileges reception contexts over the original production context. While it is difficult to fault biographers for privileging the latter—except where doing so encourages obvious errors of fact or judgment—we can be grateful to James Vest for demonstrating how crucial the reception context can be, as it helps to determine the films that are actually produced, but also as it affects subsequent receptions and understandings through time. Hitchcock's own discomfiture with the oracular assessments of his work by the young *Cahiers* Turks is thus a sign of the necessary contingency of all interpretive acts. That the terms of debate established by the New Wave generation in reference to Hitchcock (identification, transference, transgression, the gaze, and so on) are still deeply pertinent—if only to judge by the recent work of Slavoj Žižek—is thus all the more remarkable. Indeed, on this account Vest's *Hitchcock and France* is more aptly compared to *Hitchcock: The Making of a Reputation*, by Robert Kapsis, than to the more comprehensive biographies. The Vest book is a worthy "prequel" to the Kapsis volume for treating a crucial decade to which Kapsis devotes scant attention. *Hitchcock and France: The Forging of an Auteur* is well researched, crisply written, and a truly significant contribution to Hitchcock studies. *L'auteur! L'auteur!*

Robert Kolker, ed., *Alfred Hitchcock's* Psycho: *A Casebook*. New York: Oxford University Press, 2004. 272 pp. $18.95 paper.

MICHAEL HEALEY

In a fit of college-age hubris, while arguing that *Vertigo* and *The Birds* are superior films, I was once foolhardy enough to claim that *Psycho*, though no doubt superb, gave up its secrets too easily. Perhaps the narration's willingness— even hunger—to reveal itself, to structure itself with an eye toward the viewer's habitual complacency, allowed me to believe that the film's humor and artistry offered the possibility of redemption, or at least escape, from its unforgiving depiction of postwar American life. I should instead have heeded the film's own warning: the smug and self-satisfied are exposed to being attacked when they least expect it, vanquished by the forces of the irrational, and sent reeling backward down a steep flight of stairs. Had I not already come to my senses, reading *Alfred Hitchcock's* Psycho: *A Casebook*, edited by Robert Kolker, would be enough to convince me that this picture's mysteries are bottomless, and the perspectives one can apply to it practically innumerable.

Oxford University Press's *Casebooks in Criticism* series has been primarily a literary venture, concentrating on novels by modernist authors such as James Joyce and William Faulkner. The publishers would have been hard-pressed to select a more appropriate film for this inaugural foray into cinema, and Kolker wisely constructs this volume to illustrate the development of cinema studies itself in the years since the picture's release in 1960. Familiar material, such as excerpts from Robin Wood's and Raymond Durgnat's auteurist studies, as well as from the Hitchcock/Truffaut interview book, offers new possibilities for reflection and expansion when placed in such close proximity both to one another and to strong subsequent work by critics such as Kolker and Linda Williams.

Fully half of this volume is comprised of essays published within the past decade. Kolker's selection implies that the 1970s-vintage psychoanalytic approach remains of little more than historical interest to today's readers; the one essay derived from that theoretical model, the epilogue to *Hitchcock's Bi-Textuality: Lacan, Feminisms, and Queer Theory* by Robert Samuels (originally published in 1998), is surely the collection's weakest. Samuels' reliance on Freudian theory causes him to jump to conclusions without presenting sufficient evidence: "We can read the name 'Norman' as a condensation of the 'normal man.' What is normal, then, is for the male subject to be divided in half between his identifications with his mother and her desire and his identification with his father" (152). But in what sense is Norman Bates (Anthony Perkins) representative of a "normal" man?

This is a major question, and the strictly Freudian explanation is just too limited. (A Jungian reading, with Norman as Persona and "Mother" as Shadow, though not entirely sufficient, might be more accurate.) Admittedly, Norman's deviance has its origins in matters of sexual insecurity and parental dependence all "normal" people have to deal with. Hitchcock fills the early scenes with overbearing parents, such as the obnoxious millionaire who uses his wealth to keep his "baby" under his thumb or the mother who procures tranquilizers for her daughter's wedding night. While he thus prepares us for the relationship between Norman and his mother (as our acceptance of Marion's crime paves the way for Norman's) the director does not suggest that all of these are equivalent. Just as we cannot write *Psycho* off as a mere case study, it will not do to claim that Norman is therefore an Everyman. He is a homicidal graverobber, who argues aloud with his mother's corpse—and often loses, although he provides both voices. Even before he murders Marion Crane (Janet Leigh), he is seen to be jittery, childish, threatening, and a peeping tom. Every character who comes in contact with Norman recognizes sooner or later that there is something disturbing lurking underneath his attempts to appear ordinary. The genius of the narrative is in the way it tricks us into first accepting the character as "normal"—an unfortunate young man in thrall to a difficult mother—but in order to comprehend the film's moral stance, we must recognize the extent to which we have been deceived, as Marion does in the parlor scene. Granted, *Psycho* establishes a troubling connection between the banality of daily life and the horror that lurks beneath, but to say that Norman Bates represents a "normal . . . male subject" is to disregard that the narrative clearly modulates from the former to the latter.

Samuels also overlooks a major element of the film's construction: its humor. He points out that after she decides to steal the $40,000—an impulsive act presented in a manner far more complex and problematical than Samuels admits—Marion is costumed in black lingerie, which contrasts with the white she wears in the opening scene. Yet Samuels fails to mention the Hitchcockian irony: Marion, whose mid-afternoon tryst with Sam Loomis (John Gavin) appears more stifling than erotic, was not so innocent to begin with.

Of course, it remains virtually impossible to discuss this film without reference to its Freudian underpinnings, but most of the essays reprinted in this collection attempt to examine the manner in which Hitchcock manipulates Freudian tropes to achieve his own, distinct objectives. Jean Douchet sets a fine example in "Hitch and His Audience" (1960): the French critic deals explicitly with key psychoanalytic concepts such as voyeurism and the projection of desire, yet admits, "I don't think this is enough to explain the invention of the forms and their internal dynamics" (72). He uses the term "occultism" to refer to those aspects of the film that psychoanalytic readings cannot hope to clarify. Although each arrives at a different conclusion, nearly all of the subsequent essays follow Douchet's lead and investigate *Psycho*'s formal structure in hopes of unpacking the mysterious elements that keep us coming back to the picture, even after countless analyses and viewings.

A majority of the critical essays included here revolve around the same topics (viewers' identification/complicity; images of eyes and related circular compositional elements; frequent character doubling; the relationship between sex and money established during the opening scenes; the police psychologist's "explanation" of Norman's character), yet there is little consensus as to how they should be interpreted. Occasionally, a critic's diction will signal that his or her essay may be a deliberate response to a forerunner, as in Durgnat's repeated use of the term "hysteria." Writing two years earlier, Wood had claimed that the narrative's "sardonic humor" allows for the dramatization of "desolation . . . [and] the ultimate horrors without hysteria, with a poised, almost serene detachment" (84). (This judgment provides crucial support for Wood's thesis that Hitchcock should be considered one of the twentieth century's great moral artists.) On the contrary, Durgnat contends that the meaning of the humor resides in its implication of hysteria: "we must be mad to be laughing at a joke like this" (91). He further argues that the hysterical condition extends beyond issues of tone to the narrative itself, as with the viewer's divided reaction to Lila Crane's (Vera Miles) exploration of the Bates house: "As we can't make up our mind whether the danger is coming from in front of her (Mom) or from behind her (Norman), we're no longer thinking very coherently . . . we yield to a helpless hysteria" (93). Neither writer is incorrect, which is a testament not only to *Psycho*'s complexity but also to the value of Kolker's collection for creating a forum in which we can appraise this diversity of critical perspectives.

Kolker's admirable, overriding concern in selecting essays for inclusion in this volume seems to have been: Can this writer improve our understanding of how we, as spectators, experience *Psycho*? Film criticism, no matter how erudite, is worth very little if it does not address the complicated manner in which viewers may respond to the work at hand. Hitchcock clearly—and rightly—understood cinema as a mass art; hence his stated wish to play the audience "like an organ" (16). Throughout the oft-cited interview with Truffaut, a section of which appears as the introductory item in this collection, the director speaks repeatedly and unequivocally of his pleasure that the film "caused audiences all over the world to react and become emotional," and his conviction that "it won't necessarily get you the best notices, but you have to design your film just as Shakespeare did his plays—for an audience" (21). The comparison to Shakespeare is especially interesting. (Wood regularly invokes the playwright in the seminal first edition of *Hitchcock's Films* [1965].) Though now held up as a paragon of high art, Shakespeare's plays were among the great popular spectacles of their time, chock-full of shocking incidents such as *King Lear's* grisly blinding scene. In making reference to Shakespeare, Hitchcock was not only sneaking in an admission of his own greatness—the likes of which he never would have permitted himself to state baldly—but also suggesting that his films' popularity should not exclude them from consideration as serious works of art. Although many aspects of Hitchcock's artistic personality betray affinities with high Modernism, the director certainly does not disdain the public.

Linda Williams' "Discipline and Fun: *Psycho* and Postmodern Cinema" represents a significant advancement in our understanding of such popular reception with respect not only to this film but also to a whole style of movie-going that came to an end soon after *Psycho's* release. Previous critics generally took their lead from Hitchcock's statement that the spectators "were aroused by pure film" (20), and they tend to follow one of two approaches. The first, as with the aforementioned chapters by Wood and Durgnat, is to review the entire narrative with an eye toward Hitchcock's careful manipulation of audience identification throughout. The second approach is to choose either one sequence (most famously, the shower scene) or a single motif or narrative element and to perform a close reading. (Examples from this volume include Royal S. Brown's technical, yet still accessible, study of Bernard Hermann's score and George Toles's gaze theory essay, " 'If Thine Eye Offend Thee . . .': *Psycho* and the Art of Infection.") But Williams has introduced a third tactic: her imaginative, historicized article locates *Psycho's* originality in its creation of a new type of collective viewing experience rather than strictly in the film's departure from classical narrative form.

In Williams' hands, *Psycho* becomes one of the half dozen or so most important films since the invention of the sound cinema to have influenced the ongoing development of the theater-going ritual. She does not make reference to these pictures, but after reading Williams' article—sure to take its rightful place among the best written on the complicated subject of the audience—I feel that *Psycho* can be understood as perhaps the most significant film (from a theatrical perspective) to appear between the release of *Gone With the Wind* (1939) and the emergence of the summer blockbuster in the latter half of the 1970s. The wit of Hitchcock's ad campaign, insisting "that no one be admitted late to the film" (183)—not even the Queen of England or the theater manager's brother—has been noted, as has its effectiveness in drumming up enthusiasm for the picture. However, Williams argues that the experience of seeing *Psycho* in 1960 theaters "fundamentally altered viewing habits" (165), which had previously been defined by the fact that, unlike the audience of a play or a symphony, moviegoers arrived whenever it suited them and had no objection to picking up a film at the midpoint or beyond. Incorporating an impressive array of extra-cinematic reference points ranging from Disneyland to Michel Foucault's *Discipline and Punish* (1978), she details the spectators' willing, surprising submission to the new guidelines—both to waiting in line and, after seeing the film, to keeping its secrets. These self-consciously strict policies were all part of the fun, and she argues that the audience responded by interacting with the film—screaming, mostly—to an extent it never had before. Williams declares it "the beginning of an era in which viewers began going to the movies to be thrilled and moved in quite visceral ways" (172). She gathers diverse yet apposite support for her argument, including a digression on the habits of Cincinnati, Ohio orchestra patrons circa 1873, as well as a collection of photographs taken of the audience during *Psycho*'s first run at London's Plaza Theater. Most appreciated, however, is the fact that she never loses sight of the film itself, a flaw to which other cultural studies theorists frequently succumb.

Finally, Kolker concludes the volume with his own lengthy visual analysis, "The Man Who Knew More Than Too Much: The Form, Structure, and Influence of *Psycho*," an expanded version of his essay "Algebraic Figures: Recalculating the Hitchcock Formula." (Much of the "Influence" section, particularly as it pertains to Martin Scorcese, will also be familiar to readers of Kolker's book *The Cinema of Loneliness* [2000].) He makes a strong case, supported by dozens of stills, for the presence of an abstract design based on a system of vertical and horizontal lines underlying not merely Saul Bass's credit sequence but the entire film's *mise-en-scène*. Thus, prominent circular elements such as characters' eyes or the showerhead, usually interpreted symbolically, are conceived also as deviations from the narrative's governing photographic scheme. Kolker's conception is carefully worked out and "open" enough to account for the appearance of diagonal lines at significant moments, such as the staircase in the Bates house or the chain that exhumes Marion's car from the swamp in the picture's final shot. While it may seem pedantic when reduced to just a few sentences, Kolker's argument succeeds both as a contribution to the wealth of scholarly work on *Psycho*'s cinematic form and as a fitting conclusion to this particular volume, which had obviously been lacking a systematic analysis of the film's visuals.

My only complaint about this collection is the relative lack of material on those sections of the film centered on Arbogast (Martin Balsam) or Sam and Lila. One cannot really fault the editor for this, though, as the vast majority of commentators tend to focus on *Psycho*'s first hour and its concluding moments. However, much remains to be said about the "detective movie" passages positioned between the sinking of Marion's car and the climactic revelation of Norman-as-"Mother." Nevertheless Psycho: *A Casebook* should be a welcome addition to any film lover's library, either as a teaching tool or as a handy collection of notable essays published in the years since David Bordwell's overview of criticism on *Psycho* in *Making Meaning* (1989).

Murray Pomerance, *An Eye for Hitchcock*. New Brunswick, NJ: Rutgers University Press. 2004. 306 pp. $22.95 paper.

CHARLES L.P. SILET

In the penultimate chapter of *An Eye for Hitchcock*, on *I Confess*, Murray Pomerance remarks that the moral of the film is ''how to watch a film.'' He adds that ''moving from place to place and point to point won't help if we can't see in the first place'' (187). This pretty well sums up his approach to the films covered in this book. *An Eye for Hitchcock* is a study in close watching by a scholar with a keen eye for detail and a supple mind for making sense out of what he sees.

In his introduction, Pomerance discloses his method: inquiry not statement, play not analysis, so as to take pleasure in the ''Hitchcockian moment.'' He proposes a personal approach to the films, to write what he calls an ''unconventional'' book about his subject, not one relying on the director's biography or on traditional ways the films here considered have been read. He wants to avoid strictly ideological and psychological readings, although there are some of both in his deliberations. Pomerance devotes a chapter each to six films: *North by Northwest, Spellbound, Torn Curtain, Marnie, I Confess,* and *Vertigo*. None of these chapters provides a comprehensive reading of the film, but in keeping with his stated purpose, each offers a personal assessment, a playful and insightful consideration, of some of the more neglected details of the films.

One of the central themes that Pomerance follows throughout his analysis is ''verticality,'' the reflection of class hierarchy, as Hitchcock elaborates and develops this idea. His focus is not on a simple recounting of the structure of class, but rather on the vital verticality embedded in Hitchcock's films, encompassing such things as ''social scales in which powerlessness struggles under power; climbing; falling; precarious rest in gravity; architectures suggesting, and founded upon, upward thrust; camera movement in the vertical lines, especially shooting from above and below; geographical upness and downness; the moral scale'' (12).

Perhaps Pomerance's discussion of verticality in *North by Northwest* best illustrates his procedure. In a section titled "High Society" he traces the various risings and fallings that Roger O. Thornhill experiences during his journey of discovery, north-northwest, in search of the illusive George Kaplan. Pomerance argues that much of the aggression and humiliation Thornhill suffers is expressed vertically. The film begins with his descent from the heights of a Manhattan office building, a locus of power that suggests his status, narcissism, and his control over imagery through advertising, representing his ability to manipulate knowledge and belief, an ability the film will challenge at its every turn. The descent to street level will expose Thornhill visually to threats posed by Vandamm and his cronies. Following Hitchcock's use of low- and high-angle shots, not to mention his dramatic overhead shot of Thornhill fleeing the United Nations building, Pomerance traces the various moments of aggression and humiliation Hitchcock's protagonist is subjected to until he arrives at Mount Rushmore and must scramble across the presidents' faces with Eve Kendall in tow, finally to be resolved in the night train sequence when Thornhill pulls Eve, the new Mrs. Thornhill, up into the upper berth of the sleeping compartment. Throughout the film, Thornhill is constantly rising and falling, and it is Pomerance's task not only to trace these ups and downs but also to assign them meaning.

The second large-scale theme Pomerance elaborates is "anticipatory following," which he describes as "learning by imitating" the cues taken from others, a process that helps to define the self and its appropriate behavior in any given situation (15). Each of the central characters in the six films he examines must sort out a "true" self from among the various disparate selves defined by others. In this context the films all become journeys of discovery for Hitchcock's focal characters. The most obvious example of this is, of course, the journey, both physical and psychological, undergone by *Spellbound's* John Ballantine. With the help of Salvador Dalí and a smattering of Freudian dissection, Hitchcock subjects

Ballantine, a.k.a. Dr. Edwardes and J.B. ("John Brown"), to a series of psychoanalytical sessions, which eventually unlock his real personality from the various anticipatory personalities projected onto him by the others in the film.

It would be unfair to Pomerance to suggest that his book is only a "theme" book arranged around these two broad-based ideas. It is much more far-ranging than this, although these two main points do provide a center of sorts. The lack of a controlling idea or theme speaks to both the book's weaknesses and its strengths. By avoiding a central theme, the book escapes the strait jacket that often restricts the scope of books so arranged, but by the same token this book often feels a bit scattered in its approach, and the risk is that the reader will come away without any coherent sense of the book's purpose. Since Pomerance states early on that he wishes to keep his narrative free-flowing, unrestricted, and personal, an ongoing questioning of the film's texts, he puts the reader on notice. And in general *An Eye for Hitchcock* succeeds in doing what it sets out to do. It is just that the reader has to work a bit to bring the multitude of insights and observations together to understand precisely what its author is trying to say about Hitchcock and his films.

Nevertheless, the strength of the book resides in the detailed readings Pomerance gives not only to the individual films but also to the individual sequences and scenes within them. A good example of this is his detailed and masterfully clever dissection of the painting scenes in *I Confess*, made all the more useful and important because the film is so infrequently mentioned by Hitchcock scholars and is so underrated. *I Confess* is set in Québec, and revolves around a murderer (Keller) who confesses his crime to a priest (Father Logan) whose vows of silence and confidentiality prevent him from revealing the details even when he is accused of the crime. After playing around with the sight/seeing motifs of the film, Pomerance turns his attention to three scenes which make up the priest's sitting-room painting sequence, a sequence seemingly of minor interest in the film both because it is given so little space in it and because it first appears to be of only tangential importance to the murder-confession plot.

Pomerance describes these scenes as the elegant and simple statement of the film's optical paradox because they are devoted to an "elementary configuration of opticality" (197), namely the painting of a room. In the first of these scenes, two priests discuss the painting project that is being carried out by Logan and Keller. Pomerance points out that painting is, in its "simplest essence, a cover-up" (200), obviously related to the cover-up of the murder. Pomerance's discussion hinges on his analysis of French-speaking Father Milet's mispronunciation of painting as "pain-ting," and his preoccupation with the noxious smell of the paint and its relations to noxious moral problems and their cover-up. Scene two has Father Milet and the policeman, Detective Murphy, discussing the covering properties of paint with Milet, assuring the detective that the church does not cover up dirt with paint. The walls are spotless underneath. The third scene, which Pomerance describes as one of the central scenes of the film, involves Logan on a ladder painting, and Keller and his wife below as they discuss the murder. Here Logan is placed visually in a vertically superior position reflecting that he knows, through his confession, that Keller is the killer, and that Keller and his wife are afraid he will tell the police and violate the sanctity of the confessional.

Pomerance then takes these three scenes and spins them out to reveal several more issues inherent in the film: social status, the power of the church (and state), tensions between Anglo- and Francophone Québec, and the molding power of Hitchcock's lens. As an instance of film analysis through the exposition of an apparently minor element in a film, it is a *tour de force*, and it is an example of the kind of thing Pomerance does, and does well, throughout the book.

In spite of all of the book's strong points there are a few omissions. For example, Pomerance makes occasional reference to Erving Goffman's *The Presentation of Self in Everyday Life*, but he never really spells out Goffman's general set of ideas, so the references do not have much resonance in his discussion. In addition, although Pomerance footnotes other scholarly work on the films he examines, he provides scant discussion of it, which would have been helpful in assessing his own insights. These omissions do not vitiate his insights or his approach, but they do detract somewhat. A final caveat is a stylistic one. Too frequently Pomerance resorts to long lists of modifiers that are not examined in any systematic way. But all of these caveats are minor defects in an otherwise impressive book.

In *An Eye for Hitchcock*, Murrray Pomerance provides, in his idiosyncratic way, a deft discussion of six of the director's films. Students of Hitchcock will benefit from both his personal and playful method and his perceptive, detailed, and wide-ranging insights into the meaning of the films. This is especially true of his reasoned analysis of *Torn Curtain* and *I Confess*, two of Hitchcock's films that have received less close attention than they deserve from film scholars and commentators. The same might be said too for his treatment of *Spellbound* and *Marnie*, films that have attracted some attention but not nearly enough. *North by Northwest* and *Vertigo* have been much analyzed, but even with these films Pomerance manages to give them a fresh reading. All in all, *An Eye for Hitchcock* is a fine piece of work, and through Pomerance's emphasis on social class and institutional power relationships as well as his close reading of Hitchcock's visual style, the book expands our knowledge of this master filmmaker's vision.

Irving Singer, *Three Philosophical Filmmakers: Hitchcock, Welles, Renoir*. Cambridge: MIT University Press, 2004. x + 279 pp. $32.95.

WILLIAM G. SIMON

Irving Singer's *Three Philosophical Filmmakers: Hitchcock, Welles, Renoir* is a most curious and frustrating book. Singer presents productively illuminating interpretations of the three directors in question. At the same time, the limitations of his critical methodology and his manner of explication raise numerous questions.

In what sense does Singer construe Hitchcock, Welles, and Renoir as *philosophical* filmmakers? Singer identifies himself through a strong affinity for traditional liberal humanism. At a key point in his book he declares, "As a pluralist and humanist philosopher, I revel in the explorations of Renoir" (220). In his introductory discussion, he implies that the goal of entertainment understood as art is to provide "relevant and possibly profound insights about humanity as it searches for values that give meaning to life" (7). For Singer, "philosophy permeates the aesthetic fabric of the work" and "formal expression becomes the expression of an outlook."

Singer evaluates and explicates his three filmmakers in terms of the degree to which they exemplify this very generalized conception of philosophy in their own works. In Singer's argument, Renoir and Welles comfortably satisfy the criteria of humanism and pluralism, and his analyses of their films are distinguished at points by their interpretative acuity and by their attention to seldom discussed films, such as Renoir's *Picnic on the Grass* and Welles's *The Immortal Story* and *F for Fake*. Hitchcock presents a more problematic figure for his argument, and we shall subsequently consider his struggle with Hitchcock's films.

Singer's analysis of each filmmaker is largely devoted to thematic exposition along fairly familiar lines. Consistent with his humanist and pluralist emphasis, he praises Renoir for his thematic of human contact and harmony. Such harmony, the motif of unity of mankind, exists among characters within the films' stories and between characters and nature. It also exists in the films' address to their spectators, in what Singer formulates as a ''conversation'' between film and viewer. He also devotes extensive discussion to the role of artists in Renoir's work and to the relationship between sexual love and artistic achievement.

The discussion of Welles focuses on the theme and representation of time, specifically on motifs of pastness, evanescence, and death. He also presents valuable insights on performance and the concept of magic in Welles. And, as he does with Renoir, he considers in detail the complexities of narrative perspective within the films, praising the presence of ambivalence and ambiguity, presumably consistent with Singer's valuation of pluralism.

Before considering Singer's discussion of Hitchcock, it is useful to consider several aspects of his critical methodology. Firstly, in laying out his interpretations of each director's philosophy, Singer refers a great deal to the filmmakers' statements posed in interviews and memoirs. This automatically raises the issue of directorial intentionality, especially because he frequently takes the interview material as the key to his interpretations.

This strategy leads to some problematic evaluations. For instance, in discussing performance in Hitchcock, Singer largely accepts the director's account of the importance of montage in overcoming the inexpressivity of the actor's face. I would argue that recent work on performance in Hitchcock (for example, James Naremore's chapters in *Acting in the Cinema* on Cary Grant in *North by Northwest* and James Stewart in *Rear Window*) should put to rest the myth of lack of agency in Hitchcockian actors. Any consideration of Anthony Perkins' and Janet Leigh's contribution to the parlor scene in *Psycho*, both in facial expression and line readings, should further emphasize the collaborative contribution of actors to Hitchcock's work. Singer fails to question critically the formulations that Hitchcock's interviews suggest through independent consideration of the films' texts.

Additionally, Singer's use of interview and autobiographical materials almost invariably relies on texts from late in the directors' careers. From my own experience of reading filmmakers' interviews and memoirs, I would note that there is often a discrepancy accounts written around the time of a film's production and those written late in a career. The former frequently address the specificity of a film's political, social, and cultural context, whereas the latter tend to obscure specificity and context in the mists of memory and to universalize the total career output.

This tendency in the interviews and memoirs Singer draws on is consistent with the idealist humanist thrust of his interpretations. There is minimal attention to political and cultural context, and scant account of it in the interpretation of films. The Popular Front context of Renoir's mid- and late-1930s films, which figures so prominently in critical work on Renoir by Christopher Faulkner and Jonathan Buchsbaum, as well as the Cultural Front account of Welles work, so prominent in Michael Denning's work, figures only peripherally in Singer's accounts of these directors' careers. Indeed, one can protest that the reliance on late interviews and memoirs is complemented by a neglect and lack of engagement with recent critical literature and debate on all three directors. Predictably, Bazin and Truffaut are the only critics who are significantly referenced.

A second aspect of Singer's critical methodology involves a tendency to relate the films' philosophy to the avowed working methods of each of the directors. For instance, in regard to both Renoir and Welles, considerable attention is devoted to the directors' use of actorly improvisation and the concomitant degree of collaboration in the making of the films. This working method is related in an almost causal way to the thematic of human harmony in the stories of the films and to the conversational address to the spectator that Singer attributes to the films.

In regard to Hitchcock, Singer emphasizes the degree of meticulous pre-production for the films. This, he suggests, produces a strong formalist emphasis in the work and an address to the spectator which is significantly manipulative and opposed to Renoir's and Welles's methods. While this is argued in an interesting way at points, it seems misguided to infer a direct correlation between the films and the specifics of their production methods.

A third and final aspect of Singer's critical methodology has to do with his emphasis on story events and character interaction as the basis for his interpretation of films. While his declared intent is to examine how "philosophy permeates the aesthetic fabric of the work," his conception of "aesthetic fabric" is very limited. While Singer makes some reference to formal cinematic narrational issues (montage in Hitchcock, deep focus in Welles, "open" shooting style in Renoir), these aspects of his discussion are underdeveloped. He does not sufficiently consider the degree to which the filmmakers' philosophies are embedded in or represented through the cinematic signifier or the narrative discourse. The scale of this review does not allow the development of an elaborate argument on the significance of form and narrative. Suffice it to say that a great deal could be written, for example, about the dynamic dialogue of camera movement, editing, camera position, music, and narrative perspective in the scene of the burning of Rosebud in *Citizen Kane*. These formal and narrative parameters have to do with the representation of evanescence and persistence, temporal qualities of the sort Singer attributes to Welles's philosophy. His analyses would be much richer if he paid more attention to these qualities in the "fabric" of his three directors' films.

Beyond these limitations in Singer's methodology which apply to his analyses of all three filmmakers, the most problematic aspect of his book has to do with the chapter on Hitchcock. Where Renoir and Welles are made to conform to Singer's brand of humanism convincingly, Hitchcock resists a satisfactory place within his schema. Singer treats Hitchcock as a formalist who harmonizes his formalism to a concern with the ordinary and quotidian. His reservations about Hitchcock are especially inferred by the term "manipulative," used to describe Hitchcock's influence over his audience. In his most revealing statement, in the summation to his chapter, he contends that "Hitchcock never develops the epistemological ramifications of his skepticism about the ordinary. Instead, he deploys it as a means of orienting the story in each film toward whatever emotional effects his technology can evoke'' (24).

One can argue that a central theme of Hitchcock criticism from Rohmer, Chabrol, and Wood to the present has centered on appreciating and critically examining ways that Hitchcock explores the ''epistemological ramifications of his skepticism about the ordinary.'' Singer's contention especially suggests the limitations of his book in trying to force all three filmmakers into a single if very broad philosophical schema and in restricting his sources to the filmmakers' own pronouncements.

Contributors

Richard Allen is Associate Professor of Cinema Studies at New York University. He is author of *Projecting Illusion* and co-editor of five books on cinema and the philosophy of film, including *Alfred Hitchcock: Centenary Essays* and *Hitchcock: Past and Future*, both with Sam Ishii-Gonzalès. He is still completing a book on Hitchcock, now with Columbia University Press, entitled *Hitchcock's Romantic Irony: Story-telling, Sexuality, and Style*.

Charles Barr teaches at the University of East Anglia in England, and is director of the Masters programs there in Film Studies and in Film Archiving. His books include *English Hitchcock*, the BFI Film Classics volume on *Vertigo*, and *The Film at War: British Cinema 1939-1945* (forthcoming in 2006). He has published two articles related to the 2005 centenary of Michael Powell's birth: on *The Spy in Black* for *The Cinema of Michael Powell* (BFI), and on Hitchcock and Powell for the special issue of *Screen* magazine on Powell (volume 46, number 1).

Michael Healey is currently pursuing a Master of Arts degree in New York University's Cinema Studies program. He reviews films regularly for the online culture magazine, PopMatters.com.

Mark M. Hennelly, Jr., is Professor of English and former Department Chair at California State University, Sacramento. He has published in *Journal of Popular Film* and regularly teaches a course on Hitchcock. Primarily, though, his focus is Victorian fiction, on which he has published widely, including carnivalesque readings of Dickens, George Eliot, and Thomas Hardy. His most recent work appears in *Victorian Literature and Culture*, *Journal of Dracula Studies*, *Dickens Studies Annual*, *Contemporary Literature*, and *Text and Performance Quarterly*.

Leland Poague teaches film in the Department of English at Iowa State University. He is co-editor of *A Hitchcock Reader*, and most recently edited *Frank Capra: Interviews* for the University Press of Mississippi.

Charles L.P. Silet teaches film and contemporary literature at Iowa State University. His current book, *The Films of Woody Allen: Critical Essays*, will be published in 2006.

William G. Simon is Associate Professor of Cinema Studies at New York University. He is author of *The Films of Jean Vigo* and numerous articles on American cinema.

James M. Vest is Professor of French, interdisciplinary studies, and cinema at Rhodes College in Memphis, Tennessee. Author of several articles on Hitchcock's French connections, he has recently published a book on the subject, *Hitchcock and France*, with Praeger.

Michael Walker is a retired teacher who is on the editorial board of *Movie* magazine. He has contributed to *The Movie Book of Film Noir* (1992) and *The Movie Book of the Western* (1996), and to the BFI anthology *Alfred Hitchcock: Centenary Essays* (1999). His book *Hitchcock's Motifs* will be published by Amsterdam University Press in Fall 2005.

Robin Wood is a film teacher and scholar who resides in Canada. He is an editor of the Canadian cinema journal *CineAction*. His most recent books are *Hollywood from Vietnam to Reagan* (revised and expanded edition, 2003), *Hitchcock's Films Revisited* (revised edition, 2002), *Sexual Politics and Narrative Film: Hollywood and Beyond* (1998), *The Wings of the Dove* (1999), and *Rio Bravo* (2003).

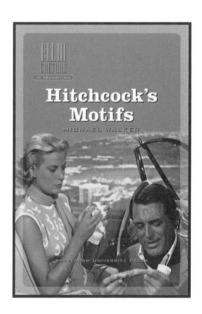

I Know That You Know That I Know
Narrating Subjects from *Moll Flanders* to *Marnie*
George Butte

"George Butte's *I Know That You Know That I Know* is a major contribution to narrative theory and to the interpretation of novels and films. This brilliant book is the product of many years of research and teaching."
—J. Hillis Miller, UCI Distinguished Research Professor of English and Comparative Literature, University of California, Irvine

In *I Know That You Know That I Know*, Butte explores how stories narrate human consciousness. Butte locates a historical shift in the representation of webs of consciousnesses in narrative—what he calls "deep intersubjectivity"—and examines the effect this shift has since had on Western literature and culture. The author studies narrative practices in two ways: one pairing eighteenth-and nineteenth-century British novels (*Moll Flanders* and *Great Expectations*, for example), and the other studying genre practices—comedy, anti-comedy and masquerade—in written and film narratives (Jane Austen and Hitchcock's Cary Grant films, for example, and *His Girl Friday*).

Butte's second major claim argues for new ways to read representations of human consciousness, whether or not they take the form of deep intersubjectivity. Phenomenological criticism has lost its credibility in recent years, but this book identifies better reading strategies arising out of what the author calls poststructuralist phenomenology, grounded largely in the work of the French philosopher Merleau-Ponty. Butte criticizes the extremes of transcendental idealism (first-wave phenomenological criticism) and cultural materialism (when it rules out the study of consciousness). He also criticizes the dominant Lacanian framework of much academic film criticism.

$ 44.95 cloth 0-8142-0945-9 $ 9.95 CD 0-8142-9027-2

The Ohio State University Press
800-621-2736 www.ohiostatepress.org